CW01666563

STARTING YOUR OWN BUSINESS

2nd edition

Ron Immink
Brian O'Kane

Downloads and additional information available @
www.startingabusinessinireland.com

Researched and written by
Ron Immink and Brian O'Kane.

Published for the
Department of Enterprise, Trade and Employment by
Oak Tree Press
19 Rutland Street, Cork.
http://www.oaktreepress.com
http://www.startingabusinessinireland.com.

© 1997 and 2001
Minister for Enterprise, Trade and Employment.
Revised 2005

ISBN 1-86076-224-7

Printed in Ireland by ColourBooks.

Acknowledgements

Production of this guide was assisted by the European Commission through the Community SME Initiative under Measure 4 of the Small Business Operational Programme.

The authors gratefully acknowledge the assistance they received from the organisations mentioned in this guide, the staff of the Department and the many others who have contributed to the research.

Disclaimer

The contents of this guide are believed to be correct at the time of printing but no responsibility can be taken by the authors, publisher or Department of Enterprise, Trade and Employment for any errors herein.
Readers should take professional advice before entering into any legally binding commitments or investing any funds.

Sometimes, you just have to allow things to speak for themselves ...

www.startingabusinessinireland.com
information, advice & resources for entrepreneurs

STARTING YOUR OWN BUSINESS?

Why not contact your local County or City Enterprise Board for:-

• Information • Advice • Financial Incentives • Business Skills Training
• Management Development • Networking • eBusiness Supports
• Exhibition Opportunities

For information on the full range of supports available from your local Enterprise Baoard visit: www.enterpriseboards.ie

NDP NATIONAL DEVELOPMENT PLAN

EUROPEAN UNION STRUCTURAL FUNDS

County & City Enterprise Boards are funded by the Irish Government and EU Structural Funds under the National Development Plan 2000-2006

County & City Enterprise Boards

FOREWORD

Department of Enterprise, Trade and Employment

Entrepreneurship is an exciting, difficult and worthwhile calling, which needs to be fostered if our present economic performance is to be maintained. Aspiring entrepreneurs represent an untapped resource with great potential for future development. They can be discouraged by the effort required to pull together all the information they need to get started. A degree of mystery surrounds the process of starting a business. The purpose of this guide, which has been revised and updated to include new sections on technology, e-business and working from home, is to provide that information in one source and, thus, to demystify the process. This guide will help prepare potential entrepreneurs and stimulate the establishment of new businesses in an innovative and vital way.

Small business people lead busy, even hectic lives. The range of skills and knowledge they require may seem daunting for an aspiring entrepreneur. Production, marketing, accounting, finance, customers, employees and business regulations are but a few areas of vital importance. In brief, entrepreneurs need to be all things, not only to all people, but also to themselves.

This guide not only addresses these needs in a focused and dynamic fashion but in a style and language that is easily understood and encourages the reader. Time is of the essence in the business world and this start-up guide addresses this from the outset. It is constructed as a self-assessment workbook so that potential entrepreneurs literally will have carried out all the necessary steps in setting up their business by the time they have finished the guide. In keeping with the Department's move towards implementing e-Business in everyday transactions, the text of the guide and updates to the information contained within it will be available on a website, **www.startingabusinessinireland.com**.

I would like to wish all would-be entrepreneurs success in their endeavours and I hope this guide will ease the path to establishing successful enterprises.

Mary Harney TD
Tánaiste and Minister for Enterprise, Trade and Employment

INTRODUCTION

The harsh reality is that too many new businesses fail – many more than ought to. Why? Because of lack of planning. They do not plan to fail, but they certainly fail to plan.

Preparation – in the form of careful and considered planning – is the most important thing you can do to ensure that your fledgling business gets off the ground and continues flying. You can never eliminate **all** risk but you can reduce it significantly – to the point where the odds are in your favour.

This guide is all about preparation – preparing you for what you will face as an entrepreneur, for the obstacles, hurdles and blockages that will be placed in your way, for the new skills that you will have to learn, for the tasks that you will have to handle, for the rules, regulations and form-filling that may trip you up, right through to the agencies – State and private sector – which can help you make your dream a success.

The first edition of this guide was developed for the Department of Enterprise, Trade and Employment under Measure 4 of the Government's Operational Programme for Small Business, which was funded by the European Commission.

It was designed to take a potential entrepreneur through the whole process of starting a business, from first thoughts about self-employment to the practicalities of start-up.

The guide consists of three chapters:

- **READY** – The first chapter, covering preparation, self-assessment, ideas generation, market research and training for entrepreneurs
- **STEADY** – The bulk of the guide, covering business planning, raising finance, sources of assistance, choosing premises, recruiting staff, marketing, book-keeping and management issues
- **GO** – When everything has been thought through and you are ready, this section provides the remaining information you need to get started.

As you work through the guide, you will find checklists, flowcharts and questionnaires designed to make you think about your proposed business. The aim is not only to give you the theory behind setting up a business but also to give you the practical tools to actually do it. It all adds up to a turn-key package – a "business in a box".

Each chapter in this guide is introduced by a number of **KEY QUESTIONS** – searching questions that the entrepreneur needs to consider carefully before moving ahead. Think through your answers to the key questions (but do not write them down yet) before you read the chapter. When you have completed the chapter, read all the sections and worked through all the checklists and questionnaires, you should then come back to the key questions and complete your answers in writing.

In each section of the guide, you will find clearly-stated **OBJECTIVES** set out beside the section heading. These summarise what you can expect to learn from the section.

Read them before you begin, to decide whether the section is relevant to your needs. And when you have finished the section, go back, read the objectives again and check them off.

And then, when you have reached the end of the guide, you have filled in and sent out all the forms that are necessary, you have written your business plan, your funding is in place, and all the preparations are made – it's time to rock and roll!

To help you even more, this second edition of the guide is linked to a web-site – **www.startingabusinessinireland.com** – where you will find spreadsheets and templates to download, as well as updated and additional information and resources.

Good luck.

Ron Immink, Dublin
Brian O'Kane, Cork
June 2001

you think having the **best business start-up** package is worth shouting about

so do we

for a further meeting of minds with the start-up specialists, let's talk

Every day, more and more entrepreneurs start their businesses with the help of Bank of Ireland - for some very good reasons. Among the many benefits on offer are **a range of current account banking services free of charge for two years*, reduced tarriffs on mobile calls and line rental from O2, a free Golden Pages listing, 50% off ISME and the SFA membership fees** in the first year and an **hours' free consultation with an ACCA-qualified accountant.**

Our Business Start-Up offers add up to a package worth **€2,150** and has been described as one of the "most comprehensive start-up packages available"**. So if you're about to become your own boss, call in and talk to your local Bank of Ireland branch, phone **1890 365 222** or visit **www.bankofireland.ie**

Bank of Ireland

Understanding Business

*Two Years means a two year period from the date of opening a business current account with Bank of Ireland.

**Source - Business Banking Board 2005. Terms and Conditions apply. Bank of Ireland is regulated by the Financial Regulator.

PERFORMANCE+
Business Solutions for Tourism Enterprises

Welcome to Fáilte Ireland

Fáilte Ireland, the national tourism development authority, is a "one stop shop" which delivers services to the tourism industry embracing Enterprise and Skills Development, Research, Marketing and Product Development.

Developing a tourism enterprise has many challenges, such as identifying your market, satisfying your customer and managing the key processes of your business. We have a range of self-help products and training programmes designed to assist you in developing your management skills and in achieving service excellence, operational efficiency and improved profitability.

Whether you run a tourism business, large or small, or are about to start your own business in the tourism industry, we can provide a business solution to suit your needs.

Please contact:
Enterprise Development Division
Fáilte Ireland
88-95 Amiens Street, Dublin 1
Tel. (01) 884 7700
Fax: (01) 855 6821
Email: solutions@failteireland.ie

Visit our Corporate Website: www.failteireland.ie

Visit our Performance Plus business solutions website:
www.failteireland.ie/performanceplus

Fáilte Ireland
National Tourism Development Authority

Developing Tourism in Ireland

CONTENTS

Welcome to…

PREMIER CONNECTION

- **Are you** starting up your own business?
- **Are you** working from home?
- **Are you** renting office space that you don't really need?
- **Are you** an overseas company looking at the possibility of setting up an office in Dublin?
- **Are you** operating in Ireland and looking to test the Dublin market?

Premier Connection is a **cost effective** and **efficient** way to run your business allowing you to have the benefits of operating from a fully serviced office, **without actually being in an office**.

With a Virtual Office you have a prestigious mailing address and dedicated phone answering in your company name **from as little as €130** per month.

Premier Business Centres are offering **3 months** free when you sign up for a minimum period of **12 months**. Please mention "Starting Your Own Business: A Workbook" when calling.

PREMIER BUSINESS CENTRES

Contact us at
Premier Business Centre
12 Lower Hatch Street, Dublin 2
Tel: +353 1 639 1100 Fax: +353 1 639 1102
E-mail: pbc@premgroup.com

www.premierbusinesscentres.com

Benefits and features

A prestigious business address in Dublin or Belfast

Dedicated call answering in your company name

Dedicated digital voicemail box

Daily, weekly office lets

Daily, weekly meeting room hire

Sign up for a month or a year

Progress to an office when business takes off

Standard Package includes*

Dedicated line answering in your company name

Dedicated digital voicemail box

Prime postal address

Mail handling

Fax number

*Can be tailored to suit individual needs

Price

Dublin City Centre (Hatch Street, Fitzwilliam Street)	€200 per month
Suburban Dublin (Citywest, Sandyford and Tallaght)	€130 per month
Belfast	stg£85 per month

Additional services available

Day office lets

Dublin – €100 per day, subject to availability

Meeting room hire

Competitive pricing on hourly/daily basis

Capacity 2–20

Introduction

- Almost 70% of people who become self-employed do not prepare themselves properly for their new role and responsibilities
- Specifically, almost 90% do not study their market
- As a result, on average about 50% of all businesses in Europe fail within five years of starting.

These statistics should show you the importance of preparation and of carefully considering whether entrepreneurship is right for you – though you should also balance this with Paul Dickson's quote in the page margin.

Chapter structure

This chapter takes you through:
- What makes an entrepreneur?
- Self-assessment (including assessment of your business partners)
- Developing and testing your idea
- Market research
- Identifying future trends
- Feasibility study grants
- Training for entrepreneurs
- Start-up alternatives (buying an existing business, franchising and network marketing).

Key Questions

The Key Questions in the panel are designed to focus your thoughts as you read this chapter.

Think through your answers to these questions before you start to read the chapter. Then come back and write your answers in the spaces provided before moving on to the next chapter.

KEY QUESTIONS

1. Do you have the skills/experience needed to run a business? ☐ YES ☐ NO
2. Do you have sufficient motivation to stick with it for as long as it takes? ☐ YES ☐ NO
3. Do you have the support of your family? ☐ YES ☐ NO
4. Does your business idea test out? ☐ YES ☐ NO
5. Are you eligible for a Feasibility Study Grant? ☐ YES ☐ NO
6. Is your business:
   > A start-up? ☐ YES ☐ NO
   > Buy-in of an existing business? ☐ YES ☐ NO
   > Franchise? ☐ YES ☐ NO
   > Network marketing? ☐ YES ☐ NO
7. Do you need further training? ☐ YES ☐ NO
8. Are you ready to write your business plan? ☐ YES ☐ NO

OBJECTIVES

☐ Understand importance of preparation

☐ Answer Key Questions

Ignore all the statistics that tell you that 95% of all new businesses fail in the first eight years. Not only are these "statistics" riddled with widely wrong assumptions and false failure rates, but they don't apply to you. Dwelling on the statistics is like staying up to study divorce rates on your wedding night.

PAUL DICKSON

Whatever you think it's gonna take, double it. That applies to money, time, stress. It's gonna be harder than you think and take longer than you think.

RICHARD A CORTESE,
on starting a business

WHAT MAKES AN ENTREPRENEUR?

OBJECTIVES

☐ Identify entrepreneurial traits

☐ Identify success factors

Entrepreneurs are risk-takers, willing to roll the dice with their money or their reputations on the line in support of an idea or enterprise. They willingly assume responsibility for the success or failure of a venture and are answerable for all its facets. The buck not only stops at their desk, it starts there too.
VICTOR KIAM

The "entrepreneurial state of mind" is an attitude that says, in short: "I didn't just come to play the game – *I came to win*".
GORDON BATY

Entrepreneurship is the dynamic process of creating wealth, undertaken by people who assume a risk in terms of money, energy, time and/or career commitment of creating value through the provision of some product or service. The product or service may or may not be new or unique but value must somehow be created by the entrepreneur by securing and using the necessary skills and resources.

Why do people become entrepreneurs?
Research suggests four motives:

- Dramatic change in personal situation (unemployment, divorce)
- Availability of resources (idea, money)
- Certain entrepreneurial skills
- Example of another successful entrepreneur.

Typical entrepreneurial traits
The entrepreneur is the key to the successful launch of any business. He/she is the person who perceives the market opportunity and then has the motivation, drive and ability to mobilise resources to meet it.

Although it is difficult to describe a typical entrepreneur, they share certain characteristics or traits:

- **Self-confident all-rounder** – The person who can make the product, market it and count the money
- **The ability to bounce back** – The person who can cope with making mistakes and still has the confidence to try again
- **Innovative skills** – Not an "inventor" in the traditional sense but one who is able to carve out a new niche in the market-place, often invisible to others
- **Results-orientated** – To make the business successful requires a drive that only comes from setting goals and targets and getting pleasure from achieving them
- **Professional risk-taker** – To succeed means taking measured risks. Often the successful entrepreneur exhibits a step-by-step approach to risk-taking, at each stage exposing him/herself to only a limited, measured amount of personal risk and moving from one stage to another only as each decision is proved
- **Total commitment** – Hard work, energy and single-mindedness are essential elements in the entrepreneurial profile.

Note that the entrepreneurial characteristics required to launch a business successfully are often not those required for growth and, even more frequently, not those required to manage the business once it grows to any size. The role of the entrepreneur needs to change with the business as it develops and grows. In particular, the management skills of the entrepreneur – in managing staff, managing his/her own time, and in strategic planning – become more important as the business grows.

Success factors
Research suggests that successful entrepreneurs share some common factors. Which of the success factors in the panel below do you have?

SUCCESS & FAILURE FACTORS
WHICH DO YOU HAVE?

1. Hard work ☐
2. Perseverance ☐
3. Motivation ☐
4. Social skills ☐
5. Leadership ☐
6. Good management ☐
7. Integrity ☐
8. Guts ☐
9. Good health ☐
10. Common-sense ☐
11. Luck ☐
12. Support of family ☐
13. Clear initial goals ☐
14. Creativity ☐
15. Ability to accept uncertainty ☐

Self-assessment

Before you decide to start your own business, you should know that:

- The average working week of a self-employed person is 64 hours. In almost half of those businesses, the spouse/partner is also involved for another 21 hours (total, 85 hours)
- Most people do not increase their income by becoming self-employed
- One in five entrepreneurs do not earn anything in the first 18 months
- Support of the spouse/partner is a critical factor in the success or failure of a start-up business.

Running your own business demands a lot of commitment. It is both physically and mentally demanding. Therefore, it is very important to ask yourself why you want to become self-employed. This will take some soul-searching but it is vital to the decision to go ahead. If your motivation is not strong enough, you will not last.

You also need to be sure that you have your family's support.

Self-assessment

The questions in the panel below and on the next page will help you assess your own suitability for starting and running a business. Write your answers in the spaces provided.

Copy this page and the next so that your business partners can answer the questions too.

	Is this a Strength or a Weakness? S	W
What personal motivation do you bring to the business?		
What skills do you bring to the business?		
What experience do you bring to the business?		
What training/education do you bring to the business?		

OBJECTIVES

- ☐ Need for commitment
- ☐ Need for family support
- ☐ Self-assessment

Beware of undertaking too much at the start. Be content with quite a little. Allow for accidents. Allow for human nature, especially your own.
ARNOLD BENNETT

Anyone who wants to achieve a dream must stay strong, focused and steady.
ESTEE LAUDER

I do not believe a man can ever leave his business. He ought to think of it by day and dream of it by night.
HENRY FORD

	Is this a Strength or a Weakness? S	W
What supports do you bring to the business?		
• Network of useful contacts ☐ YES ☐ NO		
• Support of your partner/spouse ☐ YES ☐ NO		
• Support of your family and friends ☐ YES ☐ NO		
• Finance € ______________ ☐ YES ☐ NO		
• Other (list)		
What personal characteristics do you bring to the business?		
• Health Good/OK/Bad		
• Endurance Good/OK/Bad		
• Flexibility Good/OK/Bad		
• Creativity Good/OK/Bad		
• Honesty Good/OK/Bad		
• Confidence Good/OK/Bad		
• Ability to handle stress Good/OK/Bad		
• Other (list)		
Good/OK/Bad		
Good/OK/Bad		
Good/OK/Bad		
What time commitments do you bring to the business?		
• Social activities ______ hrs/week		
• Family ______ hrs/week		
• Hobbies ______ hrs/week		
• Other (list)		
______ hrs/week		
______ hrs/week		
______ hrs/week		
Total time commitment outside the business ______ hrs/week		
How much could you reduce these to make time for the business? ______ hrs/week		
What financial commitments do you bring to the business?		
• Household expenses € ________/week		
• Loan repayments € ________/week		
• Savings/pension € ________/week		
• Hobbies/holidays € ________/week		
• Other (list)		
€ ________/week		
€ ________/week		
€ /week		
Total financial commitments € ________/week		
How much could you reduce these to develop the business? € ________/week		

Relationship with family

Your relationship with your family is going to change because of your new business.

You will no longer have a regular income – some months you may have no pay-check at all. Can your family survive on what your spouse/partner earns?

You will be working long hours, through weekends and at times when other people are off. Your working hours will be irregular – nothing to do for periods and then several urgent jobs all to be done at once. You will be under pressure, since you will no longer have a boss to take the final responsibility for everything – you will now be the boss.

You will have more at risk than just your money – your reputation, savings, borrowings, even your ego are also at risk.

All this will affect your relationship with your family. Are you ready?

Why not discuss the situations in the panel with your family? It will help you – and them – understand what lies ahead and how you will react to the choices that may need to be made.

Think positive

Don't be alarmed by this section on Self-assessment. It is merely pointing out the reality of self-employment. If you don't believe it, check with someone you know who has recently started their own business.

And above all – don't let this put you off. There are positive sides to running your own business:

- You can organise your own working hours
- You can do the tasks you like to do and pay other people to do the things you dislike
- You are in control of your own destiny
- You learn a lot
- You deal with all kinds of different situations
- You deal with a lot of different people
- You get a great sense of achievement
- People respect and admire entrepreneurs.

SITUATIONS TO DISCUSS WITH YOUR FAMILY

1. The kids need new shoes. The business needs a new piece of machinery that costs €100. There is only €100 in the bank. Which comes first?
2. A big order comes in (Congratulations!). For the next two weeks, you need to work at least 14 hours every day (including weekends) in order to meet the order. It is also your turn to look after the kids. What are you going to do?
3. You promised your spouse/partner a night out. That night a client insists on meeting you. Which comes first?
4. You have booked a holiday and the whole family is really looking forward to it. Suddenly, the person who was supposed to look after the business while you are away cancels. You cannot find another replacement on such short notice. What happens?
5. A deadline needs to be met. You get ill. Who will take over the running of the business while you are out sick?
6. The business is not going as well as expected. Your business needs an extra loan to survive. Your partner/spouse wants you to quit. What happens?
7. Your business has a cash flow problem. As a result, you have not been able to take out a salary for the past two months and some of your household bills (telephone, gas, electricity) are running behind. How long will that be acceptable to your partner/spouse?

Reproduced from LOOK BEFORE YOU LEAP *by permission of the Department of Enterprise, Trade and Employment and the Department of Social, Community and Family Affairs*

ANSWER THESE QUESTIONS BEFORE MOVING TO THE NEXT SECTION

Do you accept the changes the business is going to bring to your life?

Financial insecurity	☐ YES	☐ NO
Long working hours	☐ YES	☐ NO
Irregular working hours	☐ YES	☐ NO
Pressure	☐ YES	☐ NO
Risk	☐ YES	☐ NO
Relationship with family	☐ YES	☐ NO

Developing & Testing your Idea

OBJECTIVES

- ☐ Understand thinking processes
- ☐ Understand how to develop an idea

What kind of business are you thinking about?

Are you going to manufacture?	☐ YES	☐ NO
Are you starting in retail?	☐ YES	☐ NO
Are you starting in wholesale?	☐ YES	☐ NO
Are you going into import /export?	☐ YES	☐ NO
Are you starting a service?	☐ YES	☐ NO
Are you starting in leisure?	☐ YES	☐ NO

Describe your idea:

Developing your idea to its fullest potential involves creative thinking.

This section provides an overview of some of the most common creative thinking techniques. They will help you to identify new ideas, develop your existing idea and create new opportunities.

Thinking

We all think in two stages. The first stage is to look, simplify what we see, recognise and name what we see, then filter it through our experience and knowledge. In the second stage, we then judge and conclude. Unfortunately, we spend most of our time thinking in the second stage. With creative thinking, most of the time is spent in the first stage of thinking.

Look below. What do you see?

Your answer is probably: "A black dot".

Yes, there is a black dot, but there is also more text, a numbered list, etc. By jumping straight into second stage thinking, you missed all the surroundings.

You did not take time to sit back, relax and look a little bit longer. You rushed for the obvious answer. But, by taking time to step back, you will see more and, by seeing more, you will also see more possibilities. That is the idea behind creative thinking.

As an entrepreneur, it is important to spend time looking at your idea and trying to come up with new possibilities, extra features, alternatives, etc. This will not only give you an even better understanding of your idea, it will improve it and will make you more competitive. This kind of creative thinking should be an ongoing process to keep your business competitive.

Steps in creative thinking

1. *Move away:*
- Widen perception
- Question assumptions (Why not? What if?)
- Break the rules
- Make associations.

2. *Bring yourself back into the real world:*
- Evaluate
- Judge
- Tried before?
- Will it work?

Technique 1: Brainstorming

1. Get a group together (Four people is the minimum, preferably more)
2. Define a problem and discuss it
3. Redefine the problem
4. Practice run to warm up the mind – How many uses can you find for a paperclip?
5. Brainstorming
   > Aim to generate as many ideas as possible
   > All ideas are acceptable
   > The crazier the idea the better
6. Select the craziest idea and brainstorm that idea for a while.

One sound idea is all you need to achieve success.
NAPOLEON HILL

I work from details outward to the general and I don't stop developing big ideas until I have worked out the minutest detail.
RAY KROC, McDonalds

We haven't got the money, so we've got to think.
LORD RUTHERFORD

Attempt the impossible to improve your work.
BETTE DAVIS

Why should it be done at all? Why should it be done now? Why should it be done that way?
HERBERT BAYARD SWOPE

Technique 2: Attribute listing
This technique is best used when you are thinking of adapting or developing an existing product or service.

Take the particular product and list its attributes: For example, shape, size, design, materials, colour, functions and cost. Then take each attribute and try to find as many alternatives to it as possible.

Technique 3: Who, what, where, when, why, how
Tease out different perspectives and ideas with any product, service, problem or situation, using the six prompts above.

Technique 4: Assumption-smashing
List the assumptions of the problem or idea, then explore what happens if you drop assumptions. For example, why assume that this product should be made of plastic. What if it were made of something else?

Technique 5: Discontinuity
Disrupt your own patterns:

- Programme interruptions in your day
- Do something you have never done before or read something you would not normally read
- Watch some different TV programmes.

Putting it into practice
Developing an idea is only part of the battle. The idea must also work in practice. Therefore, it is important to ask yourself some critical questions about your business and your product/service. Write your answers below.

Copy this page and the next page before answering the questions, so that you can use these pages to develop and test other ideas later.

	Is this a Strength or a Weakness? S	W
1. Why is it a good idea?		
2. On what assumptions is that opinion based?		
3. How can you prove that those assumptions are correct?		
4. What types of customer will be interested in your product/service?		
5. Why?		
6. List four reasons why the idea may **not** work: • • • •		

	Is this a Strength or a Weakness? S	W
7. List four reasons why your idea **will** work:		
8. What is different about this idea from others already in the market-place?		
9. Why are those differences important?		
10. What if ... you changed the product/service in some way?		
Make a list of people you know who might be able to help you with the research or whose opinion you trust. Ask their opinion about your idea. Ask them to be critical and honest. **Name** **Opinion**		

Market Research

Marketing is about keeping your customers central in your thinking, behaviour and planning. To do that, you need a combination of information, vision and creativity. One of the techniques to get information is market research, which has three functions:

- **Informing** – Consumer behaviour, market trends, developments abroad
- **Evaluating** – Are goals achieved?
- **Experimenting** – Testing markets or products.

Why do market research?

Market research is the core of your business and business plan. It is important that you:

- Are aware of market developments
- Find out for yourself whether you can approach people at all kinds of levels
- Find out whether you can sell (if not, you will have to find someone to do it for you)
- Find out whether there is a market for your product/service, how big it is, how it can be reached, etc
- Are well prepared before you commit funds (your own or other people's) to your business
- Are able to show potential financiers that you have taken the trouble to gather the necessary information
- Are able to show that you know your stuff.

But the overwhelming reason for doing market research is to prove the commercial viability of your project.

Making your market research practical

Market research is often considered by entrepreneurs to be too theoretical to be bothered with. That's both dangerous and wrong: Dangerous because without market research you may start a business for which there is no demand; wrong because market research can be very practical.

Practical market research includes things as simple as:

- Counting the cars on your competitors' parking lot (to tell you how many customers they get and how well-off they are)
- Counting the people passing by the premises you are planning to rent (big stores like Marks & Spencer sometimes do this for months before deciding on a location for a new shop)
- Counting the waste bags outside the backdoor of a restaurant (to give you some idea of the volume of their business)
- Checking the number of trucks delivering supplies to competitors (on the basis that level of their purchases gives you an insight into their sales)
- Counting the numbers of customers walking into a competitors' office/shop
- Knocking on every door in a housing estate in which you are planning to open an outlet (to ask whether there is a demand, at what price, etc.)
- Collecting all your competitors' brochures and price lists (to find out what they are offering and at what prices)
- Checking where your competitors advertise and how big an advertisement they take.

Note that market research should be an ongoing process. It should not stop after the business has started but should become an integral part of your business.

Sources of information

When you are looking for information as part of your desk research, there is an almost endless list of sources of information, including:

- Your local library
- Central Statistics Office (**www.cso.ie**)
- Enterprise Ireland (**www.enterprise-ireland.com**)
- Government Publications Office
- Government Departments and State agencies (**www.irlgov.ie/www.basis.ie**)
- Business magazines and trade journals
- Newspapers – National and local
- Banks
- Enterprise Link – 1850 35 33 33
- Business Innovation Centres
- City & County Enterprise Boards (**www.enterpriseboards.ie**)
- Area Partnership Companies
- LEADER companies
- Professional associations/trade bodies
- Telephone directories

OBJECTIVES

- ☐ Understand market research techniques
- ☐ Apply them to own product/service

Three-quarters of all entrepreneurs start up without doing any market testing to establish whether there is demand for their product/service. Only three in ten carry out market research to determine whether a market exists for their business in the first place. Fewer still – one in five – draw up a detailed customer profile to build up knowledge about their prospective customers and their buying habits. Knowing who your customers are and why they will buy from you, rather than from your competitors, should be a crucial part in deciding how a business will fit into the market and whether it is likely to succeed. Those that do not assess their long-term market potential and overall competitive stance may risk early closure or failure.
BARCLAYS BANK

- Trade exhibitions and conferences
- Competitors' catalogues, brochures and price lists
- Professional advisers (accountants, solicitors, consultants)
- Friends
- Chambers of Commerce (**www.chambersireland.ie**)
- Customers (existing or potential)
- Local authorities
- Internet (use the examples above or the **www.startingabusinessinireland.com** website).

Many of these sources will give you information free of charge, or at very little cost. Recognise their help where you can – even with just a "Thank You". You'll be amazed at how much it will be appreciated – and how much you will benefit when you go back for more information. Remember:

- Seek information from a variety of sources, not just from the "experts"
- Get feedback from a variety of sources
- Let people play "the devil's advocate" and argue against you
- Ask "stupid" questions – You will get some very clever answers
- Look around for yourself – Don't assume anything.

Doing your own market research
Your market research should be structured to make sure you collect all the information you need. The structure depends on your product/service, your budget and the time you have available but ought to cover:

1. **Problem definition** – What do you want to find out?
2. **Desk research** – Consulting directories, magazines and newspapers and the Internet
3. **Pre-study field research** – A first test to see whether you are on the right track
4. **Concept questionnaire** – Your initial questions
5. **Testing the questionnaire** – Make sure that the questions can be understood and will give you useful answers
6. **Field research** – Asking the questions
7. **Data processing** – Processing the results
8. **Reporting** – The final stage.

Research techniques
There are many ways of researching your idea, including:

- **Qualitative/quantitative** – Quantitative involves researching figures and percentages; qualitative means researching opinions, reasons why, etc.
- **Consumer/distribution/industrial** – You can research the end user of your product, how the product is brought to the end user, or how the product is made
- **Questionnaires/observation** – You can ask people personally, by mail, by phone, or observe their behaviour (which may be different from what they tell you)
- **Ad hoc/panel** – You can do once-off research, or research a panel for a longer period of time
- **Group/single** – You can interview a group of people or every person in your sample individually
- **Open/half open/closed questions** – You can ask open questions (no control over the answer), half-open questions (give different options), or closed questions (yes or no).

The starting point is to define the problem – What do you want to know? Write it down in the space below.

When you start your desk research, collect informa-

I expect my market research to tell me:

MARKET RESEARCH: A CASE STUDY

A Japanese company had plans to build a paper factory in Georgia, USA. They thought it would be useful to know the production capacity of the local competitors. But these figures were not readily available. So the company started counting the number of train wagons leaving the factories. This gave them the volume of production. Although the wagons were closed, the residue left on the rails after the train had passed told them what the train was carrying. Volume multiplied by content gave them the production capacity of the competitors' plant.

tion from as many sources as possible. List in the panel opposite the sources of information you intend to use.

After you have completed the desk research (and only then), start designing a questionnaire for the target customer groups you have identified. This will need some research in the target groups itself (location, availability, language, level of questioning, perceptions, etc.).

Choose research techniques from the following:

- Group discussion
- Questionnaire by direct mail
- Direct questioning
- Questioning by phone.

Based on the techniques you have chosen, design a questionnaire. Go back to basics. Ask yourself: Who? What? Why? When? Where?

Make a list of questions you want to ask in the second panel. Copy the panel so that you can use it again.

Select only the most relevant questions. Depending on the approach you plan to take, you may need to take the length of the questionnaire into consideration. If the questionnaire is too long, people won't want to answer it – especially in the case of direct mail or questioning over the phone. Then test the questionnaire with a small group of people to make sure that it is clear and user-friendly. If you get a poor response here, redesign your questionnaire and test it again.

When the questionnaire is complete, you are ready to do the field research. If your aim is to get quantitative information, the number of people questioned should be sufficient to be statistically valid (minimum between 500 and 1,000).

Note that it's quite usual to get a very low response rate to questionnaires, hence the need for large numbers and some creativity.

Reporting results

It is useful to write a report on the results of your desk and field research.

When writing the report, it is important to bear in mind who it is written for.

Make sure you include:

- Definition of the problem
- Description of techniques used
- Results of research
- Reliability of the information (sources of information, validity of statistics)
- Copy of questionnaire.

Remember that the more time spent on this market research phase before you start your business, the more it will benefit you in future stages. What you are doing here is, in effect, laying the basis for your Business Plan.

POTENTIAL SOURCES OF INFORMATION

QUESTIONNAIRE DESIGN: QUESTIONS TO ASK

MARKET RESEARCH CHECKLIST

Does your market research cover:

- Market size ☐ YES ☐ NO
- Market structure ☐ YES ☐ NO
- Market trends ☐ YES ☐ NO
- Market potential ☐ YES ☐ NO
- Market share ☐ YES ☐ NO
- Competitor activity ☐ YES ☐ NO
- Competitor prices ☐ YES ☐ NO
- Competitor products/services ☐ YES ☐ NO
- User attitudes/behaviour ☐ YES ☐ NO
- Government factors ☐ YES ☐ NO
- Economic factors ☐ YES ☐ NO
- Demographic factors ☐ YES ☐ NO

Identifying Future Trends

OBJECTIVES

- ☐ Be aware of existing trends
- ☐ Consider future trends

You have to look where the (hockey) puck is going to be, not where it is now.
WAYNE GRETSKY

If you want to be in business for a long time, you need to develop a vision of the future and the place of your business in that future. You need not only to be aware of the trends in your market area (technology, competition, trade regulations, etc.) but also have a sense of the general direction in which the world is developing. Questions to consider are: What will Ireland look like in 2010 – or even in 2025? Where will your business fit? What should you be doing to prepare?

Consider these current trends:

- To protect themselves from crime and hostility, people are retreating into the safe environment of the home
- People want to do exciting things but want to be safe – emotional escape in a risk-free fantasy world. Consider changes in food (exotic meals), shopping (fun shopping), interactive movies and games, etc.
- Luxuries are no longer big purchases but include "rewards" like handmade chocolates, week-end breaks and expensive restaurant meals. Spending patterns are becoming less predictable
- Technology allows products to be focused on very specific needs
- People are less concerned about job security and more willing to change jobs several times during their careers to pursue new opportunities
- Consumers are more health-conscious and critical about the behaviour of companies and the quality of products and services
- People have higher expectations of life. They want to achieve more – often materially
- Time is a major factor in most people's lives. They feel a need to cram activities into the day (reading, movie, theatre, socialising, being a good parent or partner, do a course, make a career, etc.)
- Older people stay healthier much longer and age does not dictate the pace of life any more. Old people act young
- Society and business is more and more influenced by women.

Read science fiction. Much of what was written as science fiction 20 or 30 years ago is now part of our everyday lives.

Train yourself to watch trends. Look for:

- Changes in food, new products, trendy restaurants
- The introduction of new products (failures and successes)
- Changes in family structure
- Changes in demographics
- Changes in work environment
- Changes in environmental behaviour
- Whether there is optimism or pessimism in relation to the economy
- New cultures
- New words (Internet Nanny, search engine, dinky)
- Science fiction becoming real.

Watch for the balancing impact of the Action = Reaction principle. For example:

Action

- Rapid change of technology, increasing role of computers
- Globalisation of markets due to easy access of information and technology
- Re-engineering, jobs replaced or supported by use of new technology
- Multi-cultural influences due to all information available

Reaction

- Back to nature in response to technology
- Back to old values/culture as those things are familiar to us
- Back into our homes to protect us from the outside (hostile) world
- Filters on information (for example, the Internet Nanny)
- Simplifying information
- Escapism in movies, computer games, adventure trips, etc.
- To balance the stress, "perks" to cheer us (massage, fancy dinners, clothes, etc.).

Some other things to think about:

- The use of drugs for specific purposes (memory enhancers, warfare)
- Development of genetic engineering
- The role of computers and telecommunications in our society
- Nano-technology (machines the size of an atom).

What are your predictions for Ireland in 2010 and 2025? Write them down. Where does your business fit within this?

Feasibility Study Grants

Researching your idea before starting your business may not cost you much in cash terms but during this time you may not be earning anything. However, you may be eligible for a feasibility study grant from your local Enterprise Board, which may cover up to 50% of the agreed cost of the research stage up to a maximum of □6,000. The actual amount is dependent on the needs shown in your Business Plan or application.

Getting a grant

Your first step should be to check with your local Enterprise Board – you can access a central list of their websites at **www.enterpriseboards.ie**.

Generally, to be eligible for a feasibility grant, you must:

- Be an individual, community group or company
- Be investigating a new manufacturing product or process (CEBs fund services)
- Apply before beginning the study
- Carry out most of the work in the State
- Not repeat work that has previously produced negative results (whether carried out by you or someone else)
- Not seek aid from any other State body for the cost of this project.

If your study is in an area already known to have over-capacity, you are unlikely to be given a grant. Since these areas obviously change from time to time, check before starting work on your application.

Eligible studies currently include:

- Market research
- Preparation of costings and financial projections
- Assessment of manufacturing processes
- Assessment of suitable plant and equipment, etc.
- Sourcing of raw materials
- Negotiation with potential joint-venture partners
- Negotiation of manufacturing licences.

The application process involves providing much of the information that you would include in your Business Plan (see the next chapter, **STEADY**), an explanation of the work involved in the feasibility study, and the costs involved. Application forms vary but set out the information required.

Success

If your application is accepted (this can take up to two months during which you cannot proceed with your study), you will receive a letter of offer.

Read this letter carefully. Query any parts of it that you do not understand. It will be against this document, not your original application, that your expenditure will be checked before any grants are paid out to you. Make sure that you know what the terms of the grant-aid are and keep to them. Be sure to sign and return the letter of offer within the time-period indicated – otherwise the grant-aid may lapse.

You can then – **and only then** – start work on the study. You must not start before you get grant approval.

Claiming the grant

When the study is completed, you must submit a report and a note of your costs, including receipts. Generally, grants from Enterprise Boards are conditional on tax clearance. Form TC1 should be completed when applying to the Revenue Commissioners for a Tax Clearance Certificate. You will be given a form by the CEB, if appropriate. Note that feasibility grants, like other grants from Enterprise Boards, are not taxable as income.

Making sure you get a grant

The feasibility study grant is an important tool in developing your business. If you are eligible, it is definitely worth applying, since it spreads some of the costs of the research stage.

Like all State grants, the feasibility grant scheme is there to help winning projects to achieve success. If your project is badly researched, poorly presented and lacks verifiable evidence that it could be a winner, your grant application is likely to be unsuccessful.

Aim at a well-organised application that has as much information as possible. Ensure that the commercial potential of your project is clearly researched and presented. If possible, discuss your application with an adviser before making a formal application.

OBJECTIVES

- ☐ Understand purpose of Feasibility Grants
- ☐ Identify sources of Feasibility Grants
- ☐ Understand method of application

Training for Entrepreneurs

OBJECTIVES
- ☐ Be aware of different training needs at different stages
- ☐ Be able to prepare a training needs analysis
- ☐ Identify sources of training for entrepreneurs

Potential entrepreneurs need (or may need, depending on their circumstances) three kinds of training:
- Training in the specific stages/techniques of starting up a business
- Training in specific skills useful for a start-up, which they lack from previous experience
- Training in specific skills useful once the business is up and running, which they lack from previous experience.

Few people have the first, since training for start-ups is not on many school or college curricula. This guide, and many of the books and websites listed in **Appendix 2, Further Information**, attempt to fill the gap. There are also "Start Your Own Business" courses available from a variety of sources to meet this need.

Training Needs Analysis

Training in other skills, whether pre- or post-start-up, requires a Training Needs Analysis. This simply means that you list your present skills, compare them against the skills you believe that you need and plan to do something about the difference.

Answer the questions on the next page to prepare your own Training Needs Analysis. Your business partners should also complete this analysis – copy the page before you complete it so that they can use it too.

Sources of training

There are many organisations that provide training in specific subject areas – however, only a few provide a general training in entrepreneurship or how to start a business.

Organisations to contact for information on training (especially in relation to start-ups) available to entrepreneurs include:
- Enterprise Link (1850 35 33 33)
- FÁS (**www.fas.ie**)
- Your local City/County Enterprise Board or Area Partnership Company
- Project Development Centre (**www.pdc.ie**)
- Enterprise Platform Programmes, including: NEEPP, Regional Development Centre, Dundalk Institute of Technology, SEEPP, Waterford Institute of Technology, M50 EPP, Institute of Technology Tallaght; Genesis, Cork Institute of Technology.

Note that courses vary widely in their quality. Talk to people who have already taken the course you are considering and get their opinions. Always insist on quality in your training. Remember that the way you are trained will directly affect the quality of your business.

Remember also that you cannot know everything. Whatever your own background, you will have to buy in some expertise – from accountants, solicitors, computer experts or consultants. But to give yourself a general understanding of a range of topics, even if the detailed work is done by someone else, attend courses outside your own immediate area of inter-

TRAINING CHECKLIST

Before you commit to a course, check:
- **Time necessary to do the course versus time available** – There is no point starting a course if you don't have the time to do it
- **Entry level** – Have you got the necessary educational background/practical experience to benefit from the course?
- **Background of participants** – Who are the other people on the course? Will their needs be different from yours (and prevent you from achieving your training objectives)?
- **Course programme** – What does it cover? Is this relevant to you?
- **Costs** – How much does the course cost? Are there grants available? Do you qualify for a grant?
- **Available back-up support** – What happens if you have problems during the course? Afterwards?
- **Accreditation** – Is the course officially recognised? Do you get a certificate on completion?

TRAINING NEEDS ANALYSIS

1. List your skills: Of use to the business?

____________________	☐ YES ☐ NO
____________________	☐ YES ☐ NO
____________________	☐ YES ☐ NO
____________________	☐ YES ☐ NO
____________________	☐ YES ☐ NO

2. List your practical experience: Of use to the business?

____________________	☐ YES ☐ NO
____________________	☐ YES ☐ NO
____________________	☐ YES ☐ NO
____________________	☐ YES ☐ NO
____________________	☐ YES ☐ NO

3. What skills do you think you need to start your business?
   •
   •
   •
   •
   •

4. What skills do you think you need to run your business, once it has been started?
   •
   •
   •
   •
   •

5. What skills are you missing?
   •
   •
   •
   •
   •

6. What existing skills would you like to improve?
   •
   •
   •
   •

7. What training do you need?
   •
   •
   •
   •

START-UP ALTERNATIVES

OBJECTIVES

- ☐ Be aware of alternatives to start-up
- ☐ Understand risks of buying an existing business
- ☐ Understand how to evaluate an existing business for sale
- ☐ Understand franchise concept and advantages and disadvantages
- ☐ Understand how to evaluate a potential franchise
- ☐ Understand network marketing concept
- ☐ Understand how to evaluate a potential NM business

Never acquire a business you don't know how to run.
ROBERT W JOHNSON

If you want to run your own business, there are alternatives to starting it yourself. You can buy an existing business, or buy into a franchise or get involved in network marketing.

Buying an existing business

Buying an existing business is a sensible alternative to starting a business from scratch.

The main advantage is that you acquire a business with existing products, markets, customers, staff, etc. and do not have to build it all up yourself. The disadvantage is that you have to commit a considerable investment to acquire the business and may have to add to this to develop the business further. You also need to know why the business is being sold – it may be that the business is in trouble or is about to face major competition.

Buying an existing business needs a methodical approach. Insist on both historical figures (preferably three years or more) and future projections. Have the information checked over by a person you trust or hire an expert. Do your own SWOT (Strengths/Weaknesses/Opportunities/Threats) analysis, get feedback from clients, suppliers and competitors. Particular areas to look into are:

- Financial data
- Management and key personnel
- Recent investments (or lack of)
- Product development/improvements (or lack of)
- Innovation (or lack of)
- Use of modern technology (or lack of)
- Hidden liabilities.

You need to know how much more money you will have to put into the business, on top of the purchase price, and how risky is this investment. How long will it take to recover your investment?

When you think you are ready to buy a specific business, take out a sheet of paper and write down your answers to the questions in the checklist. Only buy when you are sure that the business is right for you. Above all, make sure that you take professional advice before committing to buying.

And remember, buying the business is only the beginning. You still need to work through the rest of this guide to develop a business plan for your "new" business – while you run it on a day-to-day basis.

BUYING A BUSINESS

1. Why is the business for sale?
2. What is the business of the company?
3. How is it organised?
4. What is its position in the market-place?
5. What are its future prospects?
6. Is there a current Business Plan? What does it tell me?
7. Does the culture of the company fit my style of working and managing?
8. How dependent is the company on the current owner/managers?

Buying into a franchise

Across the world, there are over 3,000 franchised businesses, covering almost every industry. Some are international brands like McDonald's; others are national brands like O'Brien's Sandwich bars; a few are much smaller, local opportunities.

When you buy a franchise, you are buying the right to use a specific trademark or business concept, which has been tested in practice. The chief benefit is that you are able to capitalize on the business format, trade name, and support system provided by the franchisor.

You pay an initial upfront fee for the rights to open your franchise. This fee may include things like training costs, start-up promotional costs, stock, equipment/fixtures (you may be required to purchase or lease specific equipment and fixtures from the franchisor), and any other costs that are necessary to start your business. Usually, the franchisor helps you during start-up, with selection of premises and equipment, a business plan, raising finance, and publicity. In return, the franchisor supplies a detailed operational manual, which sets out exactly how you should run the franchise.

You also have to pay ongoing fees to maintain the rights to your franchise. Most franchisors charge a royalty fee – typically a percentage of your gross sales, ranging from 1% to as much as 15%. It is also usual for franchisees to pay into a co-operative national advertising and promotional fund that

BUYING INTO A FRANCHISE CHECKLIST

1. Does the franchisor have a track record of success? ☐ YES ☐ NO
2. What will it cost me? Once current income? ☐ Twice current income? ☐ More? ☐
3. How much can I expect to make? Once current income? ☐ Twice current income? ☐ More? ☐
4. Will the franchisor give me an exclusive territory for the period of the franchise? ☐ YES ☐ NO
5. Will the franchisor assist me with:
   a) A management training programme? ☐ YES ☐ NO
   b) An employee training programme? ☐ YES ☐ NO
   c) A PR and advertising programme? ☐ YES ☐ NO
   d) Raising capital ☐ YES ☐ NO
   e) Borrowing money? ☐ YES ☐ NO
   f) Merchandising ideas? ☐ YES ☐ NO
   g) Finding a suitable location? ☐ YES ☐ NO
6. How long has the franchisor been operating? Less than 3 years? ☐ More than 3 years? ☐
7. Has the franchisor a reputation for fair dealing with its franchisees? ☐ YES ☐ NO
8. Has the franchisor enough finance itself to carry out its plans? ☐ YES ☐ NO
9. What happens when I want to leave/give up? Can I sell the business to anyone I like? ☐ YES ☐ NO
10. Has the franchiser shown me any certified figures indicating exact net profits of one or more franchisees, which I have personally checked with them? ☐ YES ☐ NO
11. Has the franchisor investigated me carefully enough to be sure that I can successfully operate at a profit to both of us? ☐ YES ☐ NO
12. Is my lawyer completely happy with the franchise contract? ☐ YES ☐ NO

Adapted from *Making Money* magazine by permission

benefits all franchises through increased exposure to the common trade name.

The advantages of buying a franchise are:

- Franchises traditionally have a much lower failure rate than other start-up businesses, since most of the problems have been discovered and solved
- You get a complete package, including trademarks, easy access to an established product, proven marketing method, equipment, stock, etc.
- You have the buying power of the entire network, which can help you against larger competitors
- Many franchisors provide financial and accounting systems, on-going training and support, research and development, sales and marketing assistance, planning and forecasting, stock management, etc.
- Some franchisors help with site selection, making sure that your business is located in an area where it can thrive
- You benefit from national or regional advertising and promotional campaigns by the franchisor.

But, as in anything, there are disadvantages, too. These can include:

- The essence of a franchise - buying and operating a proven concept - can make it seem like you're more of a manager than a boss
- It can take a good deal of cash to open and operate a franchise. Upfront costs can be significant, and ongoing royalty fees may impact on your cash flow
- Just as a franchisor's reputation can benefit you, the franchisor's problems are also your problems
- Your franchise agreement is a binding contract, and can be quite restrictive.

Although you own the business, its operation is governed by the terms of the franchise agreement. Therefore, you should have your lawyer and/or accountant review the franchise agreement before signing anything. Before you decide on a franchise, talk to other franchisees. Ask about their experiences. Would they do it again? What would they do differently? Listen carefully to their answers.

In looking for a franchise, check out **www.franchisedirect.com**.

Network marketing

As with franchising, everyone is familiar with network marketing, even though they may not know it by that name. Examples of network marketing businesses are:

- **Tupperware** – Household storage items
- **Dorling Kindersley** – Books
- **Amway** – Household products.

Network marketing skips the wholesalers and retailers and delivers a product directly from the producer to the customer. This means quick delivery, good service and that the product is sold by people who know the product since they use it themselves.

Because there are no intermediaries between producer and customer, a large margin is available to pay the distribution chain. Distributors earn this margin by selling direct to customers and also from a royalty on sales made by other distributors whom they have introduced.

The process is based on the idea that more gets sold by a lot of people each selling a little than by a small number of highly-effective salespeople on their own.

Because all distributors are self-employed and self-motivated, only the successful survive. Within the network, back-up is available to provide the members of the network with training, workshops, information materials, manuals, etc.

Unfairly, network marketing has a poor reputation – in part caused by its similarity in a number of respects to the now universally outlawed "pyramid selling".

Network marketing, according to one researcher, is not a "get rich quick" scheme – he says it is a "get rich scheme for those prepared to perform consistent, persistent, productive, income-producing activities".

Even though it can be done part-time while you work at another job or in the home (and this is one of its key attractions), network marketing needs a lot of time and commitment not only in selling but also in learning about the products, in training in how to do the presentations, in developing and maintaining a network, delivering the products, book-keeping and administration, etc.

NETWORK MARKETING CHECKLIST

1. Can I do it part-time? ☐ YES ☐ NO
2. How good are the products? Very good? ☐ Good? ☐ Just OK? ☐
3. What customer guarantees does the company give? No quibble? ☐ Money back? ☐ None? ☐
4. What is the company's track record, history, management, financial standing, etc? Very good? ☐ Good? ☐ Just OK? ☐
5. What investment must I make at the start?€ ________
6. How much do I have to sell to break-even?€ ________
7. How much time do I need to invest? ________
8. Am I prepared to do sales presentations for people I know well and recruit them for the network? ☐ YES ☐ NO
9. Have I met and discussed the scheme with existing distributors? ☐ YES ☐ NO
10. Do I believe the income figures they quote? ☐ YES ☐ NO

Therefore, it's just as important to write a Business Plan (see the next chapter, **STEADY**) for a network marketing business as for any other business idea.

Other alternatives

Other alternatives to the traditional start-up include:

- Inheriting a business from a relative – Nice, but you still have to run it afterwards
- Management or employee buy-outs – Where a group of employees buys the business they work in from the owners.

In every case, there is a need for planning. However you arrive at your chosen business, if it is to be successful, you need to work through this guide and develop your business plan. That's what the next chapter is all about.

Introduction

The Business Plan is the most misunderstood element of starting a business. Too many people believe it needs only to be prepared when you are looking to raise finance. That's not true. Certainly, it is nearly impossible to raise finance without a Business Plan but the real value of the Business Plan comes in the thinking about your business that is necessary before you can write down what you plan to do. The Business Plan is the core of this chapter – and of starting a business.

Chapter structure

This is the longest and most detailed chapter in this guide. Following on from the first chapter, **READY**, it takes you through all the steps involved in starting your own business.

In summary, these are:

- Developing a Mission Statement
- Developing a strategy
- Marketing
- Products and production
- Staff
- Deciding on a legal structure
- Taxation
- Accounting
- Premises
- Finance
- Operating Budget
- Cash-flow planning
- Sources of assistance
- The Business Plan.

Your Mission Statement and strategy set the direction for your new business. Putting the strategy into action involves a wide range of topics including marketing, staff, financing, budgeting and cashflow, which are covered in the following sections. Sources of assistance – grants, advice, training, etc – are covered next. Finally, this chapter takes you through the business planning process and helps you complete a Business Plan which will help you manage your business as well as raise finance.

Everything you have learnt in this chapter is drawn together in the Business Plan. This is the real aim of the chapter – to help work your way through the thinking you need to do to develop a clear business plan. The thinking is the main thing; writing the business plan is the last 10%. But, unless you go that last 10%, you haven't finished the job.

Some other topics, such as quality, environmental and health and safety issues, are more appropriate to the on-going business and are covered in the next chapter, **GO**.

Key Questions

The Key Questions in the panel below are designed to focus your thoughts as you read this chapter.

Think through your answers to these questions before you start to read the chapter. Then come back and write your answers in the spaces provided before moving on to the next chapter.

KEY QUESTIONS

1. Have you developed a strategy for your business? ☐ YES ☐ NO
2. Have you developed a customer profile? ☐ YES ☐ NO
3. Do you know how your business stands in the market-place? ☐ YES ☐ NO
4. Have you developed a promotion strategy? ☐ YES ☐ NO
5. Have you identified the taxes for which you must register? ☐ YES ☐ NO
6. Have you decided how to organise your accounting? ☐ YES ☐ NO
7. Have you decided on a legal structure for your business? ☐ YES ☐ NO
8. Do you know how much money you need to start your business? ☐ YES ☐ NO
9. Have you identified sources of finance to meet this need? ☐ YES ☐ NO
10. Do you know your break-even point? ☐ YES ☐ NO
11. Have you prepared an Operating Budget? ☐ YES ☐ NO
12. Have you prepared a Cash-flow? ☐ YES ☐ NO
13. Have you prepared a Business Plan? ☐ YES ☐ NO

OBJECTIVES

- ☐ Understand the steps in a business start-up
- ☐ Understand the importance of business planning
- ☐ Develop a business plan

Success, as I see it, is a result not a goal.
GUSTAVE FLAUBERT

If we have a formula for growth, it has been: Start with the best; Learn from the best; Expand slowly and solidify our position; Then horizontally diversify our experience.
MARK McCORMACK, International Management Group

The only place success comes before work is in a dictionary.
ANON

Developing a Mission Statement

OBJECTIVES
- ☐ Understand the importance of a Mission Statement
- ☐ Draft a Mission Statement

Ultimately, vision gets translated into sales and profit, growth and return on investment, but the numbers come **after** the vision. In the old-style companies, the numbers **are** the vision.
JOHN NAISBITT, Futurist

The Mission Statement sets out:
- The reason why the business exists
- What the company stands for
- What the company is about.

It is important to think carefully about the mission statement because it defines the core of the business and it strongly influences the direction of the company. It determines the strategy of the business.

For example, the mission statement determines whether a company sees itself as selling computer games or providing entertainment. Selling computer games means that the business will not develop books or videos. But if the mission is broadened to include entertainment, the company can diversify into other activities.

This is not to say that you should make your mission statement very broad – if it is too broad, you have no direction at all. Think of it as a guide to a journey. Unless you have some idea of where you want to go, you may never get there.

The mission statement communicates the philosophy of the company in relation to:
- The environment
- Business ethics – The way in which you do business
- People – Staff and customers
- The community within which it is based.

It can be used both internally (your staff and suppliers) and externally (your customers and the community you are working within). Trends show that customers are starting to take mission statements seriously and expect businesses to develop a social conscience.

For a clear example of a company that is run according to its Mission Statement, look at Body Shop which has built an international business on a very simple and clear set of values.

Developing your own Mission Statement

Start developing a Mission Statement for your own business by answering these questions. Write your answers in the spaces provided.

Why does your company exist?

What aims (other than profit) does it have?

Draft a mission statement for your business:

Copy this Mission Statement into your Business Plan, page 117.

Developing a Strategy

Developing a strategy for your business is as simple (or as complicated) as answering these questions:

- Where are we now?
- Where do we want to go?
- How and when will we get there?

Before deciding on your business' direction and course, you need to analyse the information already available to you and to collect more (see "Market Research" in **READY**). Do a SWOT analysis on the results of your market research, identifying each result as a:

- Strength
- Weakness
- Opportunity
- Threat.

Write your analysis in the panel below. Next, re-read the section "Identifying Future Trends" in **READY**. Start developing a vision of the future and a place for your business in that future.

To begin to develop a strategy, consider :

- **Focus** – On what?
- **Growth, decline, stabilisation** – How is your market developing?
- **Maintain existing markets** – Will this be enough?
- **Life cycle of the product** – What stage are you at?
- **New markets** – Where? At what cost?
- **New products** – How?
- **National or international** – What are your ambitions?
- **Broad market or niche market** – Where are you aiming?
- **Innovation** – What part will it play?
- **Small steps or big steps** – Which are you most comfortable with?
- **Mission Statement** – What is your business' Mission Statement? How does this determine your strategy?

Ask yourself the questions on the next pages. Write the answers in the space provided.

OBJECTIVES

☐ Understand strategy

☐ Develop a strategy for your business

Long range planning does not deal with future decisions, but with the future of present decisions.

PETER F DRUCKER, Management author

MARKET RESEARCH RESULTS

- ☐ S ☐ W ☐ O ☐ T
- ☐ S ☐ W ☐ O ☐ T
- ☐ S ☐ W ☐ O ☐ T
- ☐ S ☐ W ☐ O ☐ T
- ☐ S ☐ W ☐ O ☐ T
- ☐ S ☐ W ☐ O ☐ T
- ☐ S ☐ W ☐ O ☐ T
- ☐ S ☐ W ☐ O ☐ T
- ☐ S ☐ W ☐ O ☐ T
- ☐ S ☐ W ☐ O ☐ T
- ☐ S ☐ W ☐ O ☐ T
- ☐ S ☐ W ☐ O ☐ T

What do you want to achieve with your business?
Personal:

Business:

Summarise the trends in relation to your business:
Use of technology:

Copy the answers to these questions into your Business Plan, page 117.

Customer needs:

Competition:

What are the threats facing your business?

What are the opportunities available to your business?

What are your targets for year 1?

Copy the answers to these questions into your Business Plan, page 117.

What are your targets for year 5?

What are your targets for year 10?

How are you going to achieve the targets in year 1?

How are you going to achieve the targets for year 5?

How are you going to achieve the targets for year 10?

By answering the questions above, you have actually developed your strategy. You have set yourself targets and found ways of achieving them. You have probably found that you could be very specific about the first year targets, but that 5-year and 10-year targets are more aspirational. But don't be misled by the simplicity of this approach to strategic planning. It looks simple. Maybe you found it simple to do. But it is critical to your business. Every year, you should set yourself targets for the next year, keeping in mind your 10-year plan, which sets out the direction of your business. Compare it to a road map. The 10-year plan is the destination; the 1-year plans are the turns (right, left, straight, short cut, scenic route, stop-over, break for coffee, etc.). The direction you have decided needs to be checked on a regular basis to see whether your plans need adjustment.

INNOVATION

OBJECTIVES

- ☐ Understand the importance of innovation
- ☐ Understand the role of an information system
- ☐ Understand how to implement innovation in your business

Business has only two functions: marketing and innovation.
PETER F DRUCKER, Management author

You see how things are, and you ask "Why?"
But I dream of things that do not yet exist, and I ask "Why not?"
GEORGE BERNARD SHAW

Innovation is one of the key success factors in any modern business. The importance of innovation in the future is going to be even more significant due to constant change in technology, globalisation and the increased availability of information from the Internet, TV, computer, telephone and fax. To keep up with increasing competition, it is essential to be aware of those changes and constantly adjust the business to take account of new developments.

The management guru, Peter Drucker, defined innovation as "the purposeful and systematic search for change and opportunity". Thus, the techniques described in "Developing & Testing Your Idea" in **READY** are just as applicable in the management of innovation, to provide structure and continuity.

To manage innovation, it is important to create a constant flow of information through the business. To do this, you need to set up an information system. This will bring together feedback from within your own business (for example, comments from your staff, clients and suppliers – all of which links with quality management) and combines it with outside sources such as competitors, newspapers, trade magazines, etc. To prevent any restriction of vision, the information sources should be widespread and some should be unrelated to business – to help you keep an open mind.

Answering the following questions in the space provided will help you to develop your information system. Then go to the next section, "Competitiveness" and complete the "Information System Checklist".

Internal

How are you going to organise a system of feedback from your staff, clients and suppliers?

What information/comments should you be looking for?

External

What information sources are you going to access to keep informed?

Innovation should be part of the strategic plan (call it your "innovation plan" to get the message across), as well as being part of on-going product development. Within innovation, there are three main directions:

- **Adjustment** – These are small changes that do not alter the function of the product or service
- **Modification** – Maintaining the technology used but changing the function (from clock to watch)
- **Renovation** – Same function, different technology (from vinyl records to CDs).

You must decide which of these directions (or what combination) is right for your business.

Organising innovation

Innovation does not happen; it must be planned for, organised and managed, through:

- Constant feedback and direct contact with customers (client panel)
- Monthly review of information
- Regular brainstorm sessions with a group of people from different backgrounds
- A budget for innovation
- Appointing someone or making time yourself to search for new ideas (3M allows R&D workers to spend 15% of their time on their own ideas and initiatives and has a rule that 30% of turnover must come from products developed in the last five years)
- Creating an "idea box" (like a suggestions box) with cash prizes if ideas are used by the business
- Creating project teams (made up of both technicians and sales people) to work with clients on particular ideas and giving the team the power and authority to implement changes
- Creating a positive atmosphere in your business towards change.

Innovation does not have to be a "giant leap forward". It can be a small step or, better still, a series of small steps (the "continuous improvement" that is so much a part of Quality Management Systems).

Always be on the look-out for ways to improve your product or service:

- Watch people using your product for a while
- Swap jobs: Let technicians do the selling and let the sales team manage production
- Arrange service contracts with your customers to get constant feedback
- Let clients set the quality criteria.

You will always face resistance when you try to innovate. Don't let it get you down.

Without innovation, your business will stagnate and die. Don't let the excuses in the panel below be heard in your business.

COMMON EXCUSES FOR NOT INNOVATING

1. Tried it before
2. Does not work in our situation
3. Too busy
4. Our company is too small
5. Let's keep our feet on the ground
6. Why change? We are doing fine right now
7. You are right, but ...
8. Not practical
9. Impossible
10. We always did it like this.

Which of these excuses apply to YOUR business?

Anything that won't sell, I don't want to invent.
THOMAS EDISON, Inventor

I would think of another fundamental need people have, and I would answer that need by offering a cheaper and more efficient service than anybody else could.
In five years, I'd be a millionaire all over again.
HENRY FORD, Ford Motor Company

Sometimes when you innovate, you make mistakes. It is best to admit them quickly, and get on with improving your other innovations.
STEVE JOBS, Apple Computer

Competitiveness

OBJECTIVES
- ☐ Understand competitiveness
- ☐ Identify the competitive success factors in your business

I don't meet competition; I crush it.
CHARLES REVSON, Revlon Cosmetics

Competitive advantage must be gained in one of three areas:
- *Operational excellence (production efficiency)*
- *Product innovation and excellence (premium price)*
- *Closeness to customer (personal relationship)*

You must aim to excel on one, and be at least adequate on the other two.
BRIAN TRACY

Being competitive is very simple: Be better than your competitors. This gives rise to two questions.

The first is how to define "better". This depends on what is important in the market in which the business is operating. In your market, does "better" mean:

- ☐ Quicker?
- ☐ Friendlier?
- ☐ Cheaper?
- ☐ Higher quality?
- ☐ Technical back-up and after-sales service?
- ☐ A wide choice?
- ☐ Advice pre-purchase?

Does it mean all of these? Some of these? Something else entirely? You need to know, if you are to be able to achieve it.

Being competitive is closely connected with the overall strategy of the company. Some writers compare it with war, saying that the options are:

- **Deter** – Create barriers through contracts, copyright, licensing, trade agreements, agents; Exploit advantages of contacts, location, economy of scale, flexibility; Seek alliances
- **Attack** – Head on/flank through price, promotion, technology or marketing
- **Defend** – Customer database or network.

Competition forces your business to become a "lean, mean fighting machine".

The second question is who are your competitors. We'll look more closely at this in "Marketing" a few pages on but, for now, remember than your competition may not just be local but may come from abroad.

An information system

Part of being competitive is developing a system which constantly collects information about your competitors and about business trends generally. (See "Market Research" in **READY** and the previous section "Innovation".)

Now answer the questions in the checklist panel below about your information system.

Benchmarking

To assess how competitive your business is you need a benchmark. The most obvious benchmark is your competitors.

Study them and score how they are performing on criteria which are important to the market and customers (see your earlier research).

Try to identify areas in which:

- Your business is stronger
- Your business is weaker
- You can learn from your competitors
- Your business needs to improve
- Your competitors are developing and which you are ignoring.

Take all these factors into consideration as you write your Business Plan.

INFORMATION SYSTEM CHECKLIST

1. What types of decisions are you called on to make regularly?
2. What type of information do you need to make these decisions?
3. What type of information do you get regularly?
4. What type of information would you like to get that you are not getting now?
5. On which topics would you like to be kept informed?
6. What do you think would be the four most helpful improvements that could be made to your current information system?

Source: PLATO

Using Technology to Advantage

The use of technology can be a success factor for a business. As a start-up, you have a great advantage: You are starting from scratch and can design the technology around the specific needs of your business, subject only to availability of finance. Existing businesses very often have to make do with expensive, but now unsuitable, equipment purchased earlier in their development.

You should consider technology as a means of making your business:

- More competitive
- More efficient
- Better informed
- More family friendly.

Technology for competition

The kind of technology that will give your business a competitive edge depends entirely on the business you are in and is outside the scope of this guide.

Enterprise Ireland clients (larger start-ups likely to employ more than 10 people) should contact Enterprise Ireland to discuss whether a technology audit, under the National Technology Audit Programme, would be of assistance to your business.

This programme examines a business' processes to identify opportunities for:

- Increased sales
- Stock reductions
- Cost reductions
- Quality improvements
- Improvements in methods/processes.

Technology for efficiency

Technology is converging and what were only a few years ago different systems – TV, fax, telephone, E-mail, computer, voice recognition – are now being combined into multi-functional devices. These bring cost and time savings.

It is worth your while researching these developments (read any business/technology magazine) and upgrading your skills in using the emerging technology.

You should certainly be considering a computer within your business for efficiency. An obvious area for computerisation is your accounts system. Although sending out invoices using a computer takes probably just as long as doing them manually, computerisation means that, at the press of a button, you can produce a list of outstanding debtors or an up-to-date set of accounts. This can give you valuable information to help you manage your business better. And good computerised accounting systems can be found for under □ 100.

Another use for a computer is to send and receive e-mail – very useful, cost-effective and efficient, especially if you have more than one location, are out of the office a lot, or have international clients.

Technology for information

The world's largest information resource – the Internet – is now available by computer, on mobile phones (WAP) and TV (WebTV).

Beyond all the hype, Internet access is a valuable tool for many small businesses. The wealth of information on the Internet is literally unimaginable and the ease of access is improving as new software becomes available.

Using search engines (Lycos, Yahoo, etc.) is a cost-effective and fast way of finding your way to the information you need.

Use the Internet as part of your information collection process. A number of useful sites for entrepreneurs are included in **Appendix 2, Further Information.**

Technology for family friendly businesses

A trend among businesses of all sizes is the adoption of family friendly policies, that allow staff to balance between work and home. It's particularly important where there are skills shortages and employers must compete for staff.

Technology can also allow business functions to be carried out independent of location using information and communication technologies.

Two useful websites are:

- **www.ework.ie**
- **www.familyfriendly.ie**.

e-Business

A key part of using technology to advantage is to consider the extent to which your business can become an e-Business. We will consider this in more depth in a later section.

OBJECTIVES

- ☐ To understand the importance of technology in gaining competitive advantage
- ☐ To evaluate the potential for computerisation in the business

The glory went to the man who discovered electricity but it was the man who invented the electricity meter who made the money.
ANON

Computers are useless. They only give you answers.
PABLO PICASSO

MARKETING

OBJECTIVES

- ☐ Understand principles of marketing
- ☐ Understand the importance of constant research feedback
- ☐ Be aware of the 4 Ps
- ☐ Develop an outline marketing plan

The central idea of marketing is of a matching between a company's capabilities and the wants of customers in order to achieve the objectives of both parties.
MALCOLM MCDONALD, Marketing author

Business has only two functions: marketing and innovation.
PETER F DRUCKER, Management author

The philosophy behind marketing is to satisfy the needs of every customer as best you can while making a profit. The whole idea is that if you make your clients happy they will buy from you – not just once, but again and again. This section will take you through the stages in developing an outline marketing plan.

MARKET RESEARCH

Your market research should have defined the customers the business is going to target. If not, go back to the "Market Research" section in **READY** and do more research on your potential clients.

If you can answer the questions below, you will have a good understanding of your potential customers. Write the answers to each question in the space provided.

TOO SMALL FOR A MARKETING DEPARTMENT?

Whether you have a marketing department or not, marketing involves decisions about:

- The product itself
- Price
- Customer service levels
- Physical distribution
- Advertising
- Sales
- The sales force
- Information about markets.

How do **you** decide on these?

Your customers/target groups:

Who are they?

Where are they located?

How do they spend their money?

Where do they spend their money?

Where do they socialise?

Can they be put in a social class and, if so, which class?

What do they read?

What do they watch on TV?

What do they listen to on radio?

Who forms their opinions?

Find out what elements in your service or product are most important to them.

To understand fully your customers' needs, make sure to clarify exactly what the customer means by probing until you are clear what the real needs are. For example, if customers say they want "Total quality", ask "What do you mean by that?". When they answer "Quick response", you ask "What do you mean by quick response?". After asking "What do you mean?" a few times, you will establish the real need.

Write down the five elements of your product/service that are most important to your customers:

1.

2.

3.

4.

5.

If it doesn't exist, it's a market opportunity.
VERN ROBURN

The outcome of any serious research can only be to make two questions grow where only one grew before.
THORSTEIN VEBLEN

I am the world's worst salesman. Therefore I must make it easy for people to buy.
FW WOOLWORTH

Consumers are statistics. Customers are people.
STANLEY MARCUS

COMPETITION

A competitor is a business that provides the same goods or services as yours or an alternative. Your competition can be local, national or, increasingly, international. Use the questions in the panel below to identify and assess your competitors.

Your competitors:	Is this a Threat or an Opportunity? T	O
What are the alternatives for your products or services?		
Who makes/sells these alternatives?		
What range of products or services do they have?		
What kind of choices do they offer customers?		
How broad is their range?		
What are their target groups?		
What are their future prospects?		
What are they good at and what are they not so good at?		

IMAGE

As markets are becoming more competitive and businesses have the same access to technology and information, image is increasingly important as a way to distinguish your business from the competition.

You should now decide what image you want your business to convey to your customers. For example, you may want your business/office/practice/shop to appear:

- ☐ Practical, simple and objective
- ☐ Exclusive, high value and durable
- ☐ Modern, new and trend-setting
- ☐ Personal, multi-faceted and results-oriented.

Once you have chosen an image, make sure it is expressed in all aspects of your business. Think about your business' image in these areas. Tick the ones you will use:

- ☐ Interior
- ☐ Accommodation
- ☐ Pricing
- ☐ Name
- ☐ Business stationery
- ☐ Brochures
- ☐ Packaging
- ☐ Quality
- ☐ Business plan
- ☐ Advertising
- ☐ Correspondence
- ☐ Service
- ☐ Telephone answering
- ☐ Presentation
- ☐ Promotion
- ☐ Selling
- ☐ Employees.

Once you have chosen the image you want to present to your customers, you should remain committed to it in the long term. See it as an investment in the future of your business.

Image needs to be maintained and should be checked on a regular basis with the reputation the company actually has. What perception do you want to project (= image)? And what is the image of your company with your customers (= reputation)? Reputation is more important than image.

IMAGE CHECKLIST

What image do you want to present?

Why? How does this link back to your customers/target group?

How do you plan to achieve this image?

THE 4Ps OF THE MARKETING MIX

To market your product and project your image, you use a mix of techniques and tools to get the best effect. To work out your marketing mix, use the 4Ps:

- Product
- Price
- Place
- Promotion.

Within Promotion, we will look closely at Advertising, Personal selling, Public Relations, the Internet and Customer Service.

PRODUCT

For most customers, a product is not only the product itself (the core), but also the services and intangibles that surround it (the product surround). For example, a pub sells pints (core) and quick service and atmosphere (surround); a clothes shop sells clothing and appearance or personal image, a flower shop sells plants and flowers and ambience in the house. What do you sell?

The customer also wants a choice. What you have to offer consists of a range, a selection of choices, products that complement each other and make it attractive for the customer to come and buy. A pub also sells meals, a clothes shop also sells accessories, a flower shop also sells earthenware. What range of choices do you give your customers? Customers also want to know what extras come with your product. What do you do that the others do not do? Think about packaging, service, personal attention, brand articles, originality, creativity and so on. What extras do you offer?

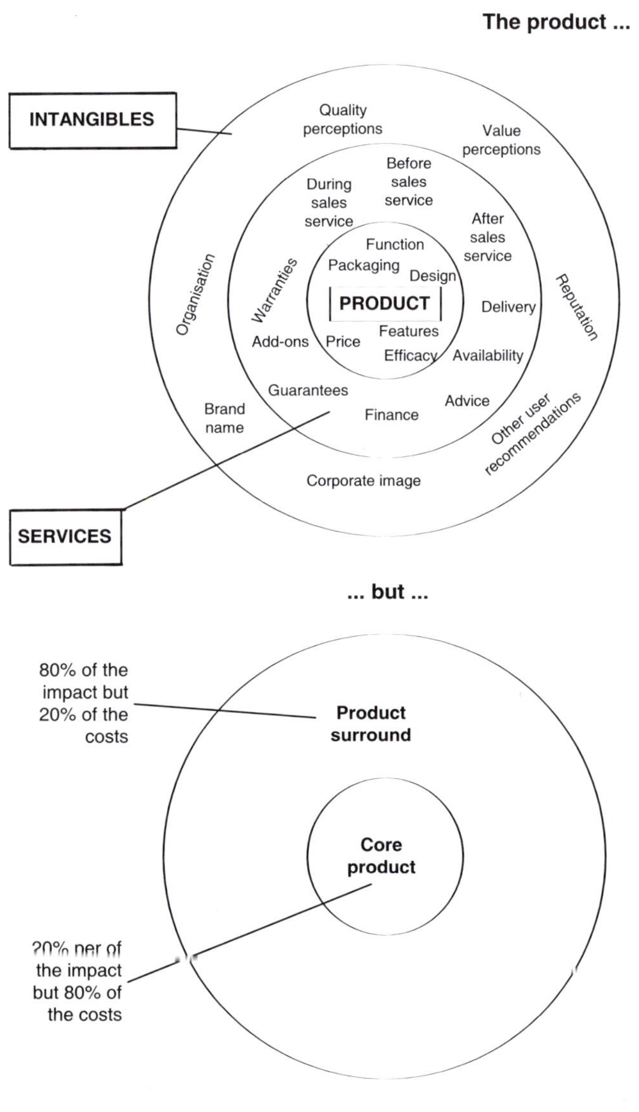

Your product:

Describe briefly the product(s) you want to launch:

Describe your product's core:

Describe your product's surround:

What choices do you offer your customers?

What extras do you offer compared to the competition?

PRICE

Pricing is important for several reasons:

- The price you charge will determine your margins and, in the end, your own salary
- Price is also closely associated with the quality and credibility of your product or service
- Once you have established your price, it is very difficult to increase it without losing customers.

To establish your price, it is important to know what your customers are used to paying, and what they are prepared to pay (see the panel below). (At this stage, price has nothing to do with cost – that comes later!)

You need to be well informed about competitors' prices. Sometimes prices are prescribed or recommended by industry organisations or professional associations. You can always deviate from established prices by means of special offers, discounts, reductions in rates, etc.

But be careful when researching price. You need to listen VERY carefully to what people say and how they say it. If your pricing is way off line, people will tell you quickly. But, if it's a little dear, and they don't want to suggest that they can't afford it, they may say the price is fine. You will only find out that it's not when you can't sell the product/service. You must also bear in mind that anyone who intends buying a product or service is unlikely to tell you if it is too cheap. Tread carefully!

When you sell a product, you have something tangible to show the customer. With services, you have nothing to show until you have done the work – and sometimes not even then. If you offer a service, when you agree a price it is a good idea to write down exactly what your customer can expect – for example:

- Details of your service
- The time to complete the service
- The time when the service will start
- The price
- The agreed method (and time) of payment
- Whether the cost of materials is included
- Whether other expenses (travel to the customer's location, for example) are included.

You also need to look at price in the context of cost. There is no point selling lots of a product if you are losing money on it! Work through the questions below to determine your pricing strategy.

Note the impact of e-Business: If your customers are on-line, they can easily compare prices with other suppliers. How will this affect your pricing strategy?

Get the confidence of the public and you will have no difficulty getting their patronage ... Remember always that the recollection of quality remains long after the price is forgotten.
H GEORGE SELFRIDGE, retailer

Price: Value plus a reasonable sum for the wear and tear on conscience in demanding it.
AMBROSE BIERCE, US Humorist

Almost anything on earth can be manufactured a little less well and be sold for a little less money.
And those who are only interested in price are the main victims of this rule.
JOHN RUSKIN, Philosopher

Your price:

What are customers accustomed to paying already?		€ ____
What are your competitors' prices (average)?		€ ____
What is your price?		€ ____
How is your price made up?		
• Materials	€ ____	
• Time	€ ____	
• Machine cost	€ ____	
• Other	€ ____	
• Total costs		€ ____
• Profit margin		€ ____
• Selling price		€ ____

Will you offer discounts? ☐ Yes ☐ No
If yes, what kind of discount?

Will you give special offers? ☐ Yes ☐ No
If yes, what will they be?

PLACE

Place means the location where your business will be established.

In some cases, a customer will never come near your place of business – for example, if you run a window cleaning or mail order business. In such cases, we only use the P for place as to mean distribution (that is, getting the product or service to the customer).

In retail businesses, place can be the most important part of the marketing mix. Important questions to ask, particularly for retail businesses, include:

- What will the customer see and experience when he or she visits your business?
- How easy is it to find you?
- Where are you situated (shopping area, a hotel or restaurant district, an office centre, in the centre or in the outskirts of town, etc.)?
- What does the area look like?
- What draws customers to your location?
- Do you provide a location map for your customers? Do you need to?
- Why did you choose this location?

Channels of distribution

You need to understand the channels of distribution that you will be using for your product. Each industry is different and fortunes have been made (and lost) on changes to the channels of distribution. Look at how Dell has changed the way people buy computers.

The diagram above summarises the main channels and the stages within them. The fewer stages, the lower the distribution cost – which is why lots of businesses try to cut out the middleman. On the other hand, the middleman provides a useful service – holding stock, sourcing customers, advising on market conditions – and cannot always be dispensed with. You need to balance distribution costs with promotion costs. Very often, sales channels with low distribution costs have high promotion costs.

Consider also alternatives to the traditional channels above – network marketing (see **READY**) and on-line distribution ("Marketing – Internet"). The latter is already making huge changes in the way people buy. How will it impact your business?

CHANNELS OF DISTRIBUTION

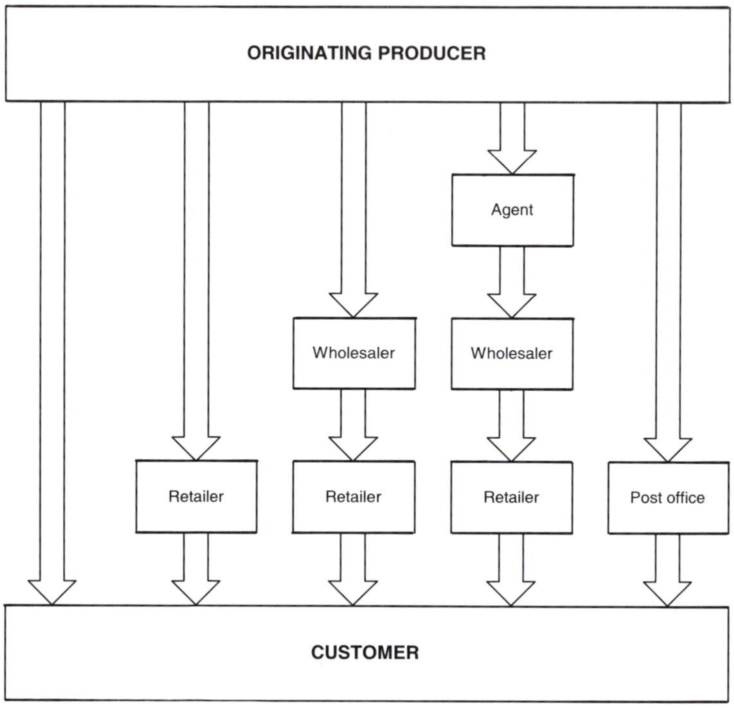

DISTRIBUTION CHECKLIST

What distribution system are you considering?

Why?

What do your competitors do?

Where are the weaknesses in your system?

How can they be corrected?

PROMOTION

This is the stage when you begin to develop your entire marketing policy. It is a mistake to think that marketing begins and ends with advertising. Advertising is just a part of the promotion policy, and it is therefore only one of the means of promotion.

What are the vehicles of your promotion policy?

- Direct mail
- Personal selling
- Public relations
- Publicity and advertising
- The Internet – see the section on "e-Business".

Each will be covered in more detail later, but below is a brief summary to set the context.

Direct mail

Use a database of the names and addresses of the customers within your target groups to send a sales letter or brochure. Make it easy for the customer to respond. Where you can, follow up with a phone call.

Personal selling

The final target is selling your product. In most cases, you are the one who is going to sell. Therefore, you must:

- Prepare your sales talk well
- Write down the buying motives of your customers and also the reasons why they do not buy
- Think of reasons to counter those objections.

Public relations (PR)

This term embraces all the activities you undertake to get positive attention for your business among the public in general. Good PR creates a positive image for your business and helps to ensure that people recognise and remember your business, especially over the long term.

Good PR is also useful for your contacts with your suppliers. If you need a quick delivery, a special order or a credit, try to make sure that your supplier will go out of their way to help you. The same applies for your neighbours, local authority, etc. Good PR will also lead to free publicity.

Advertising and publicity

The key steps in advertising are:

- Use the image you choose as the basis for ads
- Look for an aspect of the image that can be represented graphically
- Always emphasise the advantages for the customer
- Remain credible and trustworthy
- Gain attention with a headline and give sufficient information
- Raise interest with a special offer
- Motivate your public to come and buy
- Stimulate action by including something that has to be returned, an invitation, an opening, special sales days, discount coupon valid until ...

Methods of promotion

There are hundreds of ways of promoting your business and the products/services you offer. Try some of these:

- ☐ Advertise in a regional newspaper – In the classified advertising section; in Sunday papers; in a monthly magazine aimed at your target group
- ☐ Advertisement or entry in the Golden Pages (a basic line entry is free of charge)
- ☐ Design and print brochures that can be delivered house to house with the newspaper delivery or deliver them yourself; distribute brochures during large meetings or conferences, at markets, in the street, to customers, etc.
- ☐ Have posters made and hang them in strategic places
- ☐ Have a signboard made, with plastic letters or magic marker (check whether you need planning permission, depending on where you plan to locate your signboard)
- ☐ Direct mail – Send sales letters directly to potential customers and your existing customers for whom you have an address
- ☐ Participation in trade exhibitions, markets, hiring a stand at a conference. You will gain the opportunity here to demonstrate your products. Remember you will need brochures to distribute. You can also make a special exhibition offer
- ☐ Make up your front window display according to a special theme.

In practice, you will probably choose a combination of methods to make up your promotion mix.

TYPES OF PROMOTIONAL ACTIVITY UNDERTAKEN RANKED IN ORDER OF POPULARITY

Word-of-mouth	60%
Advertising in business directories	30%
Advertising in local press	30%
Advertising in trade/business press	12%
Direct mail	11%
Brochures, leaflets, point-of-sale material	5%
Telephone contact/personal visits	5%
Local radio	4%
Posters, vehicle sides, branding	4%
Seminars/conferences/exhibitions	4%
National press	3%
Sponsorship	2%
Public relations	1%

The codfish lays ten thousand eggs,
The humble hen just one.
The codfish never cackles
To tell you when she's done.
And so we scorn the codfish
While the humble hen we prize
Which only goes to show you
That it pays to advertise.
ANON

Doing business without advertising is like winking at a girl across a darkened room: You know what you are doing but no one else does.
ANON

Give them quality. That's the best kind of advertising.
MILTON HERSHEY

When business is good, it pays to advertise;
When business is bad, you've got to advertise.
ANON

Advertising: The education of the public as to who you are, where you are, and what you have to offer in the way of skill, talent or commodity.
FRANK MCKINNEY HUBBARD

ADVERTISING

Advertising is a way of communicating your product or service. Based on your market research, you know who your target groups are and how to reach them. What do you want your advertising to achieve?

- ☐ Sales
- ☐ Awareness
- ☐ Image
- ☐ Name recognition
- ☐ Introduce new product
- ☐ Introduce new service

Go back to your market research. Remind yourself of your customers' buying motives. Then decide which of your product's/service's features meet these motives and should be emphasised in your advertising.

Next begin to consider where you might advertise. You want to use an advertising vehicle (newspaper, magazine, radio, TV) that reaches your target group as economically as possible. Therefore, advertising in a national Sunday paper or on prime-time TV (even if you could afford either!) makes no sense if your market is made up of customers in your own locality. But there are now lots of local papers and radio stations, which might suit your needs much better.

Take control!

Ask for a "media pack". This will tell you not only the rates, but who the readers/listeners/viewers are, how many they are, what income groups they are in, etc. You need this information in order to decide whether a vehicle is suitable. Use the Advertising Control Sheet (see **GO** for an example) to help you place your advertising.

Don't be pressurised into advertising, either in the wrong place or at the wrong time. Most ad salespeople are on commission. They want you to buy NOW! and will give you "special discounts" – if you decide today. Don't do it until you are ready.

Don't be fooled by price either. Yes, one magazine costs □ 500 for a half-page against □ 300 for a full page somewhere else – but it goes to 20,000 of your core customers whereas the other really doesn't cover your market at all. Which is better value?

When you have placed your ads, measure the response. Unless you do this, you will never know whether your advertising works.

There is a famous advertising story of an American car manufacturer which advertised for a year in a well-respected national magazine. At the end of the year, they found that people who had not read the magazine bought more of their cars than did readers of the magazine. Their advertising was UN-selling the cars!

If it is appropriate, place a coupon (order form) or response mechanism ("Call us now for special offer details") on your advertisement. Record the number of responses you get from each ad. When people phone or call to place an order, ask them where they heard about you. This builds up invaluable information and will save you from advertising in the wrong places in future.

Writing advertisements

Writing advertisements is an art. It looks simple but it is, in fact, very hard. Keep these words by David Ogilvy, founder of Ogilvy & Mather, one of the world's largest advertising agencies, in mind:

> "I do not regard advertising as entertainment or as an art form, but as a medium of information. When I write an advertisement, I don't want you to tell me you find it 'creative'. I want you to find it so interesting that ***you buy the product.***"

The secret is to keep it simple. Be direct. Explain what you are selling, its benefits to the customer, and where they can get it.

Use your logo

If your business has a strong visual appeal, design a logo. Use it as widely as you can. Use it on:

- Envelopes
- T-shirts
- Posters
- Pens
- Van signs
- Lighters/matchboxes
- Umbrellas.

Make sure that wherever they go, your target customers are always aware that your business exists.

PERSONAL SELLING

For lots of people, selling still has a negative connotation – the image of the slick sales person pushing products down someone's neck.

Not any more. Modern-day selling is about partnership and communication. It is important to build a relationship with your customers. The customer has to trust and respect you.

Try to build a database with the names and addresses of your customers. Try to memorise the names of your customers, remember what they bought the last time, or what they asked about last time. Again, get as much information as you can about your customers' hobbies, family situation, job, etc. Use that information when you next talk to them.

The following checklists may be helpful to you in developing your personal selling techniques.

WHEN SELLING

1. Are you prepared?
2. Do you know your customers' needs (ask lots of questions)?
3. Do you listen?
4. Are you clear in your language (no jargon!)?
5. Do you talk about benefits instead of the product?
6. Do you have answers to your customers' objections (What are they?)?
7. Do you know when to close the sale?
8. Are you persistent (do not give up)?

THINGS TO ASK YOURSELF BEFORE YOU START SELLING

1. Do you know enough about the product?
2. What is the product core?
3. What is the product surround?
4. Are you talking to the right person?
5. Who are:
   - The recommenders?
   - The influencers?
   - The supporters?
   - The deciders?
6. Do you know what the customer wants?
7. Does what he wants fit with what he needs?
8. Why does the customer want it?
9. Have you had any previous experience with the customer?
10. Has the customer had experience with your competition?
11. Who is the end user of your product?
12. How will your product be used?
13. How will the customer's life be better or easier after he/she uses your product?

You should be aware that all of the above is wasted if you do not get the appointments and realise that nine out of ten appointments result in a "No". But if you get nine Nos, you also get one "Yes". Therefore self-motivation is critical. Selling – day in, day out, year in, year out – is the most underestimated element in business.

To sell
no matter what,
no matter how,
to no matter whom;
behold in these
words the whole
diplomacy of the
peasant at the fair.
JOSEPH ROUX (1834-1905)

The average salesperson spends less than 25% of their time face-to-face with their clients. Personally, I spend 90%. That's the only way to make money in sales.
EDNA LARSEN

To open a shop is easy, to keep it open is an art.
CONFUCIUS

PUBLIC RELATIONS

Public relations (PR) is not just about getting your business in the papers. Public relations is exactly what it says: Building a relationship with the public.

Let's first define public. From the perspective of where your business is located, it includes:

- Neighbours
- The neighbourhood
- The local community.

Internally, it includes:

- Staff
- Suppliers.

In a wider context, public includes:

- Colleagues
- Unions
- Government (local, regional, national)
- Politicians
- Consumer groups
- Financial institutions
- Trade organisations.

Public relations builds and maintains a good reputation. If your business is well-regarded by the groups mentioned, your marketing mix will be strengthened and it will be easier to influence people or get things done (planning permission, recruiting staff, word-of-mouth sales, etc.)

It goes back to your Mission Statement and what social profile you want to project. You have to decide which groups you want to maintain a positive relationship with and how you plan to do this. Keep it practical and within your means (both money and time).

Local newspapers are always looking for news. If you have good news about your business, make sure you let them know. Build a profile for yourself and your business through your local paper.

And while the relationship you build will not protect you totally when bad news has to be reported, it means the reporter knows and trusts you already and may go out of their way to check facts with you before going to print.

CUSTOMER SERVICE

Businesses spend a lot of money on attracting new customers. But it is cheaper to keep

Public relations is the management function which evaluates public attitudes, identifies the policies and procedures of an individual or organisation with the public interest, and executes a programme of action to earn public understanding and acceptance.
ANON

Get someone else to blow your horn and the sound will carry twice as far.
WILL ROGERS, US humorist

If you mean to profit, learn to please.
CHARLES CHURCHILL

Good service isn't a mystery – employ nice people.
KEN McCULLOCK, One Devonshire Gardens Hotel, Glasgow

PUBLIC RELATIONS CHECKLIST

Which groups are important for your company?

- ☐ Neighbours – Who are they?
- ☐ Local banks
- ☐ Local politicians
- ☐ Local authority
- ☐ Local press
- ☐ Trade organisations
- ☐ Unions
- ☐ State agencies
- ☐ Other

How will you reach them?

- ☐ Sponsorship
- ☐ Press releases
- ☐ Visits/Open Days
- ☐ Information/newsletter
- ☐ Profile in local newspapers
- ☐ Donate your services for a worthy cause

THE IMPORTANCE OF CUSTOMER LOYALTY – CALCULATE THE LIFETIME VALUE OF A CUSTOMER

Average sale value per customer	€ ______
multiplied by	
Number of sales per year per customer	______
Total sales value per year per customer	€ ______
multiplied by	
Number of years customer buys from you	______
Gross lifetime sales value per customer	**€** ______

Plus, if every satisfied customer tells one or two other people and they become customers, look how fast your sales will grow!

your existing customers than to find new ones.

Loyal customers:

- Spend more money with you than other customers
- Bring in new customers (through word-of-mouth recommendations)
- Cost less than acquiring new customers.

Use the panel opposite to calculate the lifetime value of one of your customers.

What steps will you take to keep your customers loyal to your business:

- ☐ Regular visits?
- ☐ Regular telephone contact?
- ☐ Regular direct mail contact?
- ☐ Regular evaluation of your business' performance in meeting their needs?
- ☐ Interviews with customers whose business you have lost to find out why this happened?

One way of creating and keeping loyal customers is through customer service – not just any old customer service but through superb world-class customer service.

World-class? Why not? Where's the competition? When did you last get service from any business that was so good that you would recommend someone else to use them? When did you last get service so good that you noticed?

The fact that you have only a small business makes no difference – in fact, it makes it easier for you to be close to the customer.

Customer service involves:

- Doing what you promised the customer
- Willingness to help
- Providing prompt service
- Well-trained staff
- Individual attention
- Little things which make the difference.

Research shows that businesses that provide top class customer service experience:

- Improvements in morale (reducing staff costs)
- Lower staff turnover (reducing recruitment costs)
- Longer customer retention (up to 50% longer)
- More repeat business (20-40% lower selling costs)
- More referrals (20-40% lower promotional costs)
- Higher prices (7-12% higher)
- Increased margins (7-17% more profit).

Calculate the difference this would make to your profits.

Then decide how you are going to put customer service into action in your business.

EXPORT

It may appear strange to be considering exporting when you haven't yet got your business up and running but the reality is that many Irish businesses have to consider exporting at a much earlier stage in their development than is usual in other countries.

Use the checklist below to help you plan your export strategy.

EXPORT CHECKLIST

1. How specific are your plans? Are they an integral part of your business plan and strategy for the business?
2. Which products or services do you want to export?
3. Which countries do you want to export to and in which order of priority?
4. What is your target market/segments within the market?
5. Have you done desk research on your export markets?
6. Have you actually visited the countries involved?
7. Do you have sales experience in your proposed export markets?
8. Do you have the language skills needed?
9. Have you organised your administration for foreign payments and customs/excise regulations?
10. Are you familiar with the regulations relating to your products/services in your export markets?
11. Does your product or service need adjustment? For safety, environment, quality, packaging, taste, fashion, culture or language?
12. Is your price, after calculation of the extra costs involved in exporting, still competitive?
13. What are your turnover targets: per country, per market, per segment?
14. Do you have enough time available to build and develop the export market?
15. Who will be responsible for marketing and sales abroad?
16. Is your organisation, from telephonist to after sales, ready and prepared for export and dealing internationally?
17. Can your business cope with the demands of foreign markets: Delivery times, transport, quantities?
18. Which channels are you planning to use in your export markets?
19. Do you have the right promotion and instruction materials?
20. Are your term and conditions, contracts, quotes, etc. translated and adjusted to your export markets?

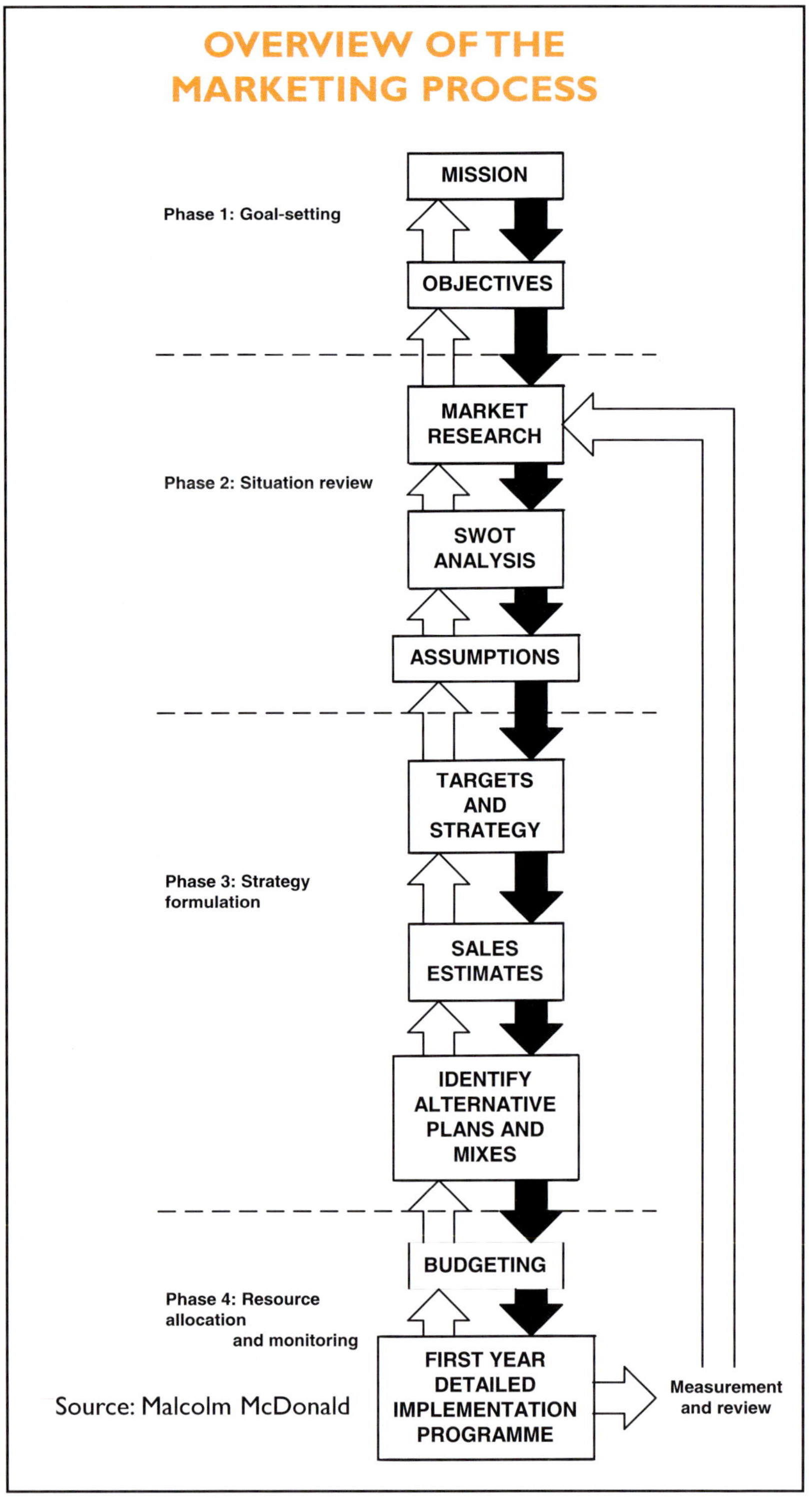

OUTLINE PLAN

At this stage, you should have enough information to be able to develop an outline marketing plan. Just as marketing is the heart of your business, so your marketing plan is the heart of your Business Plan – which is what this chapter is about.

As shown in the diagram, your plan should start with the Mission Statement, include your business and personal objectives and then summarise the results of your market research. The SWOT analysis, based on the market research, leads to assumptions, which in turn lead to the definition of targets and strategies.

Sales estimates may not be acceptable first time around, so alternatives may need to be considered.

Sales estimates can be difficult for a start-up, since you have no track-record or experience to base them on. Try to support your sales estimates with as much hard evidence – forward orders, etc – as you can.

Once sales estimates have been agreed, the budgeting process can begin – and then work begins in earnest on putting the plan into action.

Note that the diagram also includes a measurement and review loop. Marketing is a constant process.

E-Business

E-Business and the power of the Internet have significant benefits to offer small businesses. For example, the Internet lowers the barriers to entry for many markets, allowing small businesses to compete in wider geographic areas than would otherwise be possible.

Use of the Internet also facilitates a reduction in transaction costs. Some estimates suggest that the use of a B2B exchange could cut transaction costs by 90% for some businesses. Even allowing for exaggeration, there is clearly an enormous potential for cost reductions in many areas of business, which will bring benefits to the economy, individual businesses and ultimately to the consumer.

Last, all public organisations, and some bigger companies, have plans to move their purchasing on-line, so it is good to be prepared.

Some of the hype about the Internet and e-Business has been extremely positive, some very negative. As with all things, the truth is probably somewhere in the middle. What the Internet will not do is make you a millionaire overnight. It is not a magic wand. You need a good understanding of your business model and where e-commerce might fit. Where do you want to use the Internet? For:

- ☐ Communicating with your customers?
- ☐ Promotion on-line?
- ☐ Selling on-line?
- ☐ Communicating with your suppliers?

and to what effect:

- ☐ Quicker?
- ☐ Easier?
- ☐ Cheaper?
- ☐ Promotion?
- ☐ Sales?

and at what cost in terms of:

- ☐ Up-front investment?
- ☐ On-going costs?
- ☐ Time commitment?

The Internet and e-business can fit within your business model in three key areas:

- Marketing
- Production
- Administration.

Don't get bogged down with, or put off by, the technology. As any techie will tell you, it is not the technology that is the key to success, but how you use the available technology.

Getting started

To get started, you need:

- A computer
- A modem
- A telephone line
- A connection to the Internet via an Internet Service provider (ISP)
- Browser and e-mail software.

Most modern computers come with a modem and browser/e-mail software installed. In choosing an ISP, you need to decide between a "free" service that may provide a restricted service and/or charge for support, or one where you pay for the services you require – your usage of the Internet usually will determine which is better value.

E-mail

Most businesses use the Internet first for e-mail. It's a handy and cheap way of sending information all over the world for little more than the price of a local phone call. It means you can deal with queries outside normal working hours or over long distances. E-mail is also useful for marketing.

Why should you have a web-site?

A web-site offers a window onto a global networked market-place, making it easy for you to reach customers whom you would probably never have considered targeting. For example, Oak Tree Press, publisher of this guide, has a web-site (**www.oaktreepress.com**), which reaches customers around the world, through an on-line catalogue.

Software companies provide updates and new releases of software for downloading from their web-sites. Newspapers and magazines have discovered a treasure trove in their archives of material from back issues, which they can sell on-line to people looking for specific information.

Sales is one reason for establishing a web-site – and probably the best, since it most clearly recovers your investment – but there are others.

A web-site can act as an on-line brochure, attracting potential customers to

OBJECTIVES

- ☐ To understand the importance of e-Business
- ☐ To evaluate the potential for e-Business in the business
- ☐ To understand how to implement e-Business

In Internet business, profitability is for wimps. It means your business plan wasn't aggressive enough.
DOONESBURY

It's working if it makes the till ring.
DES KENNY, *Kenny's Bookshop, Galway*

The golden rule of complying with e-commerce law is: Be transparent! By being completely and fully transparent about who you are, what you are doing and how you will serve your customer, you will find that you are not only staying on the right side of the law but you are also keeping your customers happy.
CORINNA SCHULZE and JEFFREY BAUMGARTNER, *Don't Panic: Do E-commerce*

THE JARGON EXPLAINED

HTML document:
A document that can be displayed in a Web browser. HTML (hyper-text mark-up language) allows you to bring text, images, audio and video together so they can be viewed over the web.

ISP:
Internet Service Provider, providing you with access to the Internet over your telephone connection. They provide e-mail and web-site hosting.

Domain name:
This identifies your web-site on the Internet – www.yourcompanyname.com or www.yourcompanyname.ie, for example.

Web server:
A computer linked to the Internet 24 hours a day. Your site must be hosted on a Web server to allow people to access it.

Virtual server:
Owning and maintaining your own Web server is expensive and complicated. Most small web-sites are hosted on shared servers maintained by ISPs – these are called "virtual servers".

Web host:
A specialist company that provides hosting services (virtual servers). It may also be an ISP but need not be.

Web graphics:
The two main formats are: JPEGs (Joint Photographic Experts Group) for photos and GIFs (Graphic Interchange Format) for graphics.

Front end:
The part of the web-site that a user sees on screen: the text, graphics, forms and overall design.

Back end:
The part the user doesn't see, which handles communications between the user's computer and the web server. The more complex your site, the more complex the back end needed.

Shopping Cart:
Software that keeps track of your purchases on-line, allowing you to accumulate them until you are ready to complete the transaction.

Payment solutions:
At present, these are credit card-based, allowing you to accept payment by credit card for user's purchases. Electronic wallets and digital cash are under experiment.

Adapted from *Taking Your Business On-line*, Enterprise Ireland

contact you about doing business. It can also establish your credibility in a certain field, if your site is full of authoritative information on a specific topic. Last (though not a good reason for incurring the expense if that is all it is) is that it can act as a symbol of "corporate up-to-dateness".

The stages are:

- Typically, web-sites begin as an on-line brochure, simply moving the business' corporate "message" into a new medium
- The next step is to list the products and services on-line – a "catalogue" site
- Next, the business decides to allow customers buy these products or services on-line and provides some form of payment mechanism, ideally with on-line credit card clearance
- Once customers have bought from the site, it's good marketing to encourage repeat buying – so the site develops "customer retention" features, like free updates or support for registered customers
- **The final step is to integrate the web-site into the business so that it becomes the business, reducing costs because of the use of the Internet itself.**

There are many examples of the first three types – brochure, catalogue and on-line sales. Software companies, probably because they have a digital product and are tuned into the medium, have some of the best customer retention-type sites. Most integrated sites are found in the Business-to-Business (B2B) arena, where industry-specific sites for buying and selling can deliver economies of scale.

Some sites combine more than one stage of development. For example, courier companies like DHL and FEDEX allow customers track shipments on-line, giving customers more "power" but also reducing their own costs since they no longer have to field telephone enquiries.

Some of the so-called "dot-coms" are fully-integrated web-sites, where there is no business apart from the web-site. In other cases, for example, the Ryanair site, the site provides benefits to customers in terms of speed and ease of booking flights while significantly reducing Ryanair's costs, both in commission to travel agents and in handling phone bookings.

Setting up a web-site

Before you rush into setting up your own Web-site, stop and think. Ask yourself:

- **Is your business suitable?** – Are you providing goods or services that can be delivered easily world-wide (or, at least, remotely from your present location)? Or, if not, can you attract customers to come to you (hotel, tourist resort)?

- **Are your customers (and potential customers) connected to the Internet?** – Think carefully about what you need to invest, simple e-mail may be sufficient.
- **Are you clear about what you are trying to do?** – A Web-site can be used for a number of purposes (often simultaneously), including providing product support to existing customers, providing product information to potential customers, selling on-line, identifying prospects, receiving feedback from customers, advertising your business' existence, capability and excellence. Which are you doing?
- **Can you afford it – time-wise?** – Establishing a site is only the first step. You must then update it regularly. How often depends on the nature of your business and the traffic you generate. Once a month is a good target to aim for. But it all takes time
- **Can you afford it – money-wise?** – Setting up a web-site costs money. Not a lot, to be sure, but it all adds up. Domain name registration (between €50 and €150, depending on where registered), site design ("free" if you do it yourself to as much as you're prepared to spend – budget for €1,000 to €2,000), site-hosting (from €10 per month), on-line shop software (from €600), etc.

On-line sales

On-line sales can be made from a "catalogue" site, where you list or display your products and invite interested purchasers to order products by conventional means: letter, telephone, fax or email. You then handle the sale in your normal way.

The next step is to add "shopping cart" software that tracks users' purchases until they are ready to complete the transaction. This software is usually bundled with on-line credit card processing (including a merchant Internet account with a bank) as an "online shop". Typically, such software costs from €600 for simple systems capable of displaying perhaps 10 or 20 products. More sophisticated systems, with greater capabilities and more features, cost more, though prices are falling.

Adding a shopping cart and online credit card processing gives you an "e-commerce" site.

PLANNING YOUR E-BUSINESS

Consider:

- **Purpose:** Why develop as an e-business?
- **Budget:** How much will it cost?
- **Expected return:** What do you expect to get back? And when?
- **Staff:** Will all staff have access to the Internet/e-mail? What training do they need? Who is responsible for keeping the site up-to-date?
- **Marketing:** Who are your customers on-line? What impact will on-line selling have on your traditional markets?
- **Process:** Can you use the Internet to reduce costs?

TEN RULES FOR A SUCCESSFUL B2C E-COMMERCE SITE

1 Keep it simple.
2 Make it fast.
3 Build trust.
4 Give directions.
5 Welcome the shopper.
6 Create communities.
7 Service the customer.
8 Think globally.
9 Shipping must be easy.
10 Let the world know.

Source: Marco Argenti & Efrim Boritz

Security

Issues in relation to security on the web include:

- **Safety:** Whether sensitive information (credit card details, for example) is protected while it is being sent from the user's computer to the web server and onwards (if applicable)
- **Trust:** Whether commitments made on the web will be honoured (for example, will goods bought and paid for on-line be dispatched?)
- **Privacy:** Whether there are restrictions on the access to, and use of, personal information (for example, age or financial status) provided by a user as part of a web transaction.

Secure payments solutions for credit cards involve:

- A bank that provides an Internet merchant account (even if you already have a merchant account with a bank, you need an Internet merchant account)
- Software that encrypts credit card details while they are being sent form the user's computer to the bank
- A secure certificate for data encryption.

There are a number of schemes – ChamberSeal and eTrust, for example – that vet applicants before allowing them to use a logo on their web-sites signifying that they are trust-worthy.

The EU Data Protection Directive says that personal information must be:

- Obtained fairly and lawfully
- Used only for the original specified purpose
- Adequate, relevant and not excessive to purpose
- Accurate and up-to-date
- Accessible to the subject of the information
- Kept secure and destroyed after its purpose is completed.

Legislation

The Electronic Commerce Act 2000 introduced the EU's Electronic Signatures Directive into Irish law. Among other things, this means that electronic signatures and contracts have the same force as their hand-written or typed equivalents.

As a general rule, content on a website must be cleared for copyright and must avoid defamation.

Strictly, terms of trade must comply with legislation in each country in which you do business, though this may be difficult since there are few standards internationally, especially in consumer protection. The best protection is to make your terms of trade fair and clear – the "golden rule" is to be transparent. For example:

- Give your physical address
- Make it easy for people to do business with you
- Show the full price of items, including VAT and delivery costs if any
- Give a contact point where people can complain.

VAT

Under present legislation, VAT is charged (if applicable) on online transactions in the country in which the transactions originate. However, if your sales to other EU countries exceed certain limits, you may need to register for VAT in those countries. This area is still developing and new EU rulings are expected.

Domain names

A domain name identifies your business on the Internet. This is why it's important to have a name in the form www.yourcompany.com rather than www.webhost.com/~yourcompanyname. The latter is like putting "We're not a very important company" on your letterhead!

The suffix (.com or .ie) is determined by where your name is registered. Names registered with US agencies get a .com address. The reason there are so many of these (and why so many non-US web-sites have them) is that they are easy to get, with little formality beyond the credit card payment. The downside of this is that many names have already been acquired – some by people who plan to use them for their business, others by people who hope to sell them on to someone else at a profit (cyber-squatting). You can register a .com domain name at, for example, **www.networksolutions.com**.

Irish domain names, distinguished by the .ie suffix, are registered through the IE Domain Registry (**www.domainregistry.ie**). To prevent cyber-squatting, IEDR requires proof that you have an entitlement to use the name you ask for – for example, it is the name of a limited company or registered business name that you own. Since IEDR also requires hosting information, it is often easier to let your ISP register your domain name.

Just like a company name, a domain name must be distinctive and memorable. Ideally, it should be your business name but it could be a brand name or some other more general descriptive name.

On-line marketing

On-line marketing is something of a misnomer, since some of it takes place off-line. Primarily, it consists of attracting people to your web-site. You can do this by:

- Publicising your web-site address (your domain name) as widely as possible – on your letterheads, compliment slips, brochures, vans, etc
- Achieving high positions in search engine results
- "Viral" marketing – the on-line equivalent of "word-of-mouth" and the most effective (and cheapest) form of on-line marketing
- Advertising on-line on other web-sites – many sites accept advertising, though the value of online advertising is increasingly in question.

Other issues

Other e-business issues include:

- **Currency:** Good marketing practice suggests you offer products for sale in your customers' currency (usually US $ on the Web). This raises issues because of fluctuating exchange rates/differing price points.
- **Delivery:** Can you meet customers' expectations for delivery? After all, if they can find your product and order it in a few minutes, why must they wait for several weeks while it travels to them?
- **Shipping costs:** Who bears shipping costs? You will find that postage of bulky items overseas is expensive – and express couriers are not cheap.

The future

For many businesses (not all), the Web is the future. For some, it will be their business; for others, it will simply be another channel through which to reach their markets. But, for most businesses, there will be no escaping its impact. Think about it as part of your business planning.

Products and Production

Production is deliberately placed AFTER marketing in this guide because, too often, in the real world, production comes before marketing – to the detriment of the business.

This section will help you think through what you should be doing.

Start by writing down the answers to the questions below.

OBJECTIVES

☐ Understand the production process

Copy this section into your Business Plan, pages 116 and 123.

Products

Product/service	***Description***	***Price***
A ______	______	€ ______
B ______	______	€ ______
C ______	______	€ ______
D ______	______	€ ______
E ______	______	€ ______
F ______	______	€ ______

Describe your production process. Draw a flowchart on a separate page, if necessary.

What experience do you have with this process?

Are you involved with (or will you be using) new techniques or new products in your production processes? ☐ YES ☐ NO

If yes, are you receiving assistance from experts? ☐ YES ☐ NO

If yes, who are they and how are they engaged?

Develop Standards

To ensure efficient production, it might be worthwhile developing procedures and measuring your activities so that you can standardise your approach.

Standards should enable you to:

1. Do the job the easiest (and safest) way
2. Prevent errors from (re-)occuring
3. Have a benchmark to measure and improve against
4. Have objectives to work against
5. Provide a basis to train your future staff
6. Preserve the knowledge and experience you are developing as you go along.

In the same way as you analysed your idea in the **READY** chapter, you should now put your production process under the microscope. Use the panel below to help you.

Then read widely on production and manufacturing techniques, according to your needs.

PRODUCTION – OTHER ISSUES

The panel on the previous page records your production process. Look at it closely. Ask yourself:

Where are there gaps?

Where are there inefficiencies?

Where is there duplication of work?

Where is there work that could be sub-contracted out more effectively?

How could the process be improved?

Are there any capacity constraints or bottle-necks?

How can these be overcome?

How do you propose to keep your product up-to-date?

What parts of your product can be recycled?

Could it be re-designed so that more could be recycled?

At what cost?

Is your product protected by patent?

What quality assurance systems have you in place?

How do they operate?

Have the systems been certified by an external body?

STAFF

HOW MANY STAFF?

At an early stage, you need to begin to estimate how many staff you may need and how this number will grow – and where you will recruit staff from. There's not much point planning expansion if you can't get the people to do the work.

Use the panel below to estimate your initial staff numbers and how you see this developing within the first 12 months and within the first three years. These figures will help you in developing your Operational Budget (see page 85) and in making applications for employment grants, if you are eligible.

Remember that salary is not the only cost in employing someone. PRSI must be paid on their earnings (see "Taxation"); they may be entitled to bonuses, commissions, etc.; they will need training – and there will be other costs you have not thought of.

DELEGATING

Delegating is difficult for entrepreneurs. Their whole business, their way of life, is built on their own vision. What should be done, when and how are all determined by the entrepreneur. And now parts of the business, even decisions, are to be handed over to someone else. Ouch!

This is very often the way that entrepreneurs see delegating – in a negative light, as giving up control. But that's not delegating – that's giving up control!

Delegating is a specific sequence of techniques that empowers one person (the person to whom work is delegated) while freeing up the time of another (the person delegating). Delegation involves:

- **Define the task** – In terms of resources available and outcome required, not in terms of method
- **Transfer a clear understanding** – To the person who is to do the work
- **Stand back and let them do the work, while being available to help** – But only when asked
- **Careful, shared evaluation of the outcome**.

It is critical that achievement of the task is judged only in terms of the outcome – not the methods used to achieve it. You want a store-room tidied and products placed on shelves in alphabetical order. Does it matter whether the person starts by finding all the most popular items first and putting them aside? Or that the alphabetical sequence starts left of the door and not right? Or that he begins tidying at Z and not A? Just because it isn't done the way you would have done it does not make it wrong.

OBJECTIVES

- ☐ Be aware of recruitment sources and techniques
- ☐ Be aware of employment legislation
- ☐ Be aware of staff management techniques

We wanted people who were intelligent, knowledgeable and experienced but, in choosing among candidates who had these attributes, I wanted men around me who shared my enthusiasm for work.
HAROLD GENEEN

All commercial operations can, in the final analysis, be summed up in three words: personnel, products, profits. Personnel comes first. Without a good team, it is impossible to expect anything from the other two.
LEE IACOCCA

The person who figures out how to harness the collective genius of his or her organisation is going to blow the competition away.
WALTER WRISTON

STAFFING PLAN

Copy this section to your Business Plan, page 118.

Initially, how will your staffing be organised?

- You alone, while holding another wage-earning position o
- You alone, full-time o
- You and your partner: Full-time o
- You and your partner: Part-time o
- You and your business partner(s) o
- You and your business partner(s) with employees at a wage o
- How many employees full-time? ______
- How many employees part-time? ______

How do you see this expanding?	+12 months	+ 3 years
Management	______	______
Production	______	______
Sales	______	______
Marketing	______	______
Administration	______	______
Other (specify)	______	______

DELEGATION

How much does your time cost? € _____
(the standard calculation is 3 times salary,
divided by 200 days,
divided again by 8 hours in a day
= € per hour)

Do you **really** want to take work home in the evenings and weekends? ☐ YES ☐ NO

What areas do you think you must deal with yourself?

What areas are most critical to the business?

What areas are you comfortable delegating to another person?

Delegate what to whom?

Develop a profile of the right person for each task you want to delegate and match your staff to the profiles.

Reproduced from *TENBizPlan: Dynamic Business Planning for Start-ups* by Ron Immink & Brian O'Kane (Oak Tree Press).

The important points in delegation are the task definition and the evaluation. You must sit down with the person after the task is complete and talk through what they achieved. Because you have more experience, you may know faster, better, cheaper ways of doing the task – but you should let the person identify these for themself. If you tell them, they will never learn. Worse still, they will give up, saying to themselves "I did the job. Got the right result. But all the boss was concerned about was doing it his way."

The other difficulty that entrepreneurs have with delegation is a lack of recognition that their own drive differs from that of their employees. You will quite happily stay at work late into the night, work through weekends and bank holidays, but you cannot expect that your staff will always want to do the same. Good staff will be prepared to work on to get the job done – but not just for the sake of doing. You need to learn to motivate – and be reasonable in your demands.

RECRUITING

Recruiting staff is a major stumbling block for many small businesses. It takes time and effort. But the results can have an enormous impact on your bottom line. Hire the right people, and you will have a strong staff who will move your company forward. But the wrong person will pull down morale, waste your time, and cost you more than just an extra salary.

The key steps are:

- Know what you're looking for
- Finding applicants
- Interviews.

Know what you're looking for

Before you begin looking for someone to fill a vacancy, you need to know what you're looking for. You should:

- **Create a detailed job description** – Write down the specific tasks you expect this employee to perform. Think about every detail. Then summarise and put the tasks in order of priority
- **Develop a list of skills required** – What skills are essential? What skills are merely desirable?
- **Decide whether there are other things you want?** – Specific educational background? Experience in a particular industry? What else is necessary for the person to develop in your company?
- **Think about personality** – You need people who share your vision and your standards.
- **Take a reality check** – Look at what you have written down. Which areas are priorities? Where are you willing to compromise? Will you get the person you want for the salary you are offering?

Finding applicants

Requirements defined, you now need to find people to meet them. Here are some suggestions:

- **Look in your files** – A visible and successful company will have people writing in looking for jobs, even though no vacancies are being advertised. If any of these people look promising, make time to meet and find out more about them. Then, when you need a particular mix of skills, you may find the perfect candidate in your files already
- **Ask your staff** – Your own staff may know someone with the right skills whom they would be happy to recommend (for a bonus, perhaps). And they will come with a built-in guarantee, since they won't want to let down the staff-member who sponsored them
- **Ask around** – Ask everyone you know (including customers and suppliers) whether they know anyone they would recommend. Have some background information available on the job ready to give out
- **Advertising** – Make it clear what you are looking for and write the ad to attract candidates. But make sure you have the time to handle a deluge of responses
- **Use a recruitment agency** – A sensible route if you do not have the time or ability to screen

applicants, but it can be expensive. Through their contacts, agencies can often find people whom you would otherwise not reach with an advertisement

- **Look on-line** – The World Wide Web has opened up a new set of places to post your job vacancy. These are best used for high-tech vacancies
- **Contact University/IT career offices** – They are always looking for jobs for their graduates and will usually circulate your listing free of charge
- **Job fairs** – An opportunity to give your company some visibility and talk to a variety of candidates in an unpressured environment
- **Non-traditional workers** – Don't overlook older or part-time workers or those with disabilities – they can be very capable and committed
- **Recruit overseas** – Increasingly necessary as skills shortages bite (see below for more information).

Whatever route you choose, it is a good idea to insist that every candidate completes a standard application (see next chapter, **GO**). Keep the form simple but make sure that you get all the information you need to decide whether a candidate has the skills you require for the specific position. Use the candidate's CV as a back-up.

Make a shortlist

Before you start looking at CVs or application forms, write out again a summary of the main points you are looking for in a candidate. Screen quickly looking for these – and only these. Put all applications that do not meet these criteria into a separate bundle. If you want, review them later to see whether they include any candidates you might want to keep for your files. Otherwise, remove them from consideration immediately. Write to them to say that you will not be calling them to interview – from the candidate's point of view, it's better to get bad news than not to hear at all.

Concentrate on the ones that meet your criteria. Read them again more carefully. Look for little things: gaps in employment, jobs that don't quite fit a career path, hobbies that don't sit well with the personality type you are looking for, inconsistencies and even, if the job involves written communication, misspellings and poor grammar.

Make a shortlist. Decide which candidates you want to interview and contact them to arrange dates and times. Although interview candidates should do their own research on your business before coming for interview, it is helpful to include some background information on your business with the letter confirming the interview.

Overseas recruitment

Before deciding to recruit foreign workers, consider whether you can source staff locally, since overseas recruitment is usually more expensive when all costs are considered than local recruitment.

If it's necessary, you should know that:

- Workers from outside the EU or EEA (EU plus Norway, Liechtenstein and Iceland) require work permits
- Work permits are issued by the Department of Enterprise, Trade and Employment to the **employer**, not the employee
- Visas may be required of some non-EU nationals
- All non-EU nationals resident in Ireland for more than 90 days must register with the Gardai.

A Fastrack scheme, involving the issue of work visas or work authorisations, allows foreign IT, construction and medical workers obtain immigration and employment clearance in advance at Irish embassies and consultancies, provided they have a job offer and valid passport.

In such cases, the visa/authorisation is issued to the **employee**. It is valid for up to two years, during which time the employee may change employers.

Enterprise Ireland publishes a useful booklet, "Overseas Recruitment".

INTERVIEW CHECKLIST

Candidate name ____________________

Meets educational criteria?	☐ YES	☐ NO
Meets experience criteria?	☐ YES	☐ NO
Passed competence test?	☐ YES	☐ NO
Has essential skills?	☐ YES	☐ NO
Has desirable skills?	☐ YES	☐ NO
Has additional skills?	☐ YES	☐ NO
Good oral communication skills?	☐ YES	☐ NO
Good written comm. skills?	☐ YES	☐ NO
Has foreign language skills?	☐ YES	☐ NO
Good personality?	☐ YES	☐ NO
Would fit in well with other staff?	☐ YES	☐ NO
Currently employed?	☐ YES	☐ NO
Notice period needed?	____________	
Clean driving licence?	☐ YES	☐ NO
Smoker?	☐ YES	☐ NO
Good health record?	☐ YES	☐ NO
Days off in past year?	____________	
Permission to contact referees?	☐ YES	☐ NO

INTERVIEWING

When interviewing, you only have a short time to find out all you need to make an informed decision about investing in someone who should become an asset to your business. Therefore:

- **Use an interview checklist** – Develop a list of points that you want to cover during the interview (see panel above)
- **Ask open-ended questions** – Avoid questions that can be answered "yes" or "no"; use questions like "Why did you like working in sales?", "What are your strengths and weaknesses?" or "Why are you leaving your current job?"
- **Ask unconventional questions** – See how candidates think (and how fast) by asking them questions they may not have prepared for. For example, "Why shouldn't all staff be paid the same?", "If you didn't have to work, what would you do with your time?"
- **Find out what's important to the candidate** – What is he/she looking for: growth opportunities, regular hours, training, new responsibilities? Will he/she finish the job or just clock-watch?
- **Listen** – Spend 20% of the time talking and 80% listening. The purpose of the interview is to help you learn about the candidates, not to talk about yourself
- **Interview more than once** – Use the first interview to find the top two or three candidates; use the second to make sure you choose the best
- **Involve other staff** – If you are particularly pleased with a candidate, let them meet some of your existing staff with whom they will be working. Get these staff-members' opinion
- **Check references** — Ask what the relationship between candidate and referee is. Confirm previous positions, responsibilities and achievements. Ask about working habits, ability to get along with others, problems, etc.

Be open with candidates. Tell them that you are interviewing others. Give them a date by which they can expect to hear from you – one way or the other. Keep to it.

The job offer

You have already discussed the job offer with your ideal candidate at interview, before writing to offer the job – in some cases, you may make the offer at the interview and shake hands on a deal. Either way, you should write to the selected candidate and set out clearly:

- The job title and description
- The salary; how it is to be paid; and whether it includes overtime, bonuses, etc
- The normal hours of work
- Holidays
- Period of notice required on resignation/dismissal
- Grievance procedures
- Any other "house" rules.

Send two copies of this letter, both signed by you, and ask for one back, signed by the new appointee to signify their acceptance of the position on the terms offered.

EMPLOYMENT LEGISLATION

Note that there is a clear distinction, particularly for tax purposes, between employees and self-employed contractors. Check with the Department of Social, Community and Family Affairs or the Revenue Commissioners.

By law, full-time employees are entitled to:

- A written contract of employment
- Minimum wages
- Equal pay for equal work
- Protection against discrimination
- Holidays and rest periods
- Maternity, adoptive and parental leave
- Trade union membership
- Minimum notice on termination of employment
- Protection against unfair dismissal
- Protection against redundancy, and minimum payments if it should occur.

A written contract of employment

Employees are entitled to a written statement of the terms of employment, within one month of requesting it (see sample in **GO**). This must set out:

- Details of the employment
- The procedure the employer will use for dismissal
- Salary
- Deductions from salary.

Minimum wages

The National Minimum Wages Act came into force on 1 April 2000. Experienced adult workers (those over 18, more than two years employed and not a trainee) must be paid a minimum average hourly rate.

Equal pay for equal work

Where men and women perform similar work, under similar conditions, or requiring similar skills, or work of similar value or responsibility, they must be paid the same. Equality Officers of the Labour Court have the right to enter premises, examine records and seek information where an equality claim is made.

Protection against discrimination

The Employment Equality Act, 1977 bans discrimination on the basis of sex or marital status in:

- Recruitment
- Conditions of employment other than pay or pension (covered by equality legislation)
- Training and work experience
- Opportunities for promotions.

Holidays

Most employees are entitled to a minimum of 20 days annual leave, plus public holidays (8 each year). The "holiday year" runs from 1 April to 31 March and pro-rata entitlements apply for periods of less than a year.

The Organisation of Working Time Act, 1997 also requires that employees:

- Work no more than a 48-hour week, averaged over a 4, 6 or 12 month period as appropriate
- Have rest breaks while at work
- Have 11 hours rest in each 24-hour period
- Have one period of 24 hours rest per week, preceded by a daily rest period of 11 hours.

The Act applies to all workers, except Gardai and the Defence Forces. Its general provisions may be varied by collective agreement.

Maternity leave

Regardless of length of service, a pregnant employee has the right to:

- Take up to 18 weeks maternity leave
- Return to work, to her previous job or one of similar status, afterwards
- Reasonable time off for ante and post-natal care.

The Department of Social, Community and Family Affairs pays her a pay-related Maternity Allowance for 14 weeks. The remaining four weeks maternity leave are unpaid. There is no obligation on the employer to pay any salary during maternity leave.

The employee must give her employer four weeks written notice of her intention to take maternity leave and the dates of her leave. She must also give her employer four weeks written notice of her intention to return to work after maternity leave.

Adoptive leave

A women employee is entitled to 10 weeks' adoptive leave under much the same terms as maternity leave above. Similar leave is available to sole male adopters.

Parental leave

Both parents are entitled to up to 14 weeks unpaid leave to take care of a child up to five years of age.

This leave can be taken in a single block, weekly blocks, days or even hours, though the employer must be informed in writing six weeks in advance.

The Parental Leave Act, 1998 also provides for paid "force majeure" leave of up to three days in a year or five days over three days on the sudden illness/injury of an immediate family member.

Trade union membership

The Irish Constitution is an employee's ultimate assurance of the right to form or to join a trade union.

Union activities, in particular, disputes and their conduct, are covered by the Industrial Relations Act, 1990, which also established the Labour Relations Commission.

Minimum notice on termination of employment

The Minimum Notice to Terminate Employment Act, 1973, applies to employees in continuous service for 13 weeks.

Protection against unfair dismissal

Where an employee has been employed for more than 12 months, he/she is deemed to have been unfairly dismissed unless the criteria for a fair dismissal laid down in the Unfair Dismissals Act, 1977 have been met. Among other things, these require that:

- The procedures for dismissal laid down by the employer be fair
- The procedures be operated fairly.

A short-term contract must be signed by both employeee and employer and clearly state that the provisions of the 1977 Act do not apply, in order to be considered a valid reason for dismissal at the expiry of the contract term.

Protection against redundancy

Where redundancy is unavoidable, an employee is entitled to payment by the employer (or failing this, from the State). The amounts of the payments are set by law and vary according to age and length of service.

Where the employee meets certain criteria, the employer may recover 60% of the statutory redundancy payments from the Redundancy and Employers Insolvency Fund, administered by the Minister for Enterprise, Trade and Employment.

Part-time employees

Part-time workers do not have the same rights as full-time workers, although the Worker Protection (Regular Part-time Employee) Act, 1991 extended some of the benefits of full-time working to "regular" part-time employees, defined as those in continuous service for at least 13 weeks and normally expected to work at least eight hours per week.

MANAGING STAFF

Businesses go through different stages of development and the management style appropriate to one stage may not be right for another. For example, a person who runs a one-man business does not need to worry about delegating – but when he/she has a dozen employees delegating becomes more important than doing.

You should be thinking about managing long before you have anyone to manage. The starting point is your own strengths and weaknesses as an entrepreneur. Go back to the "Self-assessment" and "Training for Entrepreneurs" section in the chapter, **READY**. Refresh your memory on your skills and training needs.

Consider whether a partner or key employee could supply some of the skills you are missing. Use the panel below to identify critical areas in your business and those where a partner or key manager could make a difference. Could your business bear the financial impact of another salary? One that would make a critical difference to the speed at which your business develops? Could you reduce your own salary for a while to compensate (a real test of commitment!)?

If you are to build a strong team, you need to become a good manager yourself. There are lots of books and courses available to help you here. You need to build skills in delegation, time management, coaching, appraisal and communications to name but a few. But one of the most important points to make is that successful managers show, in lots of little but important ways, that they care for their staff, that they trust them and that they are willing to allow them to use their initiative (and to make mistakes!).

Good managers listen, they are interested in people in and outside work, they share information and knowledge, they are open to new ideas, they are enthusiastic and have a sense of humour. Check your own management style by writing the answers to the questions below in the panel below.

STAFF RETENTION

It may seem strange to consider staff retention before you have even recruited your first employee but, as in many things, forward planning pays off.

Staff are a key success factor in any business. Managing staff has implications in every part of the business as very often your staff will be responsible for implementing all the bright ideas you come up with. They can make or break your ideas. And, properly encouraged, they can produce bright ideas of their own. Therefore, a lot of time and thought should be given not only to considering whom you want to recruit but also how to keep your staff happy and productive.

To see why this is important, consider the costs of staff turnover:

- **Loss of capacity:** There's no one there to do the work, until you find a replacement
- **Loss of knowledge:** All that the person has learnt, before joining and while with your business, is gone
- **Loss of experience:** All the experience the person had is gone
- **Loss of network:** All the contacts that the person had are gone – some other employer has these now (are they a competitor of yours?)
- **Loss of training**: All the training you gave the person is gone
- **Cost of recruitment:** You will have to spend time and money recruiting a replacement and may have to pay the new person more than the person who left
- **Cost of induction:** The new person will take a little while to settle in, during which time they are producing below expected output and a drain on the time of other staff
- **Cost of new training:** You may have to train the new person.

All this means that you want to minimise staff turnover.

CRITICAL BUSINESS AREAS

Which of these areas are most critical to the development of your business? Where would a partner or key manager make the most difference?

Rank them 1, 2, 3, etc.

	Critical	Difference
Marketing	____	____
Sales	____	____
Financial control	____	____
Production	____	____
Management	____	____

YOUR MANAGEMENT STYLE

Are you a good listener?	☐ YES	☐ NO
Do you like people?	☐ YES	☐ NO
Do you mind sharing?	☐ YES	☐ NO
Do you have an open mind?	☐ YES	☐ NO
Are you enthusiastic?	☐ YES	☐ NO
Do you have a sense of humour?	☐ YES	☐ NO
Do you have clear job descriptions?	☐ YES	☐ NO
Do you know what you expect from your staff?	☐ YES	☐ NO
Are you willing to improve?	☐ YES	☐ NO

Which Legal Structure?

When starting in business, you have a choice of four main types of business entity through which to conduct your enterprise. They are: Sole trader, Partnership, Limited liability company and Co-operative.

Four things will decide which you choose:

- **The kind of business you are starting** – Some professional firms can only be formed as sole traders or partnerships
- **The expectations of those with whom you plan to do business** – Many business people expect to deal with limited companies and are wary of other forms of business entities as trading partners
- **Your attitude to risk** – In particular, to risking those of your assets that you are not planning to commit to the business. A limited liability company limits the risk of losing your capital if your enterprise is not successful.
- **How you wish to organise your tax affairs** – Certain kinds of favourable tax treatment are only available to limited liability companies.

You are taking a risk in starting an enterprise. You are risking your money, time and reputation. You are entitled to protect those of your assets that you do not wish to commit. For this reason, you are strongly advised to form a limited liability company. However, because of the tax and other implications of doing so, you should take professional help and advice before making your decision.

Sole Trader

You automatically become a sole trader by starting up a business on your own. Setting up as a sole trader needs almost nothing by way of legal formality, apart from registering with the Registrar of Business Names at the Companies Registration Office (**www.cro.ie**), which is optional.

An advantage of being a sole trader is that apart from normal tax returns, which every taxable person must make, a sole trader is not required to make public any information about the business. The downside of being a sole trader is that you have no protection if your business fails. All your assets become available to pay off your creditors.

Partnership

A partnership, essentially, is an agreement between two or more people to go into business together. It may be no more formal than a handshake or may run to a multi-page legal document.

Whichever route you take, build the following points into your planning:

- In a partnership, **each** partner is liable for **all** the liabilities of the business. If the business fails, and your partner(s) abandon(s) you, you could be left to pay for everything out of your own pocket. Before entering a partnership, decide whether you trust your partner(s)-to-be with everything you own — because that's what you will be doing.
- If you write down nothing else, write down and have all the partners sign a partnership agreement setting out how the business is to be financed, how profits and losses are to be shared, and what will happen if one of the partners decides to leave. These are important points. Failure to agree on them at an early stage can lead to difficulty later.

A limited liability company

A limited liability company is a legal entity separate from its shareholders. The shareholders are only liable, in the event of the business becoming unable to pay its debts, for any amount outstanding on their subscribed shareholdings.

Some limited companies are limited by guarantee – the guarantee being the amount that the members agree to pay in the event of the company going into liquidation. This form of company is more suitable for clubs and associations than for trading businesses.

The advantages of a limited liability company over a sole trader or partnership are:

- Limited liability status
- The possibility of obtaining credit more easily
- The only income taxable on the owners of the business is any salaries or dividends taken from the business
- Business Expansion Scheme relief for

OBJECTIVES

- ☐ Understand the options available
- ☐ Make an informed choice of structure for your business
- ☐ Understand the responsibilities of a director

One of the most fruitful sources of ruin to men of the world is the recklessness or want of principle of partners, and it is one of the perils to which every man exposes himself who enters into business with another.

SIR R MALINS

a qualifying company (to end 2006 only)
- Scope for tax planning.

The disadvantages include:
- The cost of formation expenses
- The requirement for an annual audit (not required for companies limited by shares where turnover is under €317,000, the balance sheet total is under €1.9 million and there are less than 50 employees)
- The public filing of information with the Companies Registration Office
- The need for accounts to comply with Companies Acts and auditing and accounting standards
- Business losses may not be set against personal income
- Possibility of further taxation on capital gains if appreciating assets are withdrawn from the business.

EU regulations now allow the formation of private limited companies with only one member (as against the previous requirement for two members), although two directors are still required.

Registration and other forms are available for download from **www.cro.ie**

A co-operative

A worker co-operative is where a team comes together to form and run a business according to a set of values that include self-help, self-responsibility, democracy, equality, equity and solidarity. The business is jointly owned and democratically controlled, unlike other more hierarchical business structures. Co-operative members believe in the ethical values of honesty, openness, social responsibility and caring for others. The Co-operative Principles, which provide guidelines setting out how the business should conduct itself, are:
- **Voluntary and open membership:** Co-operatives do not permit gender, social, racial, political or religious discrimination and are open to all willing to accept the responsibilities of membership
- **Democratic member control:** Co-operatives are democratically controlled by their members, who actively participate in setting policies and in decision-making
- **Member economic participation:** Members contribute equitably to the capital of their business. Surpluses are used to develop the business, benefiting members in proportion to their transactions with the co-operative and supporting activities approved by the membership
- **Autonomy and independence:** In all contracts with external bodies, co-operatives ensure that members retain democratic control and their co-operative autonomy
- **Education, training and information:** Co-operatives provide education and training for their members and employees to ensure their effective contribution
- **Co-operation among co-operatives:** Co-operatives work together through local, regional, national and international structures
- **Concern for community:** Co-operatives work for sustainable development through policies approved by their members.

Formation of co-operatives is by Model Rules, available from the FÁS Co-operative Development Unit (**www.fas.ie**). Co-operatives can be formed as limited liability companies.

Directors' responsibilities

If you are a director of a limited liability company, you take on responsibilities – and the enforcement regime for these is becoming increasingly strict – including:
- Responsibilities given under the company's Articles of Association
- Responsibilities imposed by company law
- A fiduciary duty under common law.

This means that directors act on behalf of all shareholders, not just some, and requires directors to consider the long-term implications of their actions, since they have a duty to future shareholders as well as present.

Directors owe a duty to exercise skill and diligence in their work, in line with their knowledge and experience, though they cannot be held responsible in law for errors of judgement. In certain circumstances, directors may become personally liable for the debts of a company – for example, where it can be shown that they are guilty of reckless or fraudulent trading, or where the company has failed to keep "proper books of account".

On a day-to-day basis, the Companies Acts impose requirements on directors (strictly on the company but the directors are responsible for ensuring compliance) in relation to returns of information – for example, an Annual Return each year following the Annual General Meeting. Following many years of non-compliance (or, at best, lax compliance, even among sizeable companies), the Companies Registration Office, to be backed by a Director of Company Law Enforcement, is now taking a harsher view and imposing penalties and "striking off" companies for late returns. The impact of this is that, where a company continues to trade after it has been struck off, the directors become personally liable for its debts.

In company secretarial work and your responsibilities as a director, take advice from your accountant.

Registering a Business Name

The name of a business is one of its most important assets, even though it does not appear in the balance sheet with the other assets. Choose the name of your business carefully. The right name will be:
- Unique
- Easy to remember, pronounce and spell
- Informative
- Image-creating.

If your business is going to trade as a limited company, there are some restrictions on the name you choose (see panel).

Even if your business is not going to trade as a limited company, there are still some rules to be followed. You still cannot use the name of an existing business, or one that will be confused with the name of an existing business. However, a partnership can use the same name as an existing partnership, provided the name consists only of the names of the partners. In general, follow the rules for companies above.

Registering a business name

If, trading as a limited company, you wish to trade under a name other than the company's registered name (for example as *West Cork Forest Advisory Services*, even though the company is registered as *Frank Kelly Limited*), you must register the business name.

If you are trading in one of the other business structures, it is advisable to register the name of the business.

However, note that registration of a business name does not:
- Give protection against duplication of the name (since others may be entitled to use it, though you can prevent them from "passing off" – pretending to be you)
- Imply that the name will prove acceptable as a company name (it may already be registered, or become registered later, as a company name)
- Authorise the use of the name, if its use could be prohibited for other reasons — for example, because the name proposed is the trade mark of another person.

Because of this last point, it is important to check whether someone else might have rights in the proposed name before spending money on stationery, signs etc. Check at the Companies Registration Office, Dublin.

To register a business name, you must:
- Complete Form RBN1B (available for download from the Companies Registration Office web-site)
- Send it with the prescribed fee, to The Registrar of Companies, Companies Registration Office, Parnell House, 14 Parnell Square, Dublin 1.

You can do this when you are sending in the documentation for the formation of the company.

On registration of your business name, you will be issued with a Certificate of Business Name. This must be displayed prominently at the company's registered or principal office and in every branch or premises.

Internet names

Because of abuse of the facility to register Internet "domain" names, you may now be required by the IE Domain Registry (**www.domainregistry.ie**) to provide evidence that you have some entitlement to an .ie domain name that you wish to register. A registered business name may help provide this evidence.

OBJECTIVES
- ☐ Understand the importance of choosing the right name
- ☐ Understand the importance of registering a business name
- ☐ Be aware of procedures for registration

CHOOSING A COMPANY NAME

You may not use as a name for a limited company any name which:
- Is identical to the name of an existing company
- Is identical to, or could be confused with, the name of a foreign company which conducts business in Ireland
- Is identical to a well-known trade mark
- Could be confused with the name of an existing company, because it is phonetically identical or the difference in spelling is such as to be immaterial
- In the opinion of the Minister for Enterprise, Trade and Employment, is undesirable
- Implies State sponsorship
- Uses certain restricted words, such as "Bank", "Banker", or "Banking", "Society", "Co-op", "Co-operative" or "Insurance".

Opening a Bank Account

OBJECTIVES

☐ Understand the steps involved in opening a business bank account

At least one bank account is essential for any business, however small. Don't be tempted to run your business through your own personal bank account "until it gets off the ground". That is a recipe for disaster. Open a separate bank account for your business as soon as you begin to trade.

A limited company needs to pass a resolution of the Board of Directors to open a bank account. The steps are:

- Ask your bank manager for a bank mandate form. This authorises the bank to carry out the instructions of the directors regarding the operation of the account
- Decide what instructions you want to give the bank regarding who is authorised to sign cheques on behalf of the company, and how often you want to receive statements
- Hold a meeting of the directors of the company
- Propose the resolution at the meeting in the form required by the bank – see the mandate form for the wording – and have it adopted by the directors
- Complete the mandate form
- Get sample signatures from each of the people authorised to sign cheques on behalf of the company
- Return the mandate form and sample signatures to your bank manager
- Give the bank manager a copy of each of your company's Memorandum and Articles of Association. These will be kept for the manager's files
- Show the original of the company's Certificate of Incorporation to your bank manager. A copy of this will be taken for the manager's files and on the copy will be marked the fact that the original has been seen by the manager. You will not be asked for, and you should not give the bank manager, the original Certificate of Incorporation (except in the larger city branches where the documents to open your bank account go to the Securities department for checking. In this case, your bank manager should give you a receipt for the certificate and give you a date when you can return to collect it)
- Have available some money to lodge to the new account
- Decide the name in which you want the account to be opened. You can use only the registered name of the company, unless you are trading under a registered business name. In this case, you will also need to show the bank manager the Certificate of Registration of Business Name for the company
- Depending on the bank and branch, it may take a few days or a few weeks to clear all the paperwork associated with opening your company's bank account. Allow for this in your planning
- If you need immediate access to the money you are lodging, your bank manager can usually arrange for temporary cheques to be made available while a chequebook is being printed.

OPENING A BANK ACCOUNT – CHECKLIST

When you go to the bank to open your bank account, make sure that you have:

- A completed bank mandate form ☐
- Sample signatures for all those who will sign cheques on the company's bank account ☐
- A copy of the Memorandum and Articles of Association (limited company only) ☐
- Certificate of Incorporation (limited company only) ☐
- Certificate of Business Name (if you are trading under any name other than the company's registered name) ☐
- Cash or cheques to lodge to your new account. ☐

TAXATION

Businesses in Ireland are subject to:

- **Income tax** – Sole traders and partnerships on their profits
- **Corporation tax** – Limited companies on their profits
- **Value added tax (VAT)** – All businesses with turnover in excess of €51,000 (goods) or €25,500 (services)
- **PAYE/PRSI** – All businesses with employees (including owner/directors).

Registration for tax

It is your obligation to notify the Revenue Commissioners through your local tax office of the establishment of your business and to provide them with the information required to register your business for the relevant taxes.

You must complete one of two forms, depending on your circumstances:

- Form TR1, if you are a sole trader or partnership
- Form TR2, if your business is a limited company.

Each of these forms gets you registered for all applicable taxes. They are available for download on the Revenue's web-site.

Shortly after registration, you will receive a "new Business Visit" from a Revenue official who will go through the requirements to ensure that you have proper systems in place.

CORPORATION TAX

Limited companies pay Corporation Tax. This tax is charged on the company's profits which include both income and chargeable gains.

A company's income for tax purposes is calculated in accordance with Income Tax rules. Chargeable gains are calculated in accordance with Capital Gains Tax rules.

If an individual is trading through a company, any losses arising cannot be offset against any other personal income earned. The losses can only be offset against trading income of the company or against future or past profits, subject to certain restrictions.

Self-assessment

The self-assessment system applies to companies. Preliminary Tax is payable within six months of the end of the accounting period, which is generally the period for which the company makes up its accounts. To avoid an interest charge of 1.25% per month, Preliminary Tax paid must be 90% of the final liability for the period. A company must submit a return (Form CT1) no later than 9 months from the end of the accounting period to which the return relates. If the Preliminary Tax paid was sufficient, the balance of tax is payable within one month of the issue of the assessment by the Inspector of Taxes.

There are also restrictions on the use the company can make of certain reliefs and allowances if the return is not submitted on time.

There are two rates of Corporation Tax:

- 12.5% on trading income
- 25% on non-trading income

INCOME TAX

Income tax is payable by individuals on income earned in the tax year – that is, on annual profits or gains from an individual's trade, profession or vocation and on other income, such as investment income, rental income etc.

A tax assessment is usually based on actual income earned in the tax year – from 1 January to 31 December. It is up to the individual/business to decide the date to which the accounts are prepared, usually to the same date each year.

A self-employed person will be taxed under the Self-Assessment system.

Preliminary Tax is an estimate of the income tax payable for the year. It includes PRSI and Health Contribution as well as income tax. The duty lies on the individual to calculate their own Preliminary Tax. If Preliminary Tax is not paid by the due date, or if the amount is too low, interest will be charged at a rate of 1.25% per month or part of month on the balance of tax outstanding. Failure to submit a tax return by the tax return filing date will result in a surcharge being added to the final tax bill.

Where a new business is set up, the surcharge will not be imposed if the return for the first year is made by the return filing date for the following year.

OBJECTIVES

- ☐ Understand system of taxation
- ☐ Understand basics of individual taxes

REVENUE COMMISSIONERS' MISSION

To serve the community by fairly and efficiently collecting taxes and duties and implementing import and export controls.

There's nothing so hard to understand as the income tax.
ALBERT EINSTEIN

The trick is to stop thinking of it as "your" money.
UK REVENUE AUDITOR

An explanatory booklet (IT10) on *A Guide to Self-Assessment* is available from the Revenue web-site.

Calculating taxable profits

Taxable profits are calculated by deducting allowable business expenses from turnover. Turnover is the gross amount of income earned by a business before deducting any business expenses – the total amounts from sale of goods or provision of services. If a business is registered for VAT, the turnover figure should exclude VAT.

If a business makes a loss, it is either offset against other taxable income or carried forward against the future profits of the business.

Business expenses are normally referred to as revenue expenditure, which covers day-to-day running costs (exclusive of VAT, if the business is registered for VAT), including:

- Purchase of goods for resale
- Wages, rent, rates, repairs, lighting, heating etc
- Running costs of vehicles or machinery used in the business
- Accountancy and audit fees
- Interest paid on any monies borrowed to finance business expenses/items
- Lease payments on vehicles or machinery used in the business.

Some expenses cannot be claimed as revenue expenditure, including:

- Any expense, not wholly and exclusively paid for the purposes of the trade or profession
- Any private or domestic expenditure
- Business entertainment expenditure – the provision of accommodation, food, drink or any other form of hospitality
- Expenditure of a capital nature.

For expenditure relating to both business and private use, only that part relating to the business will be allowed.

A deduction for the running expenses of a vehicle used for business purposes can also be claimed. To calculate the split of capital allowances (wear and tear) and running expenses, total mileage for the year and the total number of miles travelled for business purposes must be recorded. Journeys between home and a regular place of work are treated as private and not business mileage.

Expenditure is regarded as "capital" if it has been spent on acquiring or altering assets which are of lasting use in the business – for example, the purchase or alteration of business premises. Capital expenditure cannot be deducted in arriving at the taxable profit. However, capital allowances may be claimed on capital expenditure incurred on items such as office equipment, business plant and machinery, taking account of wear and tear on these items.

TAXPAYERS' CHARTER OF RIGHTS

In your dealings with the Revenue Commissioners, you are entitled to:

- **Courtesy and Consideration** – To expect that Revenue staff will at all times carry out their duties courteously and considerately.
- **Presumption of Honesty** – To be presumed to have dealt with your tax affairs honestly unless there is reason to believe to the contrary and subject to the Revenue Commissioners' responsibility for ensuring compliance with the law.
- **Information** – To expect that every reasonable effort will be made to give you access to full, accurate and timely information about Revenue law and your entitlements and obligations under it. So that they can do this, Revenue staff are entitled to expect that you will give them all the facts and the full co-operation which they need to deal with your affairs.
- **Impartiality** – To have your affairs dealt with in an impartial manner by Revenue staff who seek only to collect the correct amount of tax or duty, no more and no less.
- **Privacy and Confidentiality** – To expect that personal and business information provided by you will be treated in strict confidence and used only for purposes allowed by law.
- **Independent Review** – To object to a charge to tax or duty if you think the law has been applied incorrectly and to ask that your case be reviewed. If the matter cannot be resolved to your satisfaction by Revenue officials, you have rights in law to independent review.
- **Compliance Costs** – To expect that the Revenue Commissioners and their staff recognise the need to keep to the minimum necessary the costs you incur in complying with Revenue law, subject to their responsibility to carry out their functions efficiently and economically.
- **Consistent Administration** – To expect that the Revenue Commissioners will administer the law consistently and apply it firmly to those who try to evade paying their lawful share.

To arrive at the correct taxable income, the net profit should be calculated and any allowances and relief entitlements should be deducted.

Sub-contractors

Sub-contractors in the construction, forestry or meat-processing industries will have tax deducted at 35% on all payments to them by principal contractors unless they have a certificate of authorisation (C2).

The decision as to whether a person is an employee or sub-contractor is matter of fact determined by guidelines set out in an explanatory guide for sub-contractors (IT64) is available on the Revenue's web-site.

When starting a job as a sub-contractor, you must produce your C2 and sign a Form RCT1, which the principal contractor keeps. All payments to you then will be gross. Otherwise, at the end of the job, the principal contractor will issue you with a Form RCTDC, a deduction certificate, which shows how much tax has been deducted.

Whether you are paid gross, or with tax deducted, you are still liable to complete tax returns under the Self-Assessment system and pay any balance of tax due.

You can apply for a C2 at your local tax office.

PAYE/PRSI

The Pay As You Earn (PAYE) system operates on the basis that an employer deducts tax at a specified rate from an employee's pay. The system is designed so that, as far as is possible, the correct amount of tax is deducted from an employee's pay to meet his/her tax liability for the year. To achieve this, PAYE is normally computed on a cumulative basis, from the beginning of the tax year to the date on which a payment is being made.

In certain situations, it is not appropriate to operate PAYE on a cumulative basis and, therefore, tax is deducted on a "Week 1" basis.

In addition to deducting PAYE, employers are also obliged to deduct Pay Related Social Insurance (PRSI) from employees on behalf of the Department of Social, Community and Family Affairs. The employee's PRSI contribution is made up of:

- Social Insurance, which varies according to the earnings of the employee and the benefits for which the person is insured
- 2% Health Contribution.

From 6 April 2001, the old system of tax free allowances was changed in favour of a "tax credit" system, which operates as follows:

- An employee pays tax at the standard rate (20%)

COMPLETING FORMS TR1 AND TR2

Both forms register businesses for Corporation Tax, Employer's PAYE/PRSI and/or VAT, in one operation. Use Form TR1 for sole traders or partnerships, and Form TR2 for limited companies.

For either form:

- To register for Income Tax/Corporation Tax only, complete Parts A, B and C
- To register for Employer's PAYE/PRSI only, complete Parts A, B and D
- To register for VAT only, complete Parts A, B and E
- To register for ALL taxes, complete Parts A, B, C, D + E.

Whatever sections of the form have been completed, the Declaration in Part A **MUST** be signed before a company may be registered for any tax.

Make sure you give:

- The full name of the company as registered under the Companies' Acts (not the trading name)
- The name of your accountant, who will prepare the accounts and tax returns for the company
- Where a different person handles matters relating to Employer's PAYE/PRSI and/or VAT, give their name(s) and address(es).

Check with your accountant about:

- Election for registration for VAT if you are not obliged by law to register
- Election for registration for VAT in respect of certain lettings of premises where the services provided are normally exempt from VAT
- Election for cash receipts basis of accounting for VAT.

These forms are available on the Revenue's web-site.

on all his/her taxable earnings for a pay period up to the standard rate cut-off point for that period
- He/she pays tax at the higher rate (42%) on all earnings for the pay period above this point
- The total of the tax due by the employee for the pay period is reduced by tax credits due to the employee in respect of the pay period.

The amounts of the standard rate cut-off point and tax credits due to the employee are determined by the tax office and advised on a Certificate of Tax Credits and Standard Rate Cut-Off Point issued to the employee.

Employers' PAYE/PRSI

When starting in business, you must register for PAYE/PRSI if you pay:
- €8 per week (€36 a month), or more, to an employee who has only one employment
- €2 per week (€9 a month), or more, to an employee who has more than one employment.

A company must register as an employer and operate PAYE/PRSI on the pay of directors even if there are no other employees.

It is important to distinguish whether a payment, benefit, expense etc. should be regarded as "pay" and taxed under the PAYE system. There are particular areas of benefits/perks (car, medical insurance, etc.) which have different tax implications.

Expenses incurred by employees while carrying out the duties of the job and for which receipts can be produced are not generally regarded as pay.

Registration as an employer

To register for PAYE/PRSI, employers must complete form TR1 (sole trader or partnership) or TR2 (limited company). You will receive confirmation of your registration as an employer, including a registered number for PAYE purposes and detailed information regarding the operation of PAYE/PRSI.

If you become an employer and fail to register for PAYE/PRSI purposes, the Revenue Commissioners will compulsorily register you. You will have to pay the PAYE and PRSI due and interest will be charged at 1.25% per month from the date on which it should have been paid.

Payments and returns

PAYE and PRSI payments must be paid to the Collector-General within 14 days from the end of the income tax month during which the deductions were made.

A form P30 Bank Giro/Payslip is issued to the employer each month on which the figures for total tax and total PRSI contributions should be entered, together with the gross total which will equal the amount of the payment. The form P30 should be returned marked "Nil" if there is no PAYE/PRSI liability for a particular month.

Employers can arrange to pay PAYE/PRSI through a direct debit scheme and make an annual return/declaration of liability. At the end of the tax year, the employer must complete end-of-year forms P35, P35L and P35/T which are sent by the Collector-General. These forms must be returned by the due date.

Employers must also issue a Form P60 to each employee who was in employment at 31 December. This form shows total pay, tax and PRSI contributions for the year ended 31 December.

VALUE ADDED TAX

Value Added Tax (VAT) is a consumer tax collected by VAT-registered traders on their supplies of taxable goods and services in the course of business and by Customs & Excise on imports from outside the EU.

Each trader pays VAT on goods and services acquired for the business and charges VAT on goods and services supplied by the business. The amount by which VAT charged exceeds VAT paid must be paid to the Collector-General.

If the amount of VAT paid exceeds the VAT charged, the Collector-General will pay over the excess to the trader. This ensures that VAT is paid by the ultimate customer and not by the business.

Taxable persons

A taxable person for VAT purposes is an individual (other than an employee), a partnership, company etc, who supplies taxable goods and services in the course of or in the furtherance of the business.

Taxable persons are obliged to register for VAT where the amount of their annual turnover (the amount of receipts excluding VAT) exceeds or is likely to exceed:
- €51,000 – goods
- €25,500 – services.

Traders whose turnover is below these limits are not generally obliged to register for VAT but may do so if they wish.

The current rates of VAT are:
- **21% (standard rate)** – all goods and services that are not exempt or are taxable at the zero or reduced rates

HOW TO PUT A NEW EMPLOYEE ON THE BOOKS

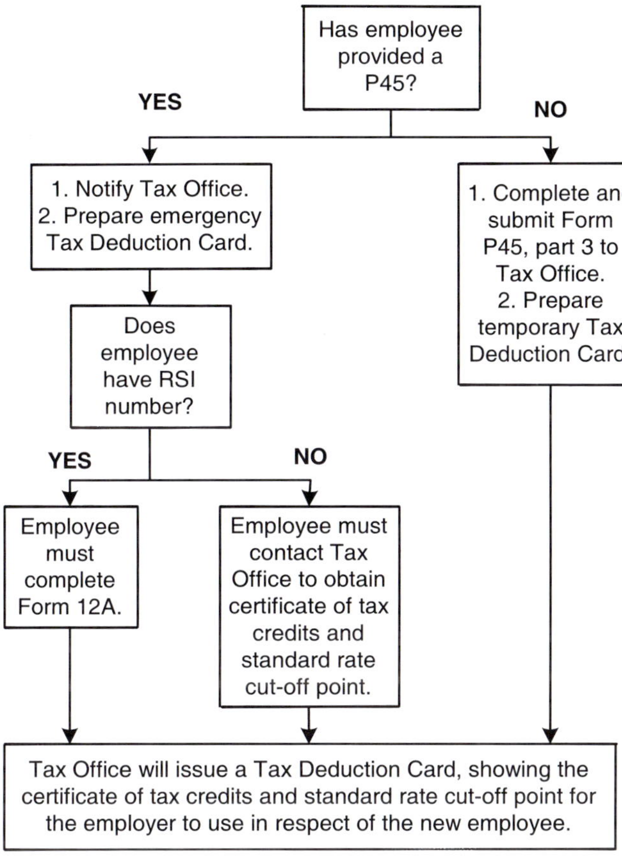

- **13.5%** – certain fuels (coal and domestic gas), building and building services, newspapers, certain other goods and services
- **4.8%** – livestock, live greyhounds and the hire of horses
- **Zero** – exports, certain food and drink (bread and milk), oral medicine, books excluding newspapers, brochures
- **Exempt** – financial, medical and educational activities.

Registration

To register for VAT, complete form TR1 (TR2 for a limited company).

Cash basis of accounting

Any registered person whose annual turnover is less than €635,000 can account for VAT on receipt of payment rather than on the issue of an invoice. This gives a significant cash-flow benefit. Applications to use the cash basis of accounting should be made to your local tax office, after discussing the matter with your accountant.

Returns

When you register for VAT, the Collector-General will send you a form VAT3 every two months. You must complete this form and return it to the Collector-General before the 19th day following the end of the two monthly period giving details of:

- VAT charged by you for the period
- VAT paid by you for the period
- VAT due to Revenue or repayable to you
- Goods supplied to/received from other EU member states.

You are required to make a VAT return even if you do not owe any VAT for the period.

An annual return of trading details is also required. This return can be prepared for any period of 12 months which best suits your accounting arrangements.

VAT may be paid through the Revenue's direct debit scheme. Any excess VAT will be repaid automatically by electronic transmission to your nominated bank or building society.

GENERAL

Record-keeping

The Revenue Commissioners have certain requirements regarding record-keeping and accounts (see "Accounting", page 72) which you must comply with.

Returns

For each of the taxes, you are required to supply the Revenue Commissioners with specific information on or by specific dates. These are called "returns" and there are severe penalties for late submission or not submitting returns at all.

Information and assistance

Comprehensive guides to all aspects of business taxation, including a "Starting in Business" guide, may be obtained from any tax office, the Revenue Forms & Leaflets Service at (01) 878 0100, or the Revenue's web-site (**www.revenue.ie**). Your accountant will also provide advice.

Revenue audits
A revenue audit is a cross-check of the information and figures shown in tax returns against those shown in a business's records, covering:

- Income Tax, Corporation Tax or Capital Gains Tax and/or
- The returns submitted for VAT, PAYE/PRSI or Relevant Contacts Tax (RCT).

The Revenue Commissioners use three methods of selection:

- Screening tax returns
- Projects on particular business sectors
- Random selection.

Generally, 14 days' advance notice in writing is given, stating the name of the person who will carry out the audit, the date and time of the audit and the year(s), accounting period(s) or VAT period(s) which are to be audited.

The auditor will examine a business' books and records to verify that the figures have been correctly calculated and that the tax returns and/or declarations for the different taxes are correct. If adjustments are required, the auditor will quantify these, discuss them with you/the appropriate person, seek agreement to the total settlement figure and issue written notification. Interest will be charged at 15% on tax underpaid where a taxpayer makes an incomplete or incorrect return and publication of an audit settlement may occur.

An explanatory booklet, *Revenue Audit – Guide for Small Business* is available from any tax office.

Taxpayers' Charter
It's not all one way, however. The Revenue Commissioners have issued a "Taxpayers' Charter" (see panel earlier), which sets out your rights as a taxpayer.

Tax clearance
Generally, grant offers from State agencies or Enterprise Boards are conditional on tax clearance. If you receive grants between €600 and €6,000, you must submit the following information:

VAT REGISTRATION FLOWCHART

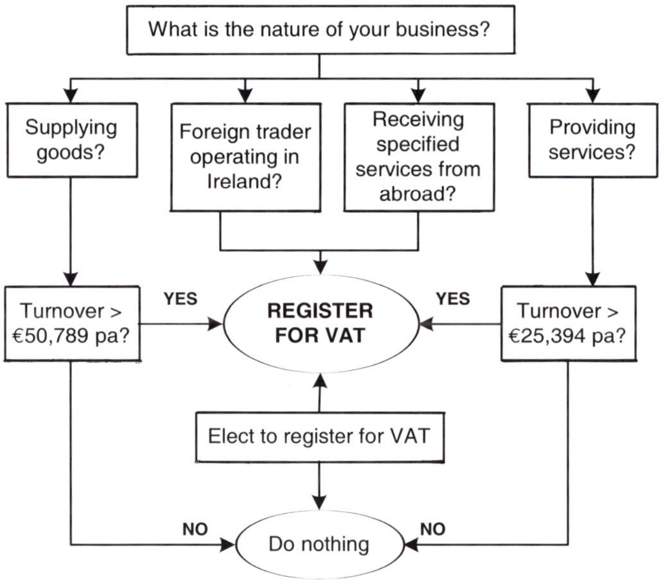

- The tax district dealing with your tax affairs
- Your tax reference number
- A signed statement indicating that, to the best of your knowledge, your tax affairs are in order.

If you receive grants of €6,000 or more, you must submit with your claim a Tax Clearance Certificate from the Revenue Commissioners confirming that your tax affairs are in order. Form TC1 should be completed when applying to the Revenue Commissioners for a Tax Clearance Certificate. You will be given a TC1 application form by the agency or Enterprise Board.

Tax clearance will also be required in respect of each contractor, where sub-contractors are employed on a construction project.

Revenue On-line Services
The Revenue Commissioners are increasingly moving on-line. Not only are all forms and publications available on their web-site but Revenue On-line Services (www.ros.ie) allows registered users to:

- View current employer taxes position on-line
- File and pay P30, P35, VAT3 forms on-line
- File P45 returns on-line.

Talk to an accountant
Because tax regulations are becoming increasingly complicated, it is worth talking to an accountant about your specific situation and needs.

ACCOUNTING

Accounting – anything to do with financial matters – is the part of being in business that most small business owners like least. So they neglect it, saying that it is more important to be "out there selling". Or they hand over responsibility for it to someone else – and forget about it.

But you wouldn't do that with any other part of your business. You wouldn't hand over responsibility for marketing, for product development or for recruiting staff to anyone else. Why do it for something as critical to your business as accounting?

Accounting consists of three steps:

- Recording transactions
- Analysing them so that they provide information
- Interpreting them so that they are useful for decision-making.

Recording transactions

First, identify what transactions you need to record. Most small businesses have:

- Purchases on credit
- Sales for credit
- Receipts – Cash into the bank account
- Payments – Cash out of the bank account
- Petty cash.

Let's start with these. For each transaction, you need to record:

- The date
- The type of transaction
- The other person involved
- The amount involved.

If you use a separate page for each type of transaction, you do not need to record the type of transaction – the page it is recorded on will tell you what type it is.

So you now have five pages for each of the transaction types with a limited amount of information recorded on each.

Analysing transactions

Next, begin to analyse the transactions to provide information.

Take purchases on credit. You might analyse the transactions under the following headings:

- **Fixed assets** – Items not for resale
- **Stock** – Items for resale
- **Overheads** – Expenses incurred in running the business (analyse these further into categories – Staff, Production, Premises, Transport, Sales and promotion, General expenses and Finance – these can be further subdivided if necessary to show the detail you need)
- **Miscellaneous/Sundry** – Items for which we can find no other obvious category or which happen so seldom that it's not worth setting up a separate analysis of them.

Sales on credit might be analysed by product/service type.

Cash into the bank account might be analysed by source, one of which will be debtors paying for goods/services bought earlier on credit. Other sources will include cash from cash sales (which should tie up on a daily basis), loans to the business, VAT and miscellaneous items.

Cash out of the bank account might be analysed by destination, one of which will be creditors from whom we bought goods/services on credit earlier. We might also have bought goods and services and paid by cheque, so we need to analyse these. We also need to include overheads, using the categories above.

Small items of expenditure are recorded as Petty cash expenses.

Value Added Tax

If your business is registered for it, recording VAT is the next step.

With certain exceptions (see the previous section, "Taxation"), VAT paid on purchases is recoverable, while you must account to the Revenue Commissioners for VAT you charge on sales. This means that, if the amount you pay for purchases includes VAT, you can reduce the cost to your business by the VAT amount. Similarly, you must deduct VAT from your sales before accounting for them in your business.

The "books"

The next chapter, **GO**, shows the very basic "books" that you must keep.

Of course, you don't need to buy

OBJECTIVES

- ☐ Understand basics of book-keeping
- ☐ Appreciate need for records and regular accounts

A Tradesman's Books, like a Christian's Conscience, should always be kept clean and clear; and he that is not careful of both will give but a sad account of himself either to God or Man.

DANIEL DEFOE (1660-1731)

expensive accounting analysis books. Ordinary paper with ruled columns will do perfectly well to start with. Keep your sheets in a folder, with dividers for each type of page.

Use an extra column – perhaps one right in at the margin – to write the number of the transactions. Keep a sequence going from the day you start. And write the transaction number onto the receipt or invoice. File all the receipts and invoices away safely in transaction number order. Then, if there are ever any queries, you will be able to find the answers quickly and easily.

These "books" are available as Excel spreadsheets to download from **www.startingabusinessinireland.com**.

Bank balance book

Your bank balance is one of the most important pieces of information in your business. You need to know what it is on a daily basis. To save time ringing the bank every day, since you have all the information you need to calculate it yourself, keep a Bank Balance Book. This is a simple ledger book (you'll find cheap versions in any stationery shop), with columns for:

- Date
- Transaction details
- Cash into the bank account
- Cash out of the bank account
- Balance.

An example of a Bank balance book appears in the next chapter, **GO**.

Record every transaction that goes through your bank account in this book, and you will always know what your balance is. Get into the habit of checking the balance before you write cheques (even if they are essential) and you will avoid unpleasant surprises. If your Bank balance book shows that writing a particular cheque will make your account overdrawn and you have no permission to do so, you have two choices:

- **Don't write the cheque** – Strictly, it's against the law to write a cheque when there isn't enough money in your account to meet it
- **Get permission** – However bad the news, it's always better to break it to your bank manager in advance than after the event, when he is in trouble with his bosses over your unauthorised overdraft.

Yes, you are duplicating some of the information on your "Cash into the bank account" and "Cash out of the bank account" pages but your Bank balance book can be written in summary form ("Cheque" will do under "Transaction details") to save time.

Transactions that originate with the bank (bank charges, interest and fees) should always be notified to you before they are charged to your account. As soon as you receive details of these amounts from your bank, write them into your Bank balance book.

Then you will be able to sleep easy at night, without worrying that the bank manager might call querying an unauthorised overdrawn situation.

Get into the habit of checking your bank statements when they arrive each month. Check to see that:

- All lodgements have been made
- All cheques cashed – You should deduct any cheques that you have written but which have not yet been cashed from the balance shown on the bank statement
- No charges or fees have been charged to your account without your knowledge.

If you find anything that you do not understand, check with the bank immediately.

"Still due" file

In addition to your bank balance, you also need to know who owes you money and how much.

A simple way of doing this is to set up a "Still due" file – a folder into which you place a copy of every invoice you send out for sales on credit. As you get paid, take out the relevant invoice and tear it up. Adding up all the invoices in the file tells you how much you are owed. And the thickness of the file provides a quick visual check of the effectiveness of your credit control procedures (see below).

"Still to be paid" file

Another piece of essential information is the amount of money you owe – particularly to suppliers, who may cut you off if they don't get paid on time.

Open a file, into which you put a copy of every invoice you receive from your suppliers for goods or services you buy on credit from them. As you pay your suppliers, take out the relevant copy invoices and staple them to the cheque you are sending. Whatever is in your "Still to be paid" file at any point is the total of what you owe. In addition, your suppliers know exactly which invoices you are paying, since you have sent them a copy. Management information in two businesses, no less!

An information system

You can begin to combine, adapt and expand the "books" and files above to provide you with an information system, following your accountant's advice.

For example, if you have very few transactions, you might put all the "books" onto a single sheet of paper which you use to record all transactions for a day or week, whatever period is appropriate. Instead of filing away the receipts and invoices, staple them onto the sheet. In this way, the sheet becomes your "books" and provides you with an immediate overview of what's going on in your business.

As you become more familiar with the financial side of your business, you will identify figures that help you understand what is happening – sales each day/week/month, for example. Organise a system to extract and report these regularly.

Interpreting the figures

What we have done so far covers recording and analysing. The next step is interpretation.

Most of this is common-sense:

- If your bank balance is always overdrawn, you are spending more than you are bringing in – and you will need to schedule another meeting with your bank manager
- If your purchases are high, and sales are low, stocks will begin to build up – and worse, you may not be able to sell the stock because it might be perishable, go out of fashion or become damaged
- If your overheads are high, you may be spending money on unnecessary items, like fancy office stationery and equipment, instead of on more productive items.

Talk to an accountant about the kind of information you need to manage your business and make sure that your system of recording and analysis provides it for you. And, of course, extracting the figures is only the starting point – you also need to do something about them.

Regular accounts

Every business is effectively required to prepare accounts once a year – some because they are limited companies and are required to do so by law, others because the tax authorities will need them to determine how much tax the business should be paying. But annual accounts are not much help in running and managing a business because:

- They are too infrequent – A year is a long time not to know what is happening to the finances of your business
- They are prepared to a different format – One that often is not helpful for decision-making.

So you need to consider preparing more regular accounts. Monthly accounts may be too much of a burden on your time and not repay you with enough useful information but quarterly accounts are essential.

In preparing accounts, all you are doing is summarising the information you have recorded and analysed – the analysis helps you with the summary. You don't need anything fancy. A simple profit and loss account to tie in with your Operating Budget (see page 85) will do. Talk to your accountant, if you need help.

Spreadsheets

If you are a computer user, you will have noted that the "books" are ideal for conversion to spreadsheets. Simply replicate the format on your spreadsheet and use its functionality to provide totals, summaries, etc.

But, if you decide to go the spreadsheet route, take some simple precautions:

- **Include a date/time on every printout** – So that you can determine which version you are looking at
- **Make back-up copies of everything** – You do not want to have to recreate your files from scratch at the end of the year or when the taxman comes calling
- **Consider locking cells** – To prevent them being overwritten by accident.

Accounting software

There are lots of accounting software packages that will do all this work for you – except the inputting of data, of course.

Some are very expensive and more suitable for larger businesses. But there are others – Big Red Book, Sage, TAS Books and MYOB – that have versions suitable for small businesses. Some of these cost under €200 so, if you have a computer, they may be worth considering.

A computerised accounting system provides information literally at your fingertips when you need it (if you have kept your inputting up-to-date!). Talk to your accountant before spending any money, to make sure you buy the right system for your needs.

Credit control

Your "still due" file is the second element in your credit control procedures – the first is sending out accurate invoices on time. If you do not send out accurate invoices, customers will complain and delay paying you.

Equally, if you do not bother to invoice customers as soon as a job is done, it suggests that you are not in a great hurry to get paid – and customers again will delay paying you.

Build a simple credit control system like this:

- Always invoice as soon as a job is done. Don't wait for the end of the month

- Make sure the invoice clearly states the date on which it is due to be paid
- File invoices in your "Still due" file in the order in which they are due to be paid. You will be able to see at a glance which invoices are overdue
- Check your "Still due" file every week for overdue invoices. Telephone to ask when you can expect a cheque. Get the name of the person who are speaking to and ask for them the next time you phone
- After three or four phone calls, write. Say that you will have to put the account into the hands of your solicitors and/or cut off supplies. Only threaten to cut off supplies when you really mean it.

Some customers only pay when they receive a "Statement of Account", a listing of all invoices due which is usually sent to them at the end of each month. Find out which customers need this and make sure you send them one.

Find out your customers' paying habits. Some businesses pay all invoices received up to the 27th day of the month in the first week of the next month. In this case, make sure your invoices are in their hands by the 27th! Fax copies, with the originals following by post.

Cash registers

If yours is a cash business with over-the-counter takings, use a cash register. Most registers will allow you to record:

- Total sales for the day
- Receipts for the day
- Analysis of sales for the day.

These daily figures can be entered directly into your books, without having to record every individual transaction.

KEEPING BOOKS AND RECORDS FOR TAX PURPOSES

You must keep full and accurate records of your business sufficient to enable you to make a proper return of income for tax purposes. These records must be kept for six years. Failure to keep proper records or to keep them for the necessary six years, where you are chargeable to tax, is a Revenue offence, punishable by fines and/or imprisonment.

The records kept must include books of account in which all purchases and sales of goods and services and all amounts received and all amounts paid out are recorded in a manner that will clearly show the amounts involved and the matters to which they relate. All supporting records such as invoices, bank and building society statements, cheque stubs, receipts etc., should also be retained.

You need to be able to account for:

- Your business takings
- All items of expenditure incurred, such as purchases, rent, lighting, heating, telephone, insurance, motor expenses, repairs, wages, etc.
- Any money introduced into the business and its source
- Any cash withdrawn from the business or any cheques drawn on the business bank account, for your own or your family's private use (drawings)
- Amounts owed to you by customers, showing the total amount owed by each debtor
- Amounts owed by you to suppliers, showing the total amount you owe to each creditor
- Stocks and raw materials on hand.

You will need to submit the following with your Tax Return:

- A **Trading Account** showing details of goods sold during the period and the cost of those goods, the difference being the gross profit/loss for the period
- A **Profit and Loss Account** showing details of gross profit and the various expenses of the trade during the period, the difference being the net profit/loss for the business for the period
- A **Capital Account** showing details of opening and closing capital, net profit/loss for the period, cash introduced and drawings (not required from a limited company)
- A **Balance Sheet** setting out details of the business' assets and liabilities at the end of the period.

Small businesses may use the Business Profile (Form BPI) which includes a simplified form of accounts. This form is available from your local tax office, from the Revenue Forms & Leaflets Service at (01) 878 0100 [24 hours a day], or www.revenue.ie.

Insurance

When you start in business, you need to consider both business and personal insurance. This section looks at what is involved.

Business insurance
The main kinds of business insurance are:
- **Fire** – To cover rebuilding costs, etc following a fire
- **Burglary/theft** – To replace stolen or damaged assets
- **All risks** – Coverage against loss of assets, however caused
- **Public liability** – Coverage against claims by members of the public
- **Product liability** – Coverage against loss relating to defective or dangerous products
- **Employer's liability** – Coverage against claims from staff
- **Motor insurance** – Coverage against driving accidents.

Most insurance companies offer these (or some combination) in a single "Office" or "Business" policy, which is more cost-effective than separate policies for each.

Other areas for which you might consider the protection of insurance include:
- Legal fees protection
- Credit insurance
- Bad debt insurance
- Computer equipement and data
- Travel
- Goods in transit
- Patents
- Business interruption.

Since insurance companies rate risks differently, it is worth talking to an insurance broker, whose job is to find you the widest coverage at the lowest price. Ask whether you can reduce the premiums by paying an excess (just like motor insurance). Ask also whether the premiums can be paid over the year rather than all at the start.

People-related insurance
If the business is dependent on yourself, or one or two key staff, it is also a good idea to take out "keyman insurance" on these people. Then, if they die or are unable to work, the insurance company will pay a lump sum to help overcome the difficulty.

You may also want to look at life assurance (to provide "death-in-service" benefits), critical illness, permanent health insurance or medical expenses insurance (VHI/BUPA) for your staff. Here cost, and whether staff value the insurance, will be major factors.

Your own insurance
What insurance you take out on yourself depends on the risk you are willing to take, your budget and your family situation. You may already have some insurance in place, in which case taking out more through the business would be duplication.

Look at the key risks:
- **You could get sick and not be able to work** – You need insurance to provide a replacement income (permanent health insurance)
- **You could get sick or die and have no one to take over the running of the business for you** – You need a replacement income plus enough extra to pay someone else to run your business (permanent health/critical illness/life assurance).

Talk to a life assurance broker about coverage against these risks. Talk to him/her also about pensions. A pension can be a tax-effective way of transferring cash from your business to yourself.

CALCULATE YOUR MONTHLY INSURANCE PREMIUMS

Business insurance

Fire	€ ______
Burglary/theft	€ ______
All risks	€ ______
Public liability	€ ______
Product liability	€ ______
Employer's liability	€ ______
Motor insurance	€ ______
	€ ______

Personal insurance

Health	€ ______
Disability	€ ______
Life assurance	€ ______
Pension	€ ______

OBJECTIVES
- ☐ Understand the different types of insurance
- ☐ Assess your need for insurance

TRADING LAWS

OBJECTIVES

☐ Be aware of key trading legislation

Don't learn the tricks of the trade.
Learn the trade.
ANON

The Single European Market removed "technical" barriers to trade and thus opened opportunities for Irish businesses to export into Europe on a scale not possible before. However, selling in Europe means meeting European product standards – increasingly, selling at home in Ireland means the same.

EU Directives set out requirements for the manufacture of a wide and growing range of products, including:

- Simple Pressure Vessels
- Safety of Toys
- Construction Products
- Electromagnetic Compatibility (EMC)
- Safety of Machinery
- Personal Protective Equipment
- Gas Appliances
- Non-Automatic Weighing Instruments
- Active Implantable Medical Devices
- Hot Water Bottles
- Motor Vehicles and their Trailers
- Low-Voltage
- The Amending Directive (bringing some of the older Directives up-to-date).

If your product falls into any of these areas, you need to meet the requirements of the relevant Directive. Compliance with these Directives is shown by the CE Marking, subject to assessment by the National Standards Authority of Ireland (NSAI).

Food labelling

The labelling of foodstuffs, in order to give accurate information to consumers, has become very important and increasingly regulated.

The basic rule is that labelling of prepackaged goods must be "clear, legible, indelible and not obscured by pictorial or written matter". It must be "in a language easily understood by the consumer" and "not mislead".

Specifically, you are required to show:

- Name of food
- Net quantity in metric
- Date of minimum durability ("Best before"/"Use by")
- List of ingredients
- Special storage instructions
- Name or business name and address of the manufacturer or packager (or seller in the EU)
- Country of origin (only where absence would mislead)
- Instructions for use
- Alcoholic strength (beverages 1.2%+ alcohol by volume)
- If irradiated, a declaration
- If packaged in a modified atmosphere, a declaration.

Certain products – jams and jellies, fruit juices, mineral waters and quick frozen foods – have additional labelling requirements.

Food labelling regulations are enforced by both Environmental Health Officers and officers of the Director of Consumer Affairs, who can enter premises where food is kept, manufactured, sold or transported, take samples, inspect documentation and take copies and examine, test and inspect products.

Most businesses involved in food preparation will have to be registered with the local Health Board and comply with the requirements of the Food Hygiene Regulations; the Environmental Health officer of your local Health Board will be able to give you details.

Licenses and registration

Most businesses can be started immediately but, in some cases, a license or registration is required.

Examples include:

- Public houses and off-licences
- Driving instructors
- Employment agencies
- Taxi drivers
- Providing credit services.

Other trading regulations

You should check with a solicitor to make sure that you are not breaking any regulations, that you are operating in line with best practices and that you are up-to-date on the latest requirements.

PREMISES

In "Marketing", we saw how important place is as part of the marketing mix (4 Ps).

In the property business, they say that only three things matter: Location, location, location. For certain kinds of business – shops, hotels, restaurants – location can make or break the business. But in all cases, the right working environment is important.

Choosing the right location

If you are looking for offices, consider somewhere that offers secretarial support (for example, telephone answering, message taking, fax, photocopying, reception, etc.) It will save you hiring a secretary until the workload justifies it. And you save buying equipment.

For workshops and factories, you need to check lay-out, logistics, transport, weight of machinery, health and safety regulations, environmental issues, availability of three-phase electricity, etc. Draw out your ideal space before starting to look for accommodation.

Picking the right location for a shop or restaurant needs lots of market research. Major retail chains like Marks & Spencer are known to spend months monitoring pedestrian traffic outside a possible location before coming to a decision.

Be prepared to spend several days standing outside what you think might be a suitable premises to check:

- Traffic flow (vehicles and pedestrians)
- Types of customers in the area
- Their spending patterns in other premises close by
- The timing of any rushes
- What other traders in the area think about the location
- What development (if any) is proposed for the area that might have an effect (positive or negative) on your plans.

Buy or rent?

This depends on how much money you have. But consider whether you are in the business of making a product/delivering a service or in the property business. It's very easy to get involved – and get your business' cash-flow involved – in improving a property you have bought, instead of getting on with making your business a success.

Leases for rented properties should be checked very carefully. They may not always include all the terms the letting agent told you about – and, by the same token, will probably include some clauses he didn't mention at all. Have the lease checked by a solicitor. And don't be rushed to sign anything until you have completed your business planning, made sure of your financing and know what you are signing.

Other issues

Wherever you locate, consider insurance premiums, compliance with food hygiene and health/safety regulations, planning permission (for signs, usage, extensions, etc), lighting, heating, alarms, signs, locks, insurance, toilets, interior decor, fittings.

OBJECTIVES

- ☐ Understand the importance of location
- ☐ Be aware of issues relating to premises

PREMISES CHECKLIST

1. How important is location for your business? Very ☐ Reasonably ☐ Not at all ☐
2. What is your budget for premises?
   - Purchase € ______
   - Rent (annual) € ______
   - Renovations € ______
   - Fixtures & fittings € ______
3. How much space do you need? ______ m^2
4. How is this to be divided between:
   - Administration ______ m^2
   - Storage ______ m^2
   - Sales ______ m^2
   - Production ______ m^2
   - Other ______ m^2
5. Will your customers visit your premises? ☐ YES ☐ NO
   - Do those visitors need to be impressed? ☐ YES ☐ NO
   - Is parking an issue? ☐ YES ☐ NO
   - Will you need space for deliveries? ☐ YES ☐ NO
6. Could your work be done from home? ☐ YES ☐ NO
   - Have you a suitable space? ☐ YES ☐ NO
   - Have you planning permission? ☐ YES ☐ NO
7. If renting, are you and your solicitor happy with the lease, as regards:
   - Period of the lease? ☐ YES ☐ NO
   - Rent (+ other charges)? ☐ YES ☐ NO
   - Your responsibilities? ☐ YES ☐ NO
   - The landlord's responsibilities? ☐ YES ☐ NO
   - Terms for renewal/termination? ☐ YES ☐ NO

Working from Home

OBJECTIVES

- ☐ Understand the benefits and drawbacks of working from home
- ☐ Be aware of legal and other requirements

Working from home is the simplest, and often the cheapest, choice in relation to premises for your business.

It suits certain kinds of business and does not suit others. Think about combining working from home with serviced offices, where you will have a professional telephone answering/message-taking service, a "business" address and access to meeting rooms for times when your customers want to come and talk to you.

Planning permission

The use of a private residence for business purposes is usually subject to planning permission. In most cases, local authorities will not require planning permission (or deny it, if it is applied for) where there is no impact on neighbouring properties. For example, a financial consultant who does his/her paperwork at home but meets clients on their own premises would expect little difficulty in relation to planning permission. But opening a garage to tune performance cars might bring complaints from your neighbours – and a refusal of the necessary planning permission.

Conditions for planning permission to work from home vary around the country. Check with your local authority's planning department before making any decision.

A dedicated workspace

If you work from home, you need to set aside a clearly-defined "workspace". In this area – and in this area only – you work. When you leave it, you are "at home". If you do not do this, you will never get a break from your business, and will burn out.

Make your workspace a "Do not disturb" zone. If you are to do your work properly, you must be able to put aside the distractions of home life (telephone calls, children, visitors, chores) while you are in your workspace (just as you would in a "proper" office).

But it's MY home!

Bear in mind that working from home becomes complicated when you have employees. It may suit you to get up late and work in your dressing-gown, but what example do you set for your staff? And what happens when you want a day off – do you have to leave home in order to get away from calls?

Other issues

Your insurers will need to be informed if you are working from home. If you have business visitors, you may need public liability cover. You are also responsible for health and safety (your own and any visitors') in your home office.

WORKING FROM HOME – ISSUES TO CONSIDER

How much space do you need and where is that space available in your home?
How will you separate home and work (think about telephone, use of computers, use of space, home duties, etc.)?
What does your family think?
What image do you want to present (meetings, telephone answering, address, etc.)?
What are the costs and cost savings (both time and money)?
Use of technology?
What happens when you are on holiday?
What about the children (holidays, after school, when they are sick, etc.)?
Can you switch off or will the home office become a constant distraction?
Do you need planning permission?

FINANCE

There are three occasions when you must pay attention to the way in which your business is financed:

- At start-up
- When you need additional finance for expansion
- All the time in between.

At start-up, you need to raise as much finance as possible in order to ensure that your business has enough money to get going yet, perversely, this is the time when it is most difficult.

The need to raise additional finance to expand a business suggests a successful business, which should have little difficulty in attracting the necessary funding – though not always.

In between start-up and second-stage fund-raising, and all along the way, your business will have a financing need that must be met day-to-day and planned in advance.

Start-up finance

There are basically only two types of finance:

- **Equity** – Capital invested in the business, usually not repayable until the business closes down finally
- **Debt** – Capital lent to the business, usually repayable at a specified date.

There are also only two sources:

- Your own money
- Someone else's money.

OWNERS' EQUITY

If you are putting equity into the business (and you MUST – if you won't, who else will!), recognise that this investment will be at risk. Decide whether there are assets you want to keep in your personal name or which you are not prepared to put up as security or to mortgage. Identify these and then look at everything else you own:

- How easily could they be sold and what would they fetch?
- Are they mortgagable assets?
- Will they be acceptable as collateral?

Before you mortgage your family home, obtain professional advice. Consider:

- Ownership of the property
- The impact of the Family Home Protection Act
- What would happen to the family home and your family if the business fails
- The approach that the banks and the courts take in such circumstances.

It is important that you raise as much as you can from your own resources, since most financiers work on a "matching funds" basis – they will invest no more than you are investing. This may mean being creative and including as part of your investment some items that would have been available to the business on an informal basis anyway. For example, if you plan to start a software business, you probably have your own PC and peripherals and probably intended using these in the business until it could afford to buy newer (and faster) machines. Put a value on them and include them as part of your investment, which might now be made up of €3,000 cash and €10,000 equipment – which looks better than just €3,000 cash!

If you can raise all the money you need from your own resources, then you can count yourself lucky and move further on in this section. Everyone else, keep reading!

OUTSIDE EQUITY

Before you raise outside equity, you need to be prepared to allow other people to own part of your business. Sounds logical, but many entrepreneurs forget this and react badly when their investors begin to want some involvement in the business in return for their investment.

If you are looking for outside equity, there are three types to consider:

- **Seed capital** – Less than €125,000, for start-ups
- **Venture capital** – Between €125,000 and €600,000, for businesses at an early stage of development
- **Development capital** – €600,000+, for companies ready to expand.

Seed capital is the one you probably want. Unfortunately, it is also the hardest to get, although the recent success of Irish technology companies means that there's plenty of funding available, sometimes linked to incubation facilities.

OBJECTIVES

- ☐ Understand the different types and sources of finance
- ☐ Calculate initial investment
- ☐ Identify possible sources of funding
- ☐ Calculate personal expenses

Small debts are like small shot: they are rattling on every side, and can scarcely be escaped without a wound; great debts are like cannon: of loud noise, but little danger.
SAMUEL JOHNSON (1709-1784)

I am convinced that the more money a new business needs to begin with, the less chance it has of success.
MARK McCORMACK, International Management Group

Before you borrow money from a friend, decide which you need more.
ANON

Seed capital is a race against insolvency.
KARL SCHUTTE, Business Innovation Fund, Dublin

You never lose money by making a profit.
ANON

The average cost of setting up in business is □11,000, one-third of which is funded externally.
The average time taken to raise external funding is one month, with 45% receiving funding within a week.
Banks are the main providers of external finance, with family and friends an important secondary source.
BARCLAYS BANK

Sources of equity
The first sources you should try are:

- **Family and friends** – Depending on your personal circumstances, this can be a fruitful source. But make sure they understand the risks involved and can afford to lose their investment. Put any agreement in writing
- **Business contacts** – It's worth checking to see whether someone you know in business will help you get started with a small investment
- **Business angels** – Professional investors who may take an active role in managing the business as well as providing finance. Enterprise Ireland, Shannon Development and Dublin Business Innovation Centre all have investor registers.

Then turn to the professionals:

- **ACT Venture Capital** – ACT operates its own fund and the ACT Enterprise Fund, aimed at the technology sector, jointly funded by Enterprise Ireland. ACT invests upwards of €600,000.
- **AWG Investment Fund** – Established by the Avonmore Waterford Group (now Glanbia) and managed by Deal Management Ltd, the fund invests between €300,000 and €600,000 in early-stage and expanding businesses.
- **Bank of Ireland Entrepreneurs Fund** – Managed by Delta Partners, the fund invests between €125,000 and €1.25 million in technology businesses.
- **The Business Expansion Scheme (BES)** – Properly called "Relief for Investment in Corporate Trades" (RICT), BES is intended to help smaller businesses. Fund-raising companies must be incorporated and resident in Ireland, must not be quoted on the Stock Exchange (except for the new Developing Companies Market), and must be engaged in a "qualifying trade". It is up to the business to find potential investors (usually through a broker or accountant) and, when it does, to obtain Revenue approval.
- **Business Innovation Fund** – Managed by Dublin BIC, the fund provides between €30,000 and €90,000 for start-up and early-stage businesses. Projects should have fewer than 10 people employed, turnover under €90,000, with significant growth potential, and meet some other conditions.
- **Campus Companies Venture Capital Fund** – This fund provides seed and early-stage development capital (€38,000 to €600,000) for businesses promoted by staff/graduates of Irish universities.
- **Cross Atlantic Capital Partners** – Cross Atlantic Capital Partners (XACP) manages a $150 million technology-focused fund.
- **Dublin Seed Capital Fund** – Managed by Dublin BIC, this fund invests from €12,000 to €250,000 in biotechnology, IT-related, industrial products, manufacturing and high-tech industries in the Dublin region
- **eircom Enterprise Fund** – This fund invests between €38,000 and €380,000 in early stage businesses with growth potential, in telecoms, media and tech.
- **Enterprise 2000 Fund** – This fund provides early-stage finance, mainly to technology businesses, ranging between €32,000 and €127,000.
- **Enterprise Equity** – Established by the International Fund for Ireland, Enterprise Equity provides venture capital of between €320,000 and €1.9 million to new and expanding businesses in the border counties of Cavan, Donegal, Leitrim, Louth, Monaghan and Sligo.
- **Growcorp Innovation Centre** – Growcorp develops businesses with leading-edge platform technologies in ICT and biosciences, through an incubation process.
- **Guinness Ulster Bank Equity Fund** – Managed by NCB Ventures, this fund focuses on small to medium-sized enterprises. The typical investment is between €95,000 and €950,000, with a maximum investment of €1.15 million.
- **Hibernia Capital Partners** – Hibernia provides equity and equity-

related finance for development capital, management buy-outs and buy-ins, and start-ups with significant scale and demonstrable market potential. Hibernia can invest up to €15 million from its own resources in any one transaction, and further funds through co-invest arrangements with partners worldwide. Equity-related funding under €2.5 million is normally referred to a sister fund, Trinity Venture Capital.

- **HotOrigin** – HotOrigin is an e-commerce and software accelerator focused on fast-tracking new e-companies. It also makes seed-stage investments of up to €380,000.
- **ICC Bank** – (now Bank of Scotland (Ireland)) Provides equity investment through a corporate finance unit and venture capital funds.
- **Irish BICs Seed Capital Fund** – Managed by Dublin BIC, this fund provides early-stage seed capital from €12,000 to €125,000. Projects should be innovative with growth potential in high-tech, biotechnology, IT-related, industrial products, manufacturing. An on-line application form is available on Dublin BIC's website.
- **Millennium Entrepreneur Fund** – Established by Bank of Ireland, LM Ericsson, McCann Group and Enterprise Ireland, this fund provides early-stage seed capital up to €125,000 to highly skilled individuals or teams with strong international experience, an identified technology-based high growth business opportunity, at least one team member currently residing overseas, but willing to return to Ireland to set up either an internationally traded manufacturing/service business.
- **The Seed Capital Scheme** – Operated by the Revenue Commissioners, the scheme repays income tax to people leaving employment to start their own businesses (only companies qualify, not sole traders or partnerships). In the year of starting their business, qualifying individuals may claim back the tax paid in respect of up to €31,750 of income in each of the previous five tax years.
- **Shannon Development** – Shannon Development's Investment Division operates a number of funds that invest between €12,000 and €600,000. It also has a "Business Angel" network.
- **Small Enterprise Seed Capital Fund** – This fund, an initiative of the Project Development Centre Network and the Bolton Trust, is a designated Business Expansion Scheme (BES) Fund.
- **Trinity Venture Capital** – Trinity provides up to €2.5 million for early stage and expanding companies. Additional capital can be sourced through Hibernia Capital Partners, a sister company.

OWNERS' DEBT

This is not a major source of finance for start-ups, since other investors prefer to see the owners' investment in the form of equity (more permanent than loans). However, it may be appropriate to put some part of your investment in the business as a loan (and thus repayable). Take your accountant's advice here.

OTHER DEBT

Debt comes in a variety of forms, from a simple loan from a friend with few conditions attached, through overdrafts, term loans, long-term loans, mortgages, etc.

Debt finance available to start-ups includes:

- **Overdraft** – The simplest form of bank finance. Basically, this is no more than permission to have a minus balance on your bank account. However, overdrafts must be cleared (and stay cleared for at least 30 days during the year, though not necessarily consecutive days) on an annual basis and the overdraft is repayable on demand
- **Term loan** – A loan for a fixed period, usually at a variable rate. Repayments include interest and capital
- **Long-term loans** – Often subsidised by Government or EU schemes, these aim to provide businesses with capital for 7 to 10 years
- **Mortgages** – Loans to buy business property, secured on the property itself, with fixed or variable rate options
- **Leasing** – A way of acquiring the use of fixed assets (for example, plant and machinery, cars, office equipment) by paying a regular monthly or quarterly payment, which is usually allowable for tax purposes. At the end of the lease, depending on the terms, you may have the option to continue using the asset for a small continuing payment or to buy it outright from the lessor
- **Invoice discounting** – A facility linked directly to sales, which maximises the cash value of current assets. The bank will pay you, say, 80% of the face value of an invoice when it is issued. The balance, less charges, will be paid to you when the invoice is paid. Useful for the company that is expanding and in danger of being choked for lack of cash.

When considering financing your business with debt, you must consider:

- Fixed or floating
- Long-term or short-term.

Fixed debt is a loan that is secured on a specific asset – for example, on premises. Floating debt is secured on assets that change regularly – for example, debtors.

"Secured" means that, in the event that the loan is

not repaid, the lender can appoint a "receiver" to sell the asset on which the loan is secured in order to recover the amount due. Thus, giving security for a loan is not something to be done lightly.

Because you have to pay interest on debt, you should try to manage with as little as possible. However, few businesses get off the ground without putting some form of debt on the balance sheet. The issues are usually:

- What is the cheapest form of debt available?
- What is the right balance between debt and equity?
- How to reduce the amount of borrowing required?
- Will borrowing be backed by personal assets?

It is a good idea to try to match the term of the loan to the type of asset that you are acquiring:

- To avoid constant renewing/restructuring problems
- To ensure that each loan is covered by the break-up value of the assets in case of disaster.

For example, a loan to buy premises should be a long-term loan, unless you can see clearly that you will have enough money within a short space of time to repay it. Taking out a short-term loan or overdraft to buy premises is a recipe for disaster. You will have to renegotiate it time and again – and, if your business runs into temporary difficulties, you run the risk of losing everything if the bank calls in the loan.

Short-term loans, or even overdrafts, are more suited to funding stock or debtors because you should be able to repay the loan once you have sold the goods or got the money in. Short-term finance is also used to fund other forms of working capital and cash flow. It should always be repaid within the year – even if at the end of the period you still need to borrow more to fund future cash flow. If you have to borrow the same sum of money against the same asset for longer than a year at a time, you should be considering longer-term finance.

If disaster strikes and you have to repay the loan, it will be much easier to do so if the value of the assets it was used to fund is roughly equivalent to the value of the loan. Thus, for instance, you would hope to sell your premises for at least as much as you borrowed to buy them. Machinery may be more difficult, as the resale price is rarely comparable with the purchase price. For this reason, unless the equipment you need is very specialised, consider buying second-hand for your start-up.

If you can, you should arrange your loans so that unrealisable (or slow to realise) assets are purchased out of your own equity, using borrowing only for realisable assets. If an asset is easily realisable, the bank is much more likely to accept it as security.

Sources of debt

Sources of debt you should try first include:

- **Family and friends** – Depending on your own circumstances, this can be a fruitful source. But make sure they understand the risks involved and can afford to lose their investment. Put any deal in writing, with professional advice on both sides
- **Business contacts** – It's worth looking to see whether someone you know in business will help you get started with a small investment
- **Banks** – The main source of start-up borrowing
- **Credit cards** – If you have a credit card with a high credit limit (and a low balance!), this may provide a source of funding (though more expensive than most). However, once your business is up and running, a company credit card not only provides an additional credit line but can cut purchasing costs and simplify administration
- **Credit unions** – Increasingly willing to help members start businesses, especially co-operatives
- **Finance companies** – Sometimes more willing to lend than a bank, as long as they can secure the loan with assets or personal guarantees. Rarely cheaper than banks, but may sometimes be prepared to lend when banks refuse.

When looking for finance, beware of "specialists" who claim that they can find you money at favourable rates of interest if only you pay an up-front fee. Don't pay **anything** until you have the money.

Often, if you only need a small amount of money, the best way to raise it is to approach a bank with which you have already built up some relationship, whether on a personal basis or in a business capacity. The larger borrower may feel it worthwhile to seek professional help to put together a more sophisticated fund-raising package. Your accountant is the best person to give you advice in this area and may have contacts that will ease your path.

Bank finance

The following banks provide loans to start-ups:

- **ACC Bank –** (Now Rabobank) A broadly-based commercial bank.
- **AIB Bank Enterprise Development Bureau** – The Enterprise Development Bureau is AIB's focal point for start-up and expanding businesses, both in manufacturing and service industries. It provides access to AIB's range of banking facilities, including overdrafts, loans, leasing, hire purchase, invoice discounting, business insurance,

credit cards and electronic banking.

- **Bank of Ireland Enterprise Support Unit** – The Enterprise Support Unit typically lends between €65,000 and €300,000. It also provides hands-on support and does not require personal guarantees. It exempts start-ups from most bank charges and fees in the first year of operation. The ESU provides access to the full range of Bank of Ireland facilities, including invoice discounting (Bank of Ireland Commercial Finance) and leasing/hire purchase.
- **Bank of Scotland (Ireland) –** Formerly Equity Bank Ltd, Bank of Scotland's services include commercial lending and SME banking, asset finance, treasury and trade finance.
- **ICC Bank** – Provides short, medium and long-term loans, tending towards short-term finance.
- **National Irish Bank** – NIB operates a New Enterprise Loan Fund, to support and assist in the creation and development of small and medium-sized businesses that have employment potential with loans of between €19,000 and €90,000. No personal guarantees are required. Access the fund at any NIB branch or the specialist regional offices.
- **TSB Bank** – (now PermanentTSB) Though geared towards the personal banking market, it offers current account facilities, overdrafts and loans to business customers.
- **Ulster Bank** – Ulster Bank has various lending schemes available including overdrafts, loans, leasing and invoice discounting, and offers Internet banking and e-commerce facilities. The Small Business Unit also offers information and assistance on franchising to franchisees and potential franchisers.

Other sources of start-up finance include:

- **Guinness Workers' Employment Fund** – Funded by Guinness workers and pensioners, the Fund provides start-up businesses with financial assistance, and supports expansion of existing businesses, usually by way of a term loan, at interest rates below those charged by the commercial banks.
- **Credit Unions –** Members of credit unions or businesses structured as co-operatives may qualify for a credit union loan. Each application is treated in confidence and will be considered on its own merits. In deciding whether to grant the loan, the member's record of saving and repayments, as well as ability to repay, and need will be taken into account.
- **Fingal Employees Youth Business Fund** – The Fund was set up by Fingal County Council staff to meet the needs of those who fall through the loopholes left by other schemes. Applicants must be aged between 18 and 30, either be from Fingal (North County Dublin) or want to start a business in Fingal, have a sound business idea, and be prepared to work to make it a success. The Fund will assist R&D, feasibility studies, start-up finance and equipment.
- **First Step –** First Step provides seed funding for projects or people with no security. It can fund up to 50% of a project's start-up costs by way of loans, though matching funds may be required. Bank of Ireland will match approved First Step projects with interest-free loans of up to €32,000. First Step's Back to Work Fund, in co-operation with the Department of Social & Family Affairs, provides small-scale seed capital for the long-term unemployed who find it difficult to raise capital.

INITIAL INVESTMENT

The rule for funding a new business is: "As little as possible, as cheaply as possible". Do not put money into the unnecessary. It is better to start your business from the attic without a loan than in a glossy, but unnecessary, high-profile office with heavy bank borrowings.

On the other hand, do adopt a realistic position on the amount of money that you need to get going. Your financing will have to be sufficient to carry the business for a reasonable period before it reaches some kind of balance, when money coming in equals money going out.

In addition to capital investment in plant, equipment and premises, your financing may have to supply most of the working capital until sales begin to generate sufficient income to give you an adequate cash flow.

Try this technique:

- **Close your eyes** – Pretend to be in your new business. Look around you. What do you see? Make a list – from carpets to lamps, from computers to phones, from equipment to signs, from stock to the van for deliveries. Make the list as long as possible
- **Put a value on each item** – How much would it cost to buy new? Could you buy it second-hand?
- **Look at the list again** – Mark off the items you already have (chair, telephone, desk, lamp)
- **Calculate the difference** – This is your initial investment in starting your business
- **Take it a stage further** – You need to buy all the items you do not have at present, but do you need to buy them all at the beginning or could some wait a few weeks or even months? What could wait?

Use the Initial Investment panel on page 82 to calculate and record what you need to start your business.

CALCULATING YOUR INITIAL INVESTMENT

	Need?	How many?	Have now	Need to buy	Cost new €	Cost 2hand €	Total cost €	Timing of purchase: Now €	Mth 1 €	Mth 2 €	Mth 3 €	Mth 4-6 €
Office:												
	Y/N		Y/N	Y/N								
	Y/N		Y/N	Y/N								
	Y/N		Y/N	Y/N								
	Y/N		Y/N	Y/N								
	Y/N		Y/N	Y/N								
	Y/N		Y/N	Y/N								
	Y/N		Y/N	Y/N								
	Y/N		Y/N	Y/N								
	Y/N		Y/N	Y/N								
	Y/N		Y/N	Y/N								
Factory/Workshop:												
	Y/N		Y/N	Y/N								
	Y/N		Y/N	Y/N								
	Y/N		Y/N	Y/N								
	Y/N		Y/N	Y/N								
	Y/N		Y/N	Y/N								
	Y/N		Y/N	Y/N								
	Y/N		Y/N	Y/N								
	Y/N		Y/N	Y/N								
	Y/N		Y/N	Y/N								
	Y/N		Y/N	Y/N								
Shop:												
	Y/N		Y/N	Y/N								
	Y/N		Y/N	Y/N								
	Y/N		Y/N	Y/N								
	Y/N		Y/N	Y/N								
	Y/N		Y/N	Y/N								
	Y/N		Y/N	Y/N								
	Y/N		Y/N	Y/N								
	Y/N		Y/N	Y/N								
	Y/N		Y/N	Y/N								
	Y/N		Y/N	Y/N								
Transport:												
	Y/N		Y/N	Y/N								
	Y/N		Y/N	Y/N								
Other:												
	Y/N		Y/N	Y/N								
	Y/N		Y/N	Y/N								
	Y/N		Y/N	Y/N								
	Y/N		Y/N	Y/N								
	Y/N		Y/N	Y/N								
	Y/N		Y/N	Y/N								
TOTAL												

INITIAL INVESTMENT ANALYSIS FOR BUSINESS PLAN

Copy this panel into your Business Plan, page 127.

1. Fixed assets	
Property	€ ______
Renovations	€ ______
Fixtures and fittings	€ ______
Transport	€ ______
Machines and equipment	€ ______
Goodwill, security deposits	€ ______
Other	€ ______
Total fixed assets	**€** ______
2. Current assets	
Stock of raw material	€ ______
Stock of finished goods	€ ______
Work in progress	€ ______
Debtors	€ ______
Other	€ ______
Total current assets	**€** ______
3. Liquid assets	
Cash	€ ______
Bank	€ ______
Other	€ ______
Total liquid assets	**€** ______
4. Start-up costs	
Prepaid expenses	€ ______
Promotion, opening	€ ______
Other	€ ______
Total start-up costs	**€** ______
5. Margin for unforeseen costs	**€** ______
Total investment	**€** ______

CHECKLIST FOR INITIAL INVESTMENT

1. Can you support the required investment in fixed assets with quotations from suppliers? ☐ YES ☐ NO
2. How did you estimate your stock levels?
3. How did you estimate the value of your debtors?
4. Do you have sufficient cash to fund on-going operational costs until sales begin to realise cash? ☐ YES ☐ NO
5. Do you have sufficient cash, or assets that can be quickly turned into cash, to cope with disappointments, delays and unexpected expenses? ☐ YES ☐ NO

Then go back through the list and take out what is not absolutely necessary. Be hard – take out anything that you don't REALLY need. But don't cut back so far that you will be unable to get the business off the ground. What you are doing is what an investor or banker who reads your business plan will be doing – challenging everything to make sure that you have done your homework. Do it yourself before it's done to you and you will find raising finance for your start-up much easier.

Next, you need to put your initial investment into a format suitable for your business plan by identifying:

- **Fixed assets** – Property, renovations, fixtures and fittings, transport, machines and equipment, etc
- **Current assets** – Stocks, debtors
- **Cash**
- **Start-up expenses** – Expenses paid before the business begins, promotion and opening costs, etc.
- **Margin for unforeseen costs** – There will always be something you have forgotten or that could not have been expected when you did your planning. Allow for it here.

Use the panel opposite and complete the checklist.

Sourcing your initial investment

Now that you know how much you need (and what for), you need to find appropriate sources of finance. Re-read this section. Then decide how you will raise the money you need. Complete the panel on page 84, showing your sources of funding. If you have some sources already agreed, indicate this in the panel.

Personal expenses

Just because you are starting a business does not mean that the real world will go away. You and your family still need to be fed, to buy clothes, to pay for food, clothing, heating, bus fares, mortgages, etc. You need to allow for this. If you haven't allowed for pension or health cover as part of your business expenses (see "Insurance", allow for them here.

Complete the panel on page 84 to calculate your personal expenses. Use whichever column – Week, Month, Year – suits your own circumstances best. When you have finished, convert all the figures into annual totals – it will be the annual personal expenses figure that you will be using in your Business Plan. This is not a target – it is what you need. It must be factored into your Operating Budget and Business Plan.

Of course, because start-ups are risky you will not be able to depend on this income. In the panel at the end of page 84 are some questions about your attitude to risk and its consequences. Make sure you discuss them (and your own answers) with your family.

INITIAL INVESTMENT
PROPOSED SOURCES OF FUNDING

Copy this panel into your Business Plan, page 128.

Personal assets available

Fixed assets	€ ______
Car	€ ______
Additional private mortgage	€ ______
Savings	€ ______
Deferred loans (family)	€ ______
Other	€ ______
Total personal assets	**€** ______

Introduced as:

Equity	€ ______
Loans	€ ______

External equity		*Agreed?*
Source	€ ______	Y/N

External debt	*Term*	*Amount*	*Agreed?*
Long/medium-term			
Mortgage	______ years	€ ______	Y/N
Loan	______ years	€ ______	Y/N
Leasing	______ years	€ ______	Y/N
Other	______ years	€ ______	Y/N
	______ years	€ ______	Y/N
Total		**€** ______	

Short-term finance	*Amount*	*Agreed?*
Overdraft	€ ______	Y/N
Suppliers' credit	€ ______	Y/N
Payments received in advance	€ ______	Y/N
Other	€ ______	Y/N
	€ ______	Y/N
Total	**€** ______	

Subsidies/grants		*Agreed?*
Agency	€ ______	Y/N
Enterprise Board	€ ______	Y/N
Area Partnership Company	€ ______	Y/N
Other	€ ______	Y/N
	€ ______	Y/N
Total subsidies/grants	**€** ______	

Total available finance	**€** ______

CALCULATE YOUR PERSONAL EXPENSES

	Week	**Month**	**Year**
Expenses			
Rent/mortgage	€ ______	€ ______	€ ______
Gas, water, ESB	€ ______	€ ______	€ ______
Food	€ ______	€ ______	€ ______
House expenses	€ ______	€ ______	€ ______
Clothing/footwear	€ ______	€ ______	€ ______
Telephone	€ ______	€ ______	€ ______
Insurance	€ ______	€ ______	€ ______
Study expenses	€ ______	€ ______	€ ______
Memberships	€ ______	€ ______	€ ______
TV licence	€ ______	€ ______	€ ______
Transport	€ ______	€ ______	€ ______
Loan repayments	€ ______	€ ______	€ ______
Holidays	€ ______	€ ______	€ ______
Replacing fridge, etc	€ ______	€ ______	€ ______
Luxuries	€ ______	€ ______	€ ______
Other expenses			
______	€ ______	€ ______	€ ______
______	€ ______	€ ______	€ ______
Sub-total (A)	**€** ______	**€** ______	**€** ______
Deductions			
Children's allowances	€ ______	€ ______	€ ______
Government benefits	€ ______	€ ______	€ ______
Rent/lease subsidies	€ ______	€ ______	€ ______
Spouse/partner's income	€ ______	€ ______	€ ______
Other income	€ ______	€ ______	€ ______
Subtotal (B)	**€ <___>**	**€ <___>**	**€ <___>**
Personal expenses (NET OF TAX) (A) less (B)	**€** ______	**€** ______	**€** ______
Allowance for tax	**€** ______	**€** ______	**€** ______
Gross taxable income needed	**€** ______	**€** ______	**€** ______

ASK YOURSELF:

Can you cope with:

Financial insecurity?	☐ YES	☐ NO
Reduced income?	☐ YES	☐ NO
Irregular income?	☐ YES	☐ NO
Unexpected financial setbacks?	☐ YES	☐ NO

Operating Budget

Budgeting is the process of estimating costs in advance, in order to:

- Ensure adequate finance for the business to achieve what it has planned
- Provide a control mechanism over subsequent spending.

With the exception of "zero-base budgeting", most budgets begin with the previous year's actual figures and make assumptions about the future:

- Adding a percentage for inflation
- Adding new costs and activities
- Deleting old costs and activities.

However, as a start-up company, you have no historical figures to work from. You can budget in two directions (often it is helpful to do both and compare the results).

"Revenue down" budgeting starts by working out how many units you expect to sell and at what price. This gives you total revenue. Then estimate what percentage of revenue is accounted for by the various costs – Cost of sales (50% perhaps), Salaries (25%), Overheads (20%), leaving a net profit margin of 5%. Be careful with this method, since it's all too easy to scale up your budget beyond the point where you have exceeded your capacity to produce.

"Cost up" budgeting starts from the cost of making the product. To this, you add a profit margin big enough to cover marketing expenses, salaries, overheads and a profit. Multiply the total of product cost and the margin by the number of units you expect to sell to get total revenue. The difficulty with this method is that your selling price is unrelated to the market. In fact, inefficiencies in production are disguised by this method – until your product reaches the market-place.

Target costing is a relatively new method of costing, introduced from Japan. Here you identify the maximum price customers will pay for the product and manufacture within this. Usually, this means that you have to look very hard at quantity, suppliers, materials used, the use of technology and alternative sources.

In the Operating Budget, you forecast:

- **Turnover** – total sales
- **Gross profit** – the difference between the turnover and its purchase cost
- **Overheads** – all the expenses incurred in order to keep the business going
- **Net profit** – the gross profit less the overheads.

In developing your Operating Budget, take into account the expenses you will incur to keep the business running and to provide you, as the entrepreneur, with an income (your personal expenses from the last section), as well as the cost of meeting repayments if you have borrowed money.

If you have a good idea of the overheads involved, you can calculate what the turnover figure will need to be, using the formula:

Turnover – Purchases = Gross Profit
Gross profit – Overheads = Net profit.

Work out what you expect to sell (turnover) and how you are going to achieve this target.

Bear in mind that, because you will have busy times and not so busy times, your turn-over will not remain constant throughout the year. Budget for peaks and troughs.

At the same time, look at the forecast in light of overheads. Test these again against the turnover forecast. For example: Does the number of visits planned to customers agree with the mileage that you have included in the Transport and travel category?

Gross profit is the difference between the total amount for sales (turnover excluding VAT) and the purchase cost of the goods you have sold.

This gross profit can also be expressed as a percentage of the turnover (excluding VAT). A gross profit percentage of 45% signifies that for every □100 of turnover, □55 is purchases and €45 is regarded as the gross profit of the business.

Overheads

This section looks at the expenses that you will have in running your business, including:

- Staff
- Production
- Premises
- Transport
- Selling and promotion
- General expenses
- Finance
- Depreciation.

OBJECTIVES

- ☐ Understand the budgeting process
- ☐ Be able to prepare an Operating Budget

Know when to spend,
And when to spare,
And you need not be busy,
And you'll never be bare.
JAMES KELLY

Spare no expense to make everything as economical as possible.
SAM GOLDWYN

Operating Budget – Overheads

Staff

These expenses are only incurred if you actually have employees working for you (full or part-time).

In addition to wages/salaries, you may (depending on the contract of employment) have to include travelling expenses, work clothes or uniforms, study expenses for employees, and so on. Bonuses, employers' PRSI and other costs associated with staff should be included here.

Production overheads

If your business has a production unit, you will have costs that cannot be directly associated with items of production – for example, heat, light and power, maintenance, etc.

Premises

This covers all expenses that are directly connected with your premises:

- Rent of premises (bear in mind the need for a good rental agreement, checked with your solicitor)
- Mortgage interest, if you own the property under a mortgage
- A percentage of your personal accommodation expenses, if you begin your business from your own house (rent or mortgage split between the part used for business and the total, expressed in m^2)
- Repairs and maintenance, depending on the condition of the premises and, if rented, the contract under which it is used
- Gas, water and electricity expenses (enquire about these at your local authority energy department)
- Business charges and taxes, including service charges (if levied by your local authority)
- Insurance – fire insurance is essential
- Cleaning expenses – cleaning consumables or the cost of hiring a cleaner
- Miscellaneous small items (for example, hand tools, kitchen equipment, etc.) that are not depreciated.

Transport and travel expenses

First, you should estimate all the journeys by public transport that you are likely to make for your business.

For car expenses, estimate the mileage that you will travel on behalf of the business. The mileage should be multiplied by the cost per mile – which should include insurance, road tax, maintenance, depreciation, etc. The Automobile Association regularly publishes cost per mile figures that you may be able to use – or use Civil Service rates.

Selling and promotion

The costs you estimate for promotion should be based on the section, "Marketing – Promotion", earlier.

General expenses

This category looks very simple but, in fact, it is frequently underestimated. General expenses include:

- **Telephone and postage** – Note that if you work from your own house and make use of your private telephone, only the business-related calls can be regarded as expenses for the business and not the line rental
- **Subscriptions and contributions** – For example, to employers' or small business representative organisations, professional and trade journals, Chamber of Commerce, etc.
- **Insurance premiums** – Excluding the premiums for private insurance
- **Administration and office expenses** – Everything that you need in order to be able to perform your bookkeeping and carry on your correspondence (business stationery, envelopes, computer supplies, filing system, etc.)
- **Accountancy expenses** – Even though you may not have an in-house accountant, a bookkeeper can easily charge you several hundred pounds annually for compiling VAT and PAYE/PRSI returns and preparing the year end accounts
- **Entertainment** – Business-related entertainment of customers or potential customers should be included here. Note that entertainment costs are not tax-deductible.

Finance costs

These cover not only the interest on the loans you have entered into but also the expenses that are associated with the loan, such as credit advice, assessment, solicitor's fees, costs of arranging credit, etc. Remember that the repayment of loans is not a business cost but must be made from net profit.

Depreciation

Depreciation expresses the annual reduction in value of your fixed assets. There are various methods of depreciation. Though your accountant will choose the best method for your accounts, you can use the "straight line" method for your operating budget. Under this method, all fixed assets are reduced each year by a fixed percentage.

For example, a machine costs €10,000, and will last for five years, when its scrap value will be €500. The annual depreciation is calculated as:

€10,000 – €500 = 9,500 / 5 = €1,900 per year.

The depreciation term is not usually changed during the depreciation period. Commonly-used depreciation terms include: Buildings – 40 years; Extensions/renovations – 10 years; Machines – 5 or 7 years; Cars – 3 or 5 years.

OPERATING BUDGET – ANALYSIS OF OVERHEADS

Staff costs	*Year 1*	*Year 2*	*Year 3*
Gross staff salaries	€ ______	€ ______	€ ______
Employer's PRSI	€ ______	€ ______	€ ______
Bonuses, etc.	€ ______	€ ______	€ ______
Staff training costs	€ ______	€ ______	€ ______
Other staff costs	€ ______	€ ______	€ ______
Total staff costs	**€** ______	**€** ______	**€** ______

Production overheads	*Year 1*	*Year 2*	*Year 3*
Use of auxiliary materials	€ ______	€ ______	€ ______
Maintenance	€ ______	€ ______	€ ______
Heat, light & power	€ ______	€ ______	€ ______
Rent/lease equipment	€ ______	€ ______	€ ______
Insurance equipment	€ ______	€ ______	€ ______
Other costs	€ ______	€ ______	€ ______
Total production costs	**€** ______	**€** ______	**€** ______

Premises costs	*Year 1*	*Year 2*	*Year 3*
Rent	€ ______	€ ______	€ ______
Heat, light & power	€ ______	€ ______	€ ______
Insurance	€ ______	€ ______	€ ______
Cleaning	€ ______	€ ______	€ ______
Maintenance	€ ______	€ ______	€ ______
Other costs	€ ______	€ ______	€ ______
Deduct: Rent received	€ <___>	€ <___>	€ <___>
Total premises costs	**€** ______	**€** ______	**€** ______

Transport costs	*Year 1*	*Year 2*	*Year 3*
Maintenance and repairs	€ ______	€ ______	€ ______
Lease costs	€ ______	€ ______	€ ______
Fuel	€ ______	€ ______	€ ______
Insurance	€ ______	€ ______	€ ______
Road Tax	€ ______	€ ______	€ ______
Public transport	€ ______	€ ______	€ ______
Air fares	€ ______	€ ______	€ ______
Deduct: Private use	€ <___>	€ <___>	€ <___>
Total transport costs	**€** ______	**€** ______	**€** ______

Selling and promotion costs	*Year 1*	*Year 2*	*Year 3*
Advertising	€ ______	€ ______	€ ______
Packaging	€ ______	€ ______	€ ______
Promotion	€ ______	€ ______	€ ______
Trade fairs	€ ______	€ ______	€ ______
Commissions	€ ______	€ ______	€ ______
Other costs	€ ______	€ ______	€ ______
Total sales and promotion costs	**€** ______	**€** ______	**€** ______

General expenses	*Year 1*	*Year 2*	*Year 3*
Telephone	€ ______	€ ______	€ ______
Postage	€ ______	€ ______	€ ______
Subscriptions	€ ______	€ ______	€ ______
Insurance	€ ______	€ ______	€ ______
Stationery	€ ______	€ ______	€ ______
Office expenses	€ ______	€ ______	€ ______
Accountancy fees	€ ______	€ ______	€ ______
Legal & other fees	€ ______	€ ______	€ ______
Other costs	€ ______	€ ______	€ ______
Total general expenses	**€** ______	**€** ______	**€** ______

Finance costs	*Year 1*	*Year 2*	*Year 3*
Interest on loans/ overdraft	€ ______	€ ______	€ ______
Mortgage interest	€ ______	€ ______	€ ______
Charges/fees	€ ______	€ ______	€ ______
Other	€ ______	€ ______	€ ______
Total finance costs	**€** ______	**€** ______	**€** ______

Depreciation	*Year 1*	*Year 2*	*Year 3*
Property	€ ______	€ ______	€ ______
Fixtures & fittings	€ ______	€ ______	€ ______

Copy to Business Plan, page 130-131, and summarise on page 88.

Downloads for this section are available @
www.startingabusinessinireland.com

Operating Budget – Sales / Profit and Loss Account

OPERATING BUDGET – ESTIMATE OF SALES AND GROSS PROFIT

Revenue by product

	Year 1	Year 2	Year 3
Cash sales			
A ____________	€ _____	€ _____	€ _____
B ____________	€ _____	€ _____	€ _____
C ____________	€ _____	€ _____	€ _____
D ____________	€ _____	€ _____	€ _____
	€ _____	€ _____	€ _____
Credit sales			
A ____________	€ _____	€ _____	€ _____
B ____________	€ _____	€ _____	€ _____
C ____________	€ _____	€ _____	€ _____
D ____________	€ _____	€ _____	€ _____
	€ _____	€ _____	€ _____
Total sales	**€** _____	**€** _____	**€** _____
Deduct			
Opening stock	€ _____	€ _____	€ _____
Purchases	€ _____	€ _____	€ _____
	€ _____	€ _____	€ _____
Less Closing stock	€ _____	€ _____	€ _____
Cost of goods sold	**€** _____	**€** _____	**€** _____
Gross profit	**€** _____	**€** _____	**€** _____
Gross profit percentage	_____ %	_____ %	_____

%

Copy to Business Plan, page 125, and summarise in the panel to the right.

OPERATING BUDGET – ASSUMPTIONS

What assumptions did you make in estimating these key figures for your operating budget?

Sales
Purchases
Stocks
Staff salaries
Production overheads
Premises costs
Transport costs
Selling and promotion costs
General expenses
Finance costs
Depreciation

Copy these Assumptions into your Business Plan, page 129.

OPERATING BUDGET – PROFIT AND LOSS ACCOUNT

	Year 1	Year 2	Year 3
Sales	**€** _____	**€** _____	**€** _____
Cost of Sales	€ _____	€ _____	€ _____
Gross Profit	**€** _____	**€** _____	**€** _____
Gross Profit %	_____ %	_____ %	_____ %
Overheads:			
Staff	€ _____	€ _____	€ _____
Production	€ _____	€ _____	€ _____
Premises	€ _____	€ _____	€ _____
Transport	€ _____	€ _____	€ _____
Selling and promotion	€ _____	€ _____	€ _____
General expenses	€ _____	€ _____	€ _____
Finance	€ _____	€ _____	€ _____
Depreciation	€ _____	€ _____	€ _____
Total overheads	**€** _____	**€** _____	**€** _____
Net Profit/(Loss)	**€** _____	**€** _____	**€** _____
Tax on profit/(loss)	€ _____	€ _____	€ _____
	€ _____	€ _____	€ _____
Drawings	€ _____	€ _____	€ _____
Profit retained in business	**€** _____	**€** _____	**€** _____

MINIMUM TURNOVER

To calculate the minimum turnover to meet all your business and personal expenses, the formula is:
Total expenses x 100/Gross profit percentage = Minimum turnover.
Calculate your own minimum turnover.

Cash-flow Planning

OBJECTIVES
- ☐ Understand the difference between profit and cash-flow
- ☐ Be able to prepare cash-flow projections

On paper you could be the richest person in the world and still not be able to pay the mortgage (or go for a pint!). That is because there is a clear distinction between cash flow and profits and between costs and expenditure.

Getting your start-up financed is one part, keeping the company financially sound is another. You need to know when money is coming in, and when it is going out. The cash is the lifeblood of the business and should be monitored rigorously. More businesses fail because they run out of cash than from almost any other cause. Even profitable businesses can fail because of lack of cash!

So think CASH, CASH, CASH.

The main pitfalls in financing a business are:

- Underestimating the investment needed (the golden rule is to double your original estimate)
- Not including room to manoeuvre in your budget for the difficult start-up time
- Forgetting your own personal financial requirement (how much do you need to take out of the business for living expenses in the start-up period?)
- Not putting aside money to pay your taxes when they are due
- Underestimating the difficulties of getting paid (the average credit period in Ireland is around three months).

When you calculated your initial investment (see "Finance", page 82), you analysed your initial investment on a time basis – some items were needed now, others could be postponed for a month or two, or even more. Cashflow planning is the same exercise applied across your entire business. It means looking at every item of income and expenditure in your budgets and estimating when it will impact the business in cash terms. Timing of cash in or out can be critical – as you will find when your first big cheque due to come in comes in late!

Initial investment

You know when your initial investment needs to be acquired; now calculate when it needs to be paid for. Pencil in the amounts under the heading "Outgoing/Initial investment" in the appropriate months in the Cash flow projection on the following pages.

Be careful of VAT. You must pay it when you buy things but, even if you are entitled to recover it, you will not get it back for some time (See "Taxation"). Your cash flow needs to be able to pay the full amount upfront.

Next, look at sources of finance that you have agreed (see "Finance, page 84). When will these come in? Pencil the amounts into your cash flow projection in the appropriate months under "Incoming/Sources of finance").

Operating Budget

Look again at your Operating Budget:

- Which items of expenditure will occur every month? (Don't forget private drawings)
- Are there any once-off payments such as legal fees, security deposit for rent, new phone lines, insurance, etc.?
- Any advance payments for suppliers, rent, etc.?

Happiness is a positive cash-flow.
FRED ADLER, US venture capitalist

Take the cash and let the credit go.
EDWARD FITZGERALD

Check your diary. Does activity in a particular month mean extra expenditure for that month? (advertising, direct mail, networking, meeting with your mentor, holiday, travel, etc.). Fill in those extra expenses.

If clients have paid you (or will pay you) in advance, put that in the appropriate month.

Do you have any forward orders? When will the product or service be delivered and when will the customer pay? Fill in the amounts in the appropriate months.

Go back to your market research and marketing plan. Are there seasonal patterns? Will some of your promotional actions increase sales in particular months? What are your expectations of how sales will develop in the first few months? Try to estimate sales for each month. Write down how you came to that estimate and on which sources and assumptions you have based it. Fill in your sales estimates in the appropriate months.

Check your cost pricing and, more importantly, the costs directly related to the sales (variable costs). Most obvious ones are purchase of materials and travel.

Fill in the variable costs, and keep the VAT separate again. Things to check include:

- Do you have to pay VAT (calculate incoming VAT minus outgoing VAT)?
- Can you claim VAT back?
- When must you pay taxes and how much?

CASHFLOW PROJECTIONS – YEAR 1

Copy this to page 133.

	M1 €	M2 €	M3 €	M4 €	M5 €	M6 €	M7 €	M8 €	M9 €	M10 €	M11 €	M12 €	Year 1 €
Opening bal.	___	___	___	___	___	___	___	___	___	___	___	___	___
Incoming													
Sources of finance	___	___	___	___	___	___	___	___	___	___	___	___	___
Cash sales	___	___	___	___	___	___	___	___	___	___	___	___	___
Debtors	___	___	___	___	___	___	___	___	___	___	___	___	___
VAT refunds	___	___	___	___	___	___	___	___	___	___	___	___	___
Other income	___	___	___	___	___	___	___	___	___	___	___	___	___
Total income	___	___	___	___	___	___	___	___	___	___	___	___	___
Outgoing													
Initial investment	___	___	___	___	___	___	___	___	___	___	___	___	___
Cash purchases	___	___	___	___	___	___	___	___	___	___	___	___	___
Creditors	___	___	___	___	___	___	___	___	___	___	___	___	___
Overheads:													
Staff	___	___	___	___	___	___	___	___	___	___	___	___	___
Production	___	___	___	___	___	___	___	___	___	___	___	___	___
Premises	___	___	___	___	___	___	___	___	___	___	___	___	___
Transport	___	___	___	___	___	___	___	___	___	___	___	___	___
Selling/promotion	___	___	___	___	___	___	___	___	___	___	___	___	___
Gen. expenses	___	___	___	___	___	___	___	___	___	___	___	___	___
Finance costs	___	___	___	___	___	___	___	___	___	___	___	___	___
Loan repayments	___	___	___	___	___	___	___	___	___	___	___	___	___
Private drawings	___	___	___	___	___	___	___	___	___	___	___	___	___
Fixed assets	___	___	___	___	___	___	___	___	___	___	___	___	___
VAT payable	___	___	___	___	___	___	___	___	___	___	___	___	___
Other taxes	___	___	___	___	___	___	___	___	___	___	___	___	___
Other expenses	___	___	___	___	___	___	___	___	___	___	___	___	___
Total expenses	___	___	___	___	___	___	___	___	___	___	___	___	___
Net cash flow	___	___	___	___	___	___	___	___	___	___	___	___	___
Final balance	___	___	___	___	___	___	___	___	___	___	___	___	___

SCRIBBLE BOX

CASHFLOW PROJECTIONS – YEAR 2

Copy this to page 134.

	M1 €	M2 €	M3 €	M4 €	M5 €	M6 €	M7 €	M8 €	M9 €	M10 €	M11 €	M12 €	Year 2 €
Opening bal.	___	___	___	___	___	___	___	___	___	___	___	___	___
Incoming													
Sources of finance	___	___	___	___	___	___	___	___	___	___	___	___	___
Cash sales	___	___	___	___	___	___	___	___	___	___	___	___	___
Debtors	___	___	___	___	___	___	___	___	___	___	___	___	___
VAT refunds	___	___	___	___	___	___	___	___	___	___	___	___	___
Other income	___	___	___	___	___	___	___	___	___	___	___	___	___
Total income	___	___	___	___	___	___	___	___	___	___	___	___	___
Outgoing													
Initial investment	___	___	___	___	___	___	___	___	___	___	___	___	___
Cash purchases	___	___	___	___	___	___	___	___	___	___	___	___	___
Creditors	___	___	___	___	___	___	___	___	___	___	___	___	___
Overheads:													
Staff	___	___	___	___	___	___	___	___	___	___	___	___	___
Production	___	___	___	___	___	___	___	___	___	___	___	___	___
Premises	___	___	___	___	___	___	___	___	___	___	___	___	___
Transport	___	___	___	___	___	___	___	___	___	___	___	___	___
Selling/promotion	___	___	___	___	___	___	___	___	___	___	___	___	___
Gen. expenses	___	___	___	___	___	___	___	___	___	___	___	___	___
Finance costs	___	___	___	___	___	___	___	___	___	___	___	___	___
Loan repayments	___	___	___	___	___	___	___	___	___	___	___	___	___
Private drawings	___	___	___	___	___	___	___	___	___	___	___	___	___
Fixed assets	___	___	___	___	___	___	___	___	___	___	___	___	___
VAT payable	___	___	___	___	___	___	___	___	___	___	___	___	___
Other taxes	___	___	___	___	___	___	___	___	___	___	___	___	___
Other expenses	___	___	___	___	___	___	___	___	___	___	___	___	___
Total expenses	___	___	___	___	___	___	___	___	___	___	___	___	___
Net cash flow	___	___	___	___	___	___	___	___	___	___	___	___	___
Final balance	___	___	___	___	___	___	___	___	___	___	___	___	___

SCRIBBLE BOX

Downloads for this section are available @
www.startingabusinessinireland.com

CASHFLOW PROJECTIONS – YEAR 3

Copy this to page 135.

	M1 €	M2 €	M3 €	M4 €	M5 €	M6 €	M7 €	M8 €	M9 €	M10 €	M11 €	M12 €	Year 3 €
Opening bal.													
Incoming													
Sources of finance													
Cash sales													
Debtors													
VAT refunds													
Other income													
Total income													
Outgoing													
Initial investment													
Cash purchases													
Creditors													
Overheads:													
Staff													
Production													
Premises													
Transport													
Selling/promotion													
Gen. expenses													
Finance costs													
Loan repayments													
Private drawings													
Fixed assets													
VAT payable													
Other taxes													
Other expenses													
Total expenses													
Net cash flow													
Final balance													

SCRIBBLE BOX

CASHFLOW – 3-YEAR PROJECTIONS

	Year 1	*Year 2*	*Year 3*
Opening balance	**€** ______	**€** ______	**€** ______
Incoming			
Sources of finance	€ ______	€ ______	€ ______
Cash sales	€ ______	€ ______	€ ______
Debtors	€ ______	€ ______	€ ______
VAT refunds	€ ______	€ ______	€ ______
Other income	€ ______	€ ______	€ ______
Total income	**€** ______	**€** ______	**€** ______
Outgoing			
Initial investment	€ ______	€ ______	€ ______
Cash purchases	€ ______	€ ______	€ ______
Creditors	€ ______	€ ______	€ ______
Overheads:			
Staff	€ ______	€ ______	€ ______
Production	€ ______	€ ______	€ ______
Premises	€ ______	€ ______	€ ______
Transport	€ ______	€ ______	€ ______
Selling/promotion	€ ______	€ ______	€ ______
General expenses	€ ______	€ ______	€ ______
Finance costs	€ ______	€ ______	€ ______
Loan repayments	€ ______	€ ______	€ ______
Private drawings	€ ______	€ ______	€ ______
Fixed assets	€ ______	€ ______	€ ______
VAT payable	€ ______	€ ______	€ ______
Other taxes	€ ______	€ ______	€ ______
Other expenditure	€ ______	€ ______	€ ______
Total expenditure	**€** ______	**€** ______	**€** ______
Net cash flow	**€** ______	**€** ______	**€** ______
Final balance	**€** ______	**€** ______	**€** ______

SCRIBBLE BOX

Downloads for this section are available @
www.startingabusinessinireland.com

Assistance – State Agencies

OBJECTIVES

- ☐ Understand the place of grants in financing your business
- ☐ Identify main sources of grant-aid and other assistance
- ☐ Understand grant-givers' criteria

There is a wide range of State bodies charged with assisting entrepreneurs and potential entrepreneurs to develop their businesses. The assistance they provide may be in the form of cash grants but increasingly includes advice, subsidies, training, workspace, etc.

Whatever form it takes, this assistance may be vital in providing the final piece of the jigsaw to get your business up and running, or it may provide just the push you need to get going. Sometimes, it may even be just the fact that someone else has confidence in you that makes it all come together.

Grant-aid, or other assistance, is a good thing. It can help your business to grow. Going through the application process, whether or not you are successful, will focus your planning. But don't let the need to meet grant-givers' criteria push your business where you don't want to go.

Too often, entrepreneurs start by asking "Where will I get a grant?". Grants are not the aim of the business – your work on developing a strategy and a Mission Statement should tell you that. Grants are an extra, which may help you do something that you couldn't otherwise have afforded. They come at the end of the financing process – not at the start of the planning process! However, if grants – or better still, relevant training courses – are available, take advantage.

This section outlines the main sources of assistance from State bodies. Other sources, including private sector organisations, appear on page 104.

Structure of State assistance

Overall responsibility for enterprise lies with the Department of Enterprise, Trade and Employment, which is responsible for promoting competitiveness in the economy and for creating a favourable climate for the creation of self-sustaining employment. It works to monitor and improve the environment for business by ensuring that the framework of law, regulation and Government policy promotes effective company performance and both public and business confidence.

It achieves this indirectly by creating an environment for enterprise and directly through the agencies it has established, which operate to stimulate industrial development at different levels:

- **Nationally** – Enterprise Ireland
- **Regionally** – Shannon Development and Údarás na Gaeltachta
- **Locally** – City/County Enterprise Boards and Area Partnerships.

Policy is determined by Forfás, which is the national Policy and Advisory Board for Enterprise, Trade, Science, Technology & Innovation. It reports to the Department of Enterprise, Trade & Employment.

IDA Ireland and Enterprise Ireland both report to Forfás and implement policy set by it. IDA Ireland focuses on inwards investment — bringing foreign multinationals into Ireland — while Enterprise Ireland is tasked with supporting indigenous (local) businesses.

There are also other State agencies whose role includes that of stimulating development, albeit often in specified sectors.

Where do I start?

Enterprise Link is an initiative of the Department of Enterprise, Trade and Employment, is operated by Enterprise Ireland, and is designed to direct would-be entrepreneurs to the information or assistance they need. It provides a single source of information for all sources of support to start-up and small businesses in Ireland, on **1850 35 33 33**.

Although there has been a huge shift away from a jobs focus among the enterprise support agencies, ironically the first question that you must answer to decide where you should look for help still relates to the employment potential of your new business.

If, within three years or so of start-up, you are likely still to employ under 10 people, you should make your way to the City/County Enterprise Boards and/or the other local support agencies.

Once you can show that you are likely to employ more than 10 people within three years or so of start-up (and meet some other criteria, including demonstrating export potential), Enterprise Ireland (or Shannon Development/Údarás na Gaeltachta, as appropriate) classifies your business as a "high potential start-up" and takes you under its wing.

City and County Enterprise Boards

City and County Enterprise Boards are probably the most important source of assistance for the start-up business. The 35 CEBs aim to encourage local initiative. Each is a company limited by guarantee, and has an executive staff, headed by a Chief Executive Officer. The 12-14 Board members are drawn from elected members of the local authority, the social partners, State agencies, ICTU, IBEC, the farming organisations, the county manager and community and other representatives.

The CEBs have responsibility for enterprise development in areas not already covered by the State industrial development agencies – specifically, enterprises employing (or likely to employ) fewer than 10 persons and service businesses. Where they receive applications for funding and advice that are more appropriate to the remit of existing agencies (say, Enterprise Ireland), such applications are directed to the appropriate agency.

Each Board has access to an Enterprise Fund which has been established to assist small projects. However, City/County Enterprise Boards do not normally consider proposals involving grant support in excess of €60,000 or projects with investment costs in excess of €125,000. Project promoters must demonstrate that:

- There is a market for the proposed product/service
- Adequate overall finance will be available to fund the project
- They possess the management and technical capacity to implement the proposed project
- Projects to be assisted will add value so as to generate income or supplement income for those involved, and will have the capacity to create new direct employment whether full-time, part-time or seasonal, or will, as a minimum, contribute directly to maintaining employment in existing small businesses
- They will comply with existing policies on tax clearance, the certification of subcontractors, and related matters.

The Boards do not fund projects which are contrary to public policy, nor do they duplicate support for projects which would be eligible for assistance from any existing sectoral or grant structure, or which involve primary agricultural production.

STATE SUPPORT FOR START-UPS: THROUGH THE MAZE

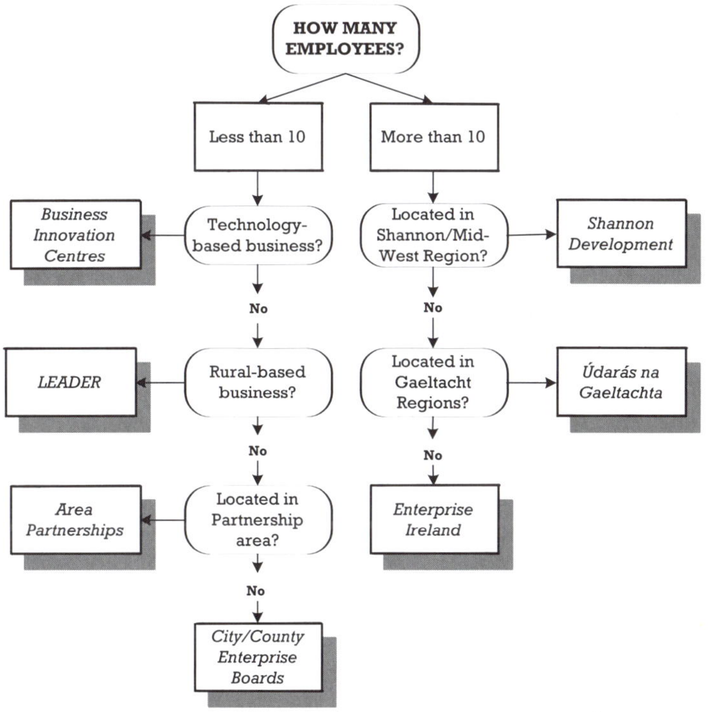

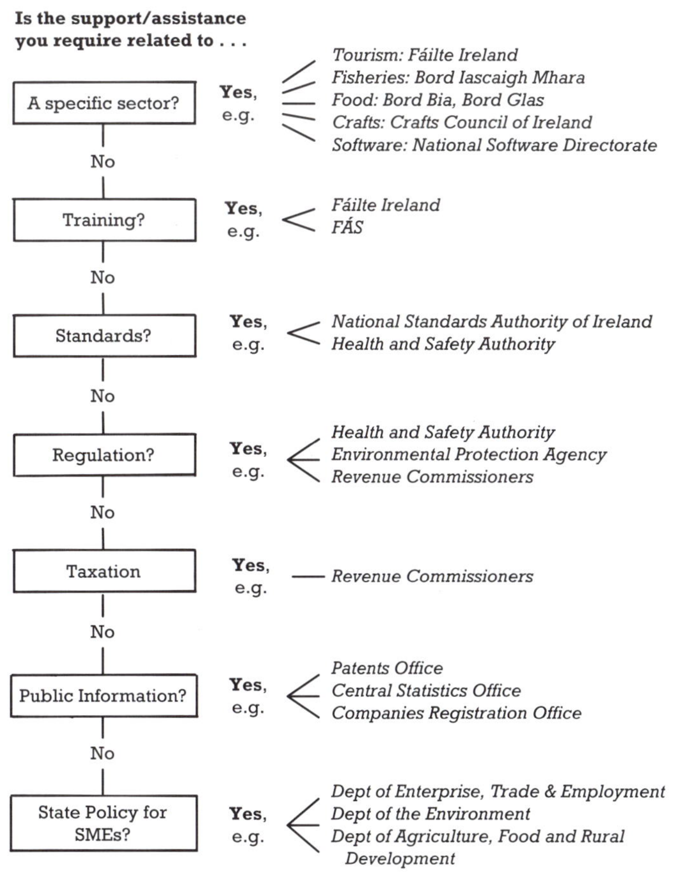

The following grants are available:

- A maximum of 50% of the cost of capital and other investment, or €60,000 – whichever is lower
- A maximum of 60% of the cost of preparing a feasibility study/business plan, subject to an overall limit of €6,000 in the case of a single project.

Assistance is not confined to grants, since the Boards have authority to provide loans and loan guarantees and to take equity stakes in businesses. In addition, the CEBs act as a source of advice and information. Many provide training and mentoring services.

The CEBs also deliver the Empower.ie e-initiative, aimed at providing e-business services and incentives to micro-businesses.

In the period 2000-2006, under the National Development Plan, the focus of the CEBs will move away from direct financial support towards a broader range of "soft" supports — training (in particular, management development), mentoring and other forms of assistance — designed to increase the survival rates of start-ups and small businesses.

Since the activities of the CEBs are tailored to the needs of their local community, you should check with your local CEB for the full range of assistance available.

CITY/COUNTY ENTERPRISE BOARDS – THE GRANT APPLICATION PROCESS

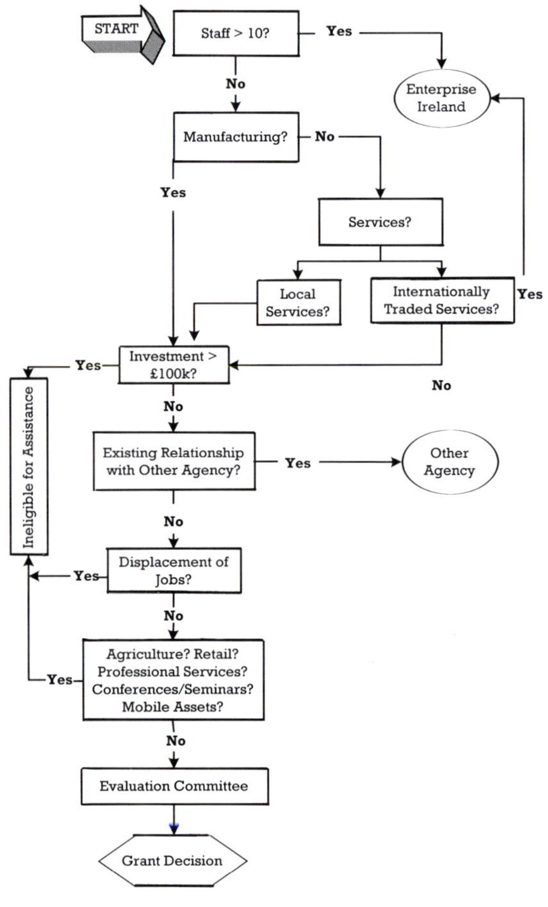

You should contact your local CEB before taking your project much beyond an initial stage. An initial informal discussion will quickly determine whether:

- The CEB can support your project
- A feasibility study grant may be available
- You should make changes to your project to make it acceptable to the CEB for assistance.

Your application should be on an official application form, obtainable from your local CEB. Read the notes with the application form carefully before completing. Almost always, except in cases where very small amounts of money are involved, CEBs will require a Business Plan with your application. A Feasibility Study Grant may help you prepare one (see the first chapter, **READY**).

Enterprise Ireland

Enterprise Ireland is the government organisation charged with assisting the development of Irish enterprise. Its mission is: "to work in partnership with client companies to develop a sustainable competitive advantage, leading to a significant increase in profitable sales, exports and employment". Its clients are mainly manufacturing and internationally-traded services companies employing more than 10 people. Its services include:

- Access to business angels and venture capital funds
- Assistance with feasibility studies
- Assistance with intellectual property and technology transfer
- Benchmarking
- Design support
- Incubation and workspaces
- Linkages with EU technology support programmes
- Market information and supports
- Mentoring
- Support for e-commerce/e-business.

Enterprise Ireland also supports a range of other initiatives targeted at developing enterprise, including the Campus Companies Venture Capital Fund, the Millennium Entrepreneur Fund, Enterprise Link, the

Innovation Relay Centre Ireland and cross-border links such as the Cross Border Technology Enterprise Start-up Programme. It also hosts an annual Student Enterprise Awards competition. More information on Enterprise Ireland's services are available at its website (**www.enterprise-ireland.com**).

Enterprise Ireland assists "high potential" start-ups:

- In manufacturing or internationally traded services
- Based on technological innovation or exploitable market niche opportunity
- Likely to achieve projected sales of at least €1.3m and 10 jobs by Year 3
- Export-oriented
- Capable in the longer term of significantly exceeding these levels
- Being established by experienced managers, academics or technical graduates.

Assistance provided by Enterprise Ireland nationally is provided in certain regions by Shannon Development or Údarás na Gaeltachta, as appropriate.

Enterprise Ireland's approach involves:

- Detailed analysis of a company's requirements
- Determination of the level of need for State support
- Targeting of funds to meet the real needs of the business
- Provision of funds to companies that are forecast to deliver strong growth in both sales and exports.

In addition to the change away from an emphasis on jobs towards sustainable competitive advantage, Enterprise Ireland has also shifted the focus of its financial support — away from grants to a mix of non-repayable grants and equity investment (in the form of preference and ordinary shares), seeking to optimise the level of repayability. The argument behind this move is that, since Enterprise Ireland's resources are limited, they must be wisely invested in businesses that give the best return. In addition, a measure of repayability provides resources that can be recycled into other companies later on.

In addition to financial support from its own resources, Enterprise Ireland can provide access to:

- Its Research, Technology and Innovation (RTI) scheme — grants to develop innovative products, awarded on a competitive basis
- Its register of "Business Angels" — private investors who usually take an active part in the business as well as an equity stake in return for their investment
- Venture capital funds, often in conjunction with other organisations.

Shannon Development

Shannon Development is the Regional Development Agency responsible for development in the Shannon Region, comprising Counties Limerick, Clare, North Tipperary and South-west Offaly and North Kerry. It offers grants and other assistance to businesses in the Shannon region, broadly in line with the assistance available nationally from Enterprise Ireland.

Shannon Development operates the National Technological Park, which includes its Innovation Centre. It also launched the Kerry Technology Park, in association with the Institute of Technology Tralee, IDA Ireland, Tralee Urban District Council and Kerry County Council. It has developed its own range of venture capital funds, the Limerick Food Centre and other facilities that make the Mid-West a prime technological base.

Údarás na Gaeltachta

Údarás na Gaeltachta combines an economic development role (that of creating sustainable jobs and attracting investment to the Gaeltacht regions) with community, cultural and language-development activities, working in partnership with local communities and organisations. Projects in manufacturing, internationally-traded services (such as software development and telemarketing/servicing) and natural resources such as mariculture are the priority for assistance. It offers grant schemes and incentives to help small and medium-sized enterprises in the Gaeltacht areas, which are broadly in line with those available nationally from Enterprise Ireland. It also provides non-financial incentives, such as advice and consultation on legal documentation.

Údarás aims to establish and develop job-creating industries and services in the Gaeltacht regions of Donegal, Mayo, Galway, Kerry, Cork, Waterford and Meath.

Area Partnerships

The 38 Area Partnerships were set up under the Programme for Economic and Social Progress (PESP) in 1993. Their activities are co-ordinated by Area Development Management Ltd. One of the Partnerships' aims is to work at local level to generate more jobs through sustainable enterprises and through the promotion of local economic projects and initiatives.

Each Partnership is autonomous and agrees different work practices. Each works on an Area Action Plan for its own region. Practical measures are taken to discriminate in favour of the long-term unemployed and those who are socially excluded.

Partnerships provide support for unemployed people setting up their own business, through:

- Support for the development of business plans

and business ideas
- Financial support, including non-repayable grants, interest subsidies, loan guarantees, small-scale investment and joint ventures
- Mentoring, including sources of advice
- Provision of workspace, including help in obtaining enterprise incubation units
- Rent subsidies
- Marketing, including identifying gaps in the market
- Training and education in enterprise, with the support of FÁS.

There is variety in what each Partnership offers, and entrepreneurs should contact the Partnership in their area for further details.

The Area Allowance (Enterprise) is payable to people who live in a Partnership area, have been unemployed for 12 months or more and have been signing the Live Register, and who have a suitable enterprise/business project within a Partnership area. The project must be one that does not displace existing enterprises/businesses, and must be approved by the Partnership. When approved, applicants will receive an allowance equivalent to their full unemployment payment, and will receive any secondary benefits to which they were entitled while in receipt of the unemployment payment. This will continue for 12 months, after which the applicant may be entitled for a further three years to the Back to Work Allowance operated by the Department of Social, Community and Family Affairs. Apply directly to your local Partnership.

Note that some of the Partnerships also operate LEADER programme in their areas, or provide support for other enterprise activities — for example, South Kerry Development Partnership hosts Carréfour Cahirciveen.

LEADER

LEADER is an EU initiative for rural development (part-funded by the Irish Government) that enables groups in rural areas to implement their own multi-sectoral integrated plans for the development of their areas.

LEADER+ is aimed at encouraging and supporting high quality and ambitious integrated strategies for local rural development, putting a strong emphasis on co-operation and networking between rural areas.

All rural areas of the EU are, in principle, eligible under LEADER+. A list of groups approved under LEADER+ is available from the Department of Agriculture, Food and Rural Development.

Typical LEADER activities include:
- Technical support to rural development including group administration
- Training and recruitment assistance
- Rural tourism
- Small firms, craft enterprises and local services
- Local exploitation and marketing of agricultural, horticultural, forest and fishery products
- Preservation and improvement of the environment and living conditions.

As each LEADER Group identifies and responds to needs within its own communities, its activities are unique to its own situation. Because of this, and the changes taking place in LEADER itself, entrepreneurs seeking assistance should make contact with their local LEADER Group to see whether and what help is available.

Business Innovation Centres

The Business Innovation Centres are primarily targeted at technology-based businesses. They encourage and foster innovation in new or existing businesses, through services directed at the development of new ideas and their conversion into real business projects.

As BIC support services may vary between centres, entrepreneurs seeking assistance should make contact with their local BIC to see whether and what help is available. There are BICs in Cork, Dublin, Galway, Limerick, Waterford and Derry.

STATE AND SEMI-STATE AGENCIES

As mentioned earlier, there are a wide range of these agencies, covering a variety of roles and responsibilities and reporting to appropriate Government Departments. Useful websites for access are:
- **www.ask-ireland.com**
- **www.irlgov.ie** – the Government web-site
- **www.basis.ie** – Business Access to State Information Services, a single information point for all Government information and services.

Arts Council

The Arts Council is the development agency for the arts in Ireland and the primary source of support for the individual creative and interpretative artist. It provides support and financial assistance for artistic purposes to individuals and organisations. It annually funds over 350 arts and non-arts organisations and makes awards to over 450 individuals across all art forms, from €750 to €10,000.

Bord Bia — The Irish Food Board

Bord Bia develops export markets for Irish food and drink companies. It provides information on exports, production, quality standards, health regulations and controls, and new developments in the industry. Its services include programmes to foster contact between international buyers and Irish companies, to protect and defend the quality and integrity of Irish food and drink, and to provide up-to-date market information. For small business, Bord Bia provides a mentoring programme, focusing on the British market.

Bord Glas - The Horticultural Development Board
Bord Glas is responsible for the development of the horticultural industry in Ireland — the amenity sector (trees, shrubs, flowers and bulbs) and the food sector (fruit and vegetables, including mushrooms, potatoes and glasshouse crops). Its programmes assist the production, marketing and consumption of horticultural produce, and help existing and new enterprises to improve standards, develop new products and markets, and plan for the future.

Bord Iascaigh Mhara - Irish Sea Fisheries Board
BIM is responsible for the sustainable development of the Irish seafood industry and stimulates investment, technological innovation, enterprise and growth. Its objective is to expand the volume, quality and value of output from the seafish and aquaculture sectors, thereby generating employment and income. BIM provides integrated development programmes providing advisory, financial, technical, marketing and training support, organised through five divisions: Aquaculture Development, Fisheries Development, Marine Services, Market Development and Secretariat.

Central Statistics Office
The CSO collects, compiles, analyses and disseminates statistical information relating to the economic and social life of Ireland. It is also responsible for co-ordinating official statistics of other public authorities and for developing the statistical potential of administrative records.

The CSOis a key source of market research information on industry and building, services statistics, labour market and vital statistics, foreign trade, agriculture, prices, National Accounts, Balance of Payments and demography. This information is available in statistical releases, publications and associated diskettes, on the CSO's website, and via a Trade Help Desk and Information Section. Special customer-tailored analyses can be provided. Many of its publications are available from the Government Publications sales office in Dublin.

The CSO attends enterprise shows and exhibitions to promote awareness of itself and statistics generally.

Companies Registration Office
The CRO is the authority for the incorporation of new companies and the registration of business names in the Republic of Ireland. It is also responsible for the receipt and registration of post-incorporation documents, for enforcement of the filing requirements of companies and for the provision of information to the public. Almost all of the information filed with the CRO is available for public inspection, usually for a small fee. Regsitration forms are available for download on the CRO's website (**www.cro.ie**).

Crafts Council of Ireland
The CCOI is the national design and economic development agency for the craft industry in the Republic of Ireland, funded by Enterprise Ireland and the EU. CCOI's services include:

- Showcase Ireland, a national trade fair
- Information services to wholesale and retail buyers on the availability of craft products, plus up-to-date, computerised information on retail outlets, courses, craftspeople and their craft products, development agencies, grant-aid bodies etc
- Business advisory service for craftspeople setting up their own craft business or craft-shop and for those already established, including grant applications and liaising with grant-aiding agencies, market research, business plans, company structure, finance and packaging
- Training and help for design enterprise through short courses, offered via local City/County Enterprise Boards, to enhance product and marketing development in craft businesses
- Training programmes in jewellery production and design skills, pottery skills, blacksmithing and forging and craft & design business development.

Department of Social & Family Affairs
The Department operates a "Back to Work" Allowance (Self-Employment) scheme to encourage people to become self-employed. To qualify, you must be:

- Setting up a self-employment business approved by a Partnership Company or Job Facilitator
- "Signing-on" for at least 12 months and getting Unemployment Benefit or Assistance
- Getting One-Parent Family Payment, Disability Allowance or Blind Person's Pension for 12 months.

You will receive support for four years (including increases for a qualified adult and child dependants), as follows:

- 100% of your weekly Social Welfare payment for Year 1; 75% for Year 2; 50% for Year 3; 25% for Year 4.

You will also retain and "secondary" benefits for the four years, provided that the combined household income for self-employment and the Back to Work Allowance is less than €317.43 per week.

ENFO — Environmental Information Service
ENFO is an environmental information service established to promote knowledge and care of the environment. It provides a query-answering service, information leaflets, reference library with computerised database with 55,000 titles, study and research facilities, educational materials, exhibitions and lectures.

Environmental Protection Agency
The EPA's responsibilities include:

- Promotion of environmentally sound practices through the use of environmental audits, eco-labelling, environmental quality objectives and codes of practice on matters affecting the environment
- Promotion and co-ordination of research
- Monitoring of environmental quality
- Licensing and regulation of large industrial and other processes (including landfills) with significant polluting potential, on the basis of integrated pollution control (IPC) and best available technologies.

Fáilte Ireland - The National Tourism Development Authority
Fáilte Ireland provides an extensive range of training and support services and business solutions to tourism enterprises, large and small, designed to develop and sustain Ireland as a high-quality competitive tourist destination.

FÁS — The Training and Employment Authority
FÁS provides a range of training and employment programmes, an employment service, an advisory service for industry, and support for co-operative and community-based enterprise.

Individuals who want to start a business can attend the Business Appraisal Training Programme, which allows them to develop business plans, enhance their technical skills and conduct market research into the viability of their business idea. The Community Enterprise Programme provides advice, training and financial assistance to community groups involved in the creation of economically viable jobs. The Social Economy Programme supports the development of social economy enterprises that will benefit the economic and social regeneration of a community. It provides up to three years' grant support to social economy enterprises providing employment opportunities for the long-term unemployed or other disadvantaged persons. Jobstart is a recruitment subsidy that offers employers financial support to meet their recruitment needs and help Jobseekers secure employment.

FÁS also assists SMEs through the FÁS Co-operative Development Unit.

FÁS Co-operative Development Unit
The FÁS Co-operative Development Unit (CDU) assists people who wish to take advantage of the Worker Co-operative structure. The CDU requires a minimum team of three persons and a commercially viable business idea before financial support can be granted. It also assists family businesses in dealing with succession planning and transfer through employee buy-outs.

Food Safety Authority of Ireland
The Food Safety Authority of Ireland's mission is to protect consumers' health by ensuring that food consumed, distributed, marketed or produced in Ireland meets the highest standards of food safety and hygiene. The Authority offers advice and information on all aspects of food safety, including the safe buying, storing, handling and preparation of food.

A Food Safety Helpline operates on **1890 33 66 77**.

Government Publications
All Government publications are available from the sales office, including Central Statistics Office reports.

Health & Safety Authority
The HSA has overall responsibility for the administration and enforcement of health and safety at work in Ireland, and:

- Monitors compliance with legislation at the workplace and can take enforcement action (including prosecutions)
- Is an expert centre for information and advice to employers, employees and self-employed
- Promotes education, training and research.

The Safety, Health and Welfare at Work Act, 1989 covers all who work, all workplaces, visitors and passers-by and also places responsibilities on manufacturers and suppliers (including designers, installers and erectors). The HSA also publishes a number of useful guides.

Irish Energy Centre
The Irish Energy Centre is Ireland's national agency for energy efficiency and renewable energy information, advice and support. EU-funded, the Centre provides guidance on the potential for more efficient use of energy in home, office, industry and municipal activities and on the development of renewable energy resources, from commercial projects to domestic applications. Practical information and advice is offered through targeted conferences, seminars, workshops and publications. In addition, the Centre offers advice on potential sources of funding for sustainable energy initiatives.

Marine Institute
The Marine Institute is the national agency responsible for undertaking, co-ordinating, promoting and assisting in marine research and development, and providing such services related to marine research and development that, in the opinion of the Institute, will promote economic development, create employment and protect the environment.

National Standards Authority of Ireland
Among NSAI's objectives are:
- To formulate, publish and sell Irish Standards, which form part of the harmonised European and worldwide system of standards in which NSAI is a designated "National Standards Body"
- To assist all sectors of industry to understand and meet the technical, quality and safety requirements of harmonised European and international standards in the domestic and overseas markets
- To provide a comprehensive quality auditing and product certification service for industry and commerce in accordance with current European and international practice
- To improve the quality of products and services through the promotion and application of the IS EN ISO 9000 series of Quality Systems Management standards
- To provide training and information on standards and their application to the certification service provided by the NSAI.

Patents Office
The principal statutory functions of the Office are:
- The granting of patents
- The registration of industrial designs & trade marks
- Providing information in relation to patents, designs and trade marks.

Registry of Business Names
By law, entrepreneurs are obliged by law to register their business with the Registry of Business Names, or the relevant body in the case of co-operatives, if it carries on a business under a name other than its own.

Registry of Friendly Societies
A co-operative society can be formed by any group of seven or more people over the age of 18, and can be registered with the Registry of Friendly Societies. The advantage of registration is limited liability. The Co-operative Development Society Ltd, Irish Co-operative Society Ltd, and National Association of Building Co-operatives Ltd have Model Rules for co-operatives that have been approved by the Registry of Friendly Societies for use by those wishing to form a co-operative.

Revenue Commissioners
Revenue's mission is to serve the community by fairly and efficiently collecting taxes and duties and implementing import and export controls. A wide range of publications and information is available from the Revenue website (**www.revenue.ie**).

Teagasc
Teagasc offers a Certificate in Rural Business for farmers exploring opportunities for starting new businesses, or expanding existing businesses, linked to the rural environment. The course covers technical and management skills as well as hands-on practical skills. Teagasc also offers a comprehensive range of training courses at its National Food Centre and Dairy Products Research Centre, aimed at strengthening in-company capabilities in quality systems, food safety and hygiene, food technology and product development/marketing. Through its Rural Enterprise Service, Teagasc provides foundation and advanced training courses for food entrepreneurs in rural areas. Teagasc research centres provide a range of technical services on a cost-recovery basis in support of the farming and food processing industries, government departments, local authorities and other clients.

Universities and Institutes of Technology
A final source of State support for enterprise are the Universities and Institutes of Technology. All have Industrial Liaison Officers or Heads of External Services or Development whose task it is to build links between the college and the business world. In many cases, this results in the college carrying out technical research for a local business or commercialising through a local business the fruits of their own research. TecNet co-ordinates and manages this for the ITs.

Frequently Asked Questions

OBJECTIVES

☐ Be aware of the questions most frequently asked of Enterprise Link

Enterprise Link is a single point of contact for all sources of support to start-up and expanding small businesses in Ireland. You can access Enterprise Link in two ways:

- By telephone on **1850 35 33 33** (this ensures that a call can be made from anywhere in Ireland for approx. €0.15)
- Via the Internet at **www.enterprise-ireland.com/enterpriselink/**

The questions most frequently asked of Enterprise Link are:

1. Are there grants for starting a business?

There is a large array of supports for starting a business including advice, information, training, mentoring, social welfare allowances and reliefs, and sometimes direct grant-aid assistance for researching a business idea, employing people or investing in equipment.

Businesses that receive grant-aid are those that have been identified as having potential for providing long-term viable jobs. Therefore, the support agencies are interested in the areas of business that are innovative, fill new market niches, replace imported products or services, demonstrate good management skills and have the financial viability necessary to succeed.

Although most start-up businesses do not receive cash grant-aid, all can avail of information and advice.

2. Why are some businesses never grant-aided?

Grant-aid assistance is targeted only at very specific sectors, regions or activities that have been identified as most likely to provide opportunities for economic and employment growth in Ireland.

Extensive research has been carried out to identify the reasons for business failures. For example, some activities have too many people in them already and cannot support more. Other activities may only be viable if the company is of a certain size or can fulfil a specific product need.

Areas such as retail trade must compete in the open market to operate successfully and, as such, are never grant-aid assisted as it would give that company an unfair advantage over others. Training in good management skills or technical improvements is often more valuable to businesses in the long-term.

3. I have an idea for a new business. Where do I start?

You need to do some basic market research to establish that a market exists, its size and how you can access it, before contacting your local Enterprise Board or Area Partnership (or Enterprise Ireland, Shannon Development or Údarás na Gaeltachta, if you expect to employ more than 10 people soon after start-up).

Next you need to do more market research and write a Business Plan.

4. Do I need to write a Business Plan?

Yes, you do.

Of course, you can start a business without a Business Plan. But you will have difficulties in raising finance or accessing support from banks or enterprise boards.

Even if you don't need finance, a Business Plan provides an invaluable framework for planning how your business will proceed and later as a benchmark for assessing the health of your business. It ensures that you know what is going on in all aspects of the business and have a method for seeing how the activities interact.

Successful entrepreneurs will tell you that planning is 90% of the effort required.

5. My business needs funding for capital equipment. Who will help?

Your local Enterprise Board may be able to help (it will not provide grant support in excess of €60,000).

If this is not sufficient for your needs, you should inquire from the State body responsible for promoting industry in your sector (for example, Bord Bia or Bord Iascaigh Mhara) whether your business qualifies for one of their schemes.

6. Where can I get a low cost or interest-free loan?

The main banks all have specialist units to support small businesses, which offer special terms (including borrowing at low rates) to start-ups.

Each of the Enterprise Boards has access

to an Enterprise Fund to support attractive projects.

First Step may be a source of finance for the entrepreneur who has unsuccessfully exhausted conventional funding sources. The Society of Saint Vincent de Paul may also help here.

7. Where can I get funding to start a creche?
Child-care is a major issue for parents and employers alike nowadays. To encourage additional child-care places, the Department of Justice, Equality & Law Reform's Equal Opportunities Childcare Section is making available grants for building, renovating, upgrading and/or equipping childcare facilities to creche operators with more than 20 children under their care.

8. Are there any grants available for B&Bs?
Grants for B&Bs may be available from your local Enterprise Board or Regional Tourism office. However, they are unlikely to be given in areas where B&Bs are already plentiful. Check first before building a grant into your plans.

9. How do I get premises in an Enterprise Centre?
Generally, you need to apply to the owner of the centre (for example, Enterprise Boards or local enterprise development groups). You may be offered premises if your business fits within the kind of activity the owners are promoting for the Centre.

10. Can I start a business in my own home?
The use of a private residence for business purposes is usually subject to planning permission. In most cases, local authorities will not require planning permission (or deny it, if it is applied for) where there is no impact on neighbouring properties. For example, a financial consultant who does his/her paperwork at home but meets clients on their own premises would expect little difficulty in relation to planning permission. But opening a garage to tune performance cars might bring complaints from your neighbours – and a refusal of the necessary planning permission.

Conditions vary around the country. Check with your local authority's planning department before making any decision. You should also check with your mortgage provider or landlord, in case they have any objections, before you start to work from home.

11. Are there grants for feasibility studies?
Generally speaking, yes.

All the enterprise support agencies subscribe to the idea that it's better to spend a little money to see whether an idea will work than to waste a lot of money only to see it fail because something was overlooked.

Enterprise Boards are the main source of feasibility grants. You should check with your local Enterprise Board for availability and conditions, as these may vary.

12. How do I register my business/business name?
You can register both with the Companies Registration Office (see Appendix for details). The CRO website (**www.cro.ie**) provides information on the process.

13. Do I have to register for VAT?
Only if your turnover is in excess of (or you expect it to be in excess of) €25,500 for services businesses or €51,000 for businesses selling physical goods.

Below these amounts, you may choose to register but you should first obtain professional advice from your accountant. The Revenue Commissioners publish a "Starting a Business" guide and other leaflets, which may be obtained from any tax office, the Revenue Forms & Leaflets Service at (01) 878 0100, or the Revenue's web-site (**www.revenue.ie**).

14. How do I source overseas employees?
EU nationals may work in any member State. Non-EU nationals require a work permit (except for some categories of workers who qualify under the "Fastrack" scheme).

FÁS may be able to help you with recruitment, through its overseas jobs fairs. "Overseas Recruitment", a booklet published by Enterprise Ireland, is essential reading.

15. I am not an Irish citizen. What must I do before starting a business in Ireland?
A non-EEA national (with some exceptions) who plans to establish a business in Ireland must apply to the Department of Justice, Equality & Law Reform with:

- Evidence to satisfy the Department that he/she has at least €300,000 available
- A business plan
- Details of professional or trade qualifications, where these are relevant to the proposed business
- A "certificate of character" from the police authority in their home state, to confirm that they do not have a criminal record, etc.

In addition, the proposed business must employ at least two non-family members, who must be Irish or EU nationals. Work permits are not required for non-EEA nationals who establish a business, though they may be required for any staff who move with the business.

Reproduced by permission of Enterprise Link.

Assistance: Other organisations

OBJECTIVES

- ☐ Understand the role of the various organisations assisting enterprise development
- ☐ Be aware of the assistance available

Small and medium-sized enterprises are defined as independent businesses (fewer than 25% of the shares held by one or more large companies), that have no more than 250 employees, and have either turnover less than □50 million or total assets net of depreciation less than □43 million.

EU definition of small and medium-sized enterprises (SMEs)

Other organisations, some State-supported, some entirely financed by the private sector, assist the potential entrepreneur in starting up and/or developing their business. This section lists some of these organisations.

For further details on each organisation and their services, contact them directly (see **Appendix 1** for addresses).

Accountants and consultants

Many accounting firms and consultants provide advice on obtaining grant-aid and on taking a business concept from viability assessment through to the production stage.

The initial meeting between a potential entrepreneur and the consultant is usually free and is used to gather information about the promoter and the business proposal. Based on the information available, the consultant will recommend appropriate action to progress the project.

Where further information is required, a structured feasibility study will be carried out, embracing key aspects such as products, markets, competitors, technology, funding etc. The consultant will prepare applications for feasibility study grant aid from an Enterprise Board, Enterprise Ireland or other appropriate bodies, and provide hands-on assistance in planning and carrying out the study. A fee should be agreed before work starts.

If the proposal is viable, the consultant will assist in the preparation of a comprehensive business plan, at a further agreed cost. The consultant will make application for grants appropriate to the project and assist in raising finance from banks or private investors. The consultant will also help to obtain commercial partners.

Professional advice on taxation, accounting and financial matters can be obtained also from a firm of accountants and auditors.

Action Tallaght

Action Tallaght was formed in 1992 as the umbrella body for five community enterprise groups in Tallaght. It provides integrated support — including sales and marketing advice, business consultancy, accountancy and legal advice, financial management and feasibility studies, business plans and funding applications — to people from Tallaght who intend to establish a business. Its Enterprise programme is supported by the Society of Saint Vincent de Paul, which provides seed capital and a professional business consultant.

Balbriggan Enterprise Development Group

BEDG operates the Balbriggan Enterprise Office, a local one-stop-shop for information and advice on market research, feasibility studies, grant applications and employment supports for new and existing businesses.

Bolton Trust

The Bolton Trust is an initiative of the Dublin Institute of Technology. It provides support for start-up enterprises and access to the resources of the DIT colleges to assist in a company's development.

It also set up the Powerhouse, which has almost 6,000 square feet of lettable office space to accommodate enterprises. Powerhouse also provides reception and secretarial services, telephones, typing, desk-top publishing, mailshots, photocopying, business address, security cards and heating – all priced on a usage basis.

Chambers of Commerce of Ireland

CCI is Ireland's largest business network with 11,000 member companies drawn from all sectors of the Irish economy. There are 55 chambers in Ireland, affiliated to CCI. Each Chamber strives for local economic development, representation of its members' interests, and the provision of market-led services to the local business community.

Co-operation Ireland

Formerly Co-operation North, Co-operation Ireland advances mutual understanding and respect by promoting practical co-operation between the people of Northern Ireland and the Republic of Ireland. It seeks to develop the capacity of small and medium enterprises in Border Counties and Northern Ireland to engage in cross-border ventures and business linkages. It funds the formation of joint venture companies, cross-border linkage companies, materials procurement programmes and cross-border studies related to economic development. It also administers EU funding to TradeNet Ireland, from the EU Special Support Programme for Peace and Reconciliation.

European Commission
To help small and medium-sized businesses (SMEs), the European Commission has funded various programmes, details of which are available from:

- **Info Points Europe**
- **Euro Info Centres**
- **Carréfours**
- **Innovation Relay Centres.**

The EU Special Support Programme for Peace and Reconciliation provides funding for a range of activities, including enterprise and community development, in the Border counties. The Commission also supports other enterprise activities, such as the Business Innovation Centres.

Excellence Ireland
Excellence Ireland, formerly the Irish Quality Association, promotes continuous improvement and business excellence among Irish companies through a range of quality/excellence schemes.

Food Product Development Centre
The Food Product Development Centre at the Dublin Institute of Technology develops innovative food concepts through investigating value-added opportunities in Irish and European markets. It provides a confidential service to clients. Its development work includes idea generation, concept and prototype development, ingredient sourcing and testing, shelf life studies, sensory assessment and market research, nutritional declaration and labelling.

Guaranteed Irish Ltd
Guaranteed Irish Limited aims to increase awareness of and demand for Irish products and services, thereby maximising employment and prosperity in Ireland through a definitive mark of excellence.

Inner City Enterprise
Inner City Enterprise is a private charity that pre-dates the Area Partnerships. It works closely with other enterprise support organisations in the inner city, including the Dublin Inner City Partnership. It provides information, advice and financial support for unemployed people in the inner city who want to start a business.

International Fund for Ireland
The International Fund for Ireland (IFI) is an international organisation established by the Irish and British Governments in 1986 to promote economic and social advancement and to encourage contact, dialogue and reconciliation between nationalists and unionists throughout Ireland. The Fund's contributions come from the United States, European Union, Australia, Canada, New Zealand and, to date, are in excess of €450m.

The IFI pursues its objectives by stimulating private investment and enterprise, supplementing public programmes and supporting voluntary efforts including self-help schemes. It runs programmes relevant to small business. The Fund also assists local community groups in providing workspace accommodation and business-loan funds to help small businesses. It has two investment companies — Enterprise Equity (NI) Ltd and Enterprise Equity (Ireland) Ltd that provide seed capital on normal commercial criteria to existing and start-up businesses.

IRD Duhallow Ltd
A Community Group established by Area Development Management, as part of its Local Development programme. It operates a Food Training Centre in Boherbue, which provides food incubation units and training.

IRD Kiltimagh
IRD Kiltimagh operates two Enterprise Centres, with incubation workspace, and has undertaken the successful implementation of a re-development programme for the Kiltimagh area in conjunction with the state and private sectors. This has included work with the Business and Tourism actors in the Kiltimagh and broader East Mayo areas. IRD Kiltimagh administers the East Mayo Local Development Programme under the auspices of Meitheal Mhaigh Eo and the LEADER Programme for East Mayo as part of the Western Rural Development Company.

Irish Business & Employers Confederation
IBEC (Irish Business & Employers Confederation) represents and provides economic, commercial, employee relations and social affairs services to some 7,000 companies and organisations from all sectors of economic and commercial activity. It works to shape policies and influence decision-making in a way that develops and protects members' interests and contributes to the development and maintenance of an economy that promotes enterprise and productive employment.

Irish Exporters Association
The Irish Exporters Association represents and promotes exporters' interests. The Association has regional branches in Cork, Dublin, Dundalk, Galway and Limerick. The Association offers a Diploma in International Trade and Marketing, as well as a series of short courses on aspects of international trade practice.

Irish Internet Association
The IIA is the professional body for those conducting business via the Internet in Ireland. IIA provides information to members on e-business, education & training, security, employer/employee rights, raising capital, marketing, design & development and languages/ platforms. The IIA website offers "iia internet resources", with catalogued links and articles within each topic.

Irish Productivity Centre
The IPC offers advice and practical assistance to businesses in solving commercial, organisational, financial and management problems and in the development of change through partnership.

Irish Small & Medium Enterprises Association
ISME's membership is composed exclusively of entrepreneurs who own and manage competitive businesses. It offers a range of services to members, including publications on wages and conditions, employers' obligations, Government-sponsored grant schemes and a member-to-member sourcing directory.

Libraries/Information Centres
Good libraries are a treasure trove for the entrepreneur conducting market research.

Check out the libraries/information centres in (phone first to check access, opening times, etc.):

- Central Business Library, ILAC Centre, Dublin
- Enterprise Ireland (Merrion Hall, Dublin)
- ENFO.

Limerick Enterprise Development Partnership
On the closure of the Krups factory in 1998 with the loss of 500 jobs, LEDP was formed to acquire it from the owners, Group Moulinex. A thriving enterprise centre now occupies the site. LEDP is a company limited by guarantee, whose members include the Limerick Enterprise Network, PAUL Partnership, Limerick Corporation, Limerick County Council, Shannon Development, IBEC and the Limerick Diocesan authorities.

Limerick Food Centre
The Food Centre provides food manufacturing and processing units, access to equipment, a full research, information and advice service, and a specialist Agribusiness and Natural Resources Support Unit. Teagasc and the National Food Centre provide research, technical, analytical and testing services. The Centre provides a range of professional, entrepreneurial support and marketing programmes for existing and potential business, linked to the wider supports, financial and investment services of Shannon Development.

MAC (National Microelectronics Application Centre)
Owned by Shannon Development, University of Limerick, and private investors, MAC's primary activity is the contract development of new and improved electronic, software, telematic and information products and processes for Irish entrepreneurs and industry. MAC can help an entrepreneur by:

- Discussing the market opportunity, concept, product, process or service idea
- Carrying out an on-line search of world databases to identify similar products, potential competitors, and competing technologies
- Designing and building a working prototype, in a feasibility study
- Designing for manufacture, sourcing appropriate state-of-the-art components, adhering to standards and regulations.

MAC normally works on fixed-price contracts to agreed schedules, so the entrepreneur's exposure is defined and can be budgeted to a grant application.

National Microelectronics Research Centre
NMRC, operating within University College Cork, is a Centre of Excellence in selected Information and Communication Technologies (ICT) fields. An advanced research division with groups in the areas of computational modelling, nanotechnology, photonics and transducers has been established to broaden NMRC's longer-term basic technological research base. NMRC provides Irish and European industry and higher education establishments with access to an extensive range of technology from advanced research to new product development and the provision of technical support services. A new Industry division provides a single entry point to industry R&D, services and training at NMRC.

National Software Centre
The Centre, in Mahon, Cork, has been funded on a public-private partnership basis, with backing from Cork Corporation, Enterprise Ireland, ICC Bank, the National Software Directorate, and private investors. It

will be managed by Cork Business Innovation Centre, and aims to become a software development hub in the southern region.

National Software Directorate
The NSD's website provides useful news on software developments, a directory of venture capital funding in Ireland, and useful publications.

Network
Network is a national organisation for women in business, management, the professions and the arts. It facilitates women in the promotion and development of their careers through regular meetings and educational seminars.

Partas
Partas (formerly Get Tallaght Working) provides enterprise support for start-up, micro and small firms. It provides a one-to-one enterprise development and business support service in Tallaght for the Tallaght Partnership, targeted at the long-term unemployed who wish to enter into self-employment. It also offers affordable office and workshop space in four centres in Tallaght, including the Brookfield Enterprise Centre. Partas also provides consulting and training for community and enterprise groups.

PLATO Ireland
PLATO Ireland is a business and management development network for owner/managers of SMEs. There are PLATO regional groups in Belfast, Cork, Dun Laoire, Louth, Newry & Mourne, Monaghan, North Dublin, South Dublin/Kildare and the South East, involving nearly 1,000 SMEs and 93 of Ireland's largest companies. An owner/manager can join the network for an initial two-year cycle and can continue to use it as a resource to meet their own needs.

Project Development Centre
The Project Development Centre is a resource centre for entrepreneurs, providing them with support and training through the start-up and growth phases of their business development. Initiated by the Dublin Institute of Technology in 1983, the Centre's aim is to assist entrepreneurs in the areas of innovation, product development and enterprise creation. PDC's courses include:

- The Fast Growth Programme, a three-pronged support system, including interactive workshops, individual strategic and investment counselling and assistance
- Prospect, a 6-month training programme to develop a strategy for commercialising university research
- Hothouse, a one-year programme to provide knowledge-intensive start-ups with the expertise, networks and tools they need to grow businesses capable of competing in global markets. Participants receive a training grant and may be eligible for a CORD grant of 50% of salary.

The PDC, in conjunction with the Bolton Trust, is a promoter of the Small Enterprise Seed Fund, a source of equity funding for small companies.

Regional Development Centre
The Regional Development Centre was established by Dundalk Institute of Technology to contribute, in partnership with State, European and international developmental organisations, to the industrial and commercial development of the East Border Region and to enhance the region's science and technology infrastructure.

The Centre acts as a commercially-oriented interface between the IT and the industrial, commercial and business life of the region, making available the Institute's expertise, facilities and resources for the wider benefit of the regional economy. It liaises with local industry and offers:

- Entrepreneurial development programmes
- Incubation facilities for knowledge and technology-based enterprises
- Industrial applied research, consultancy and information services.

Richmond Business Campus
The Richmond Business Campus offers multi-purpose premises and in-house supports — ISDN telephone system, fax, photocopying, boardroom, kitchen facilities, security, car parking — with other services being provided by external consultants.

Society of Saint Vincent de Paul
The Society of Saint Vincent de Paul is active in the area of community enterprise. One of its programmes is the Enterprise Support scheme, which provides seed capital loans on an interest-free basis (to a maximum of €5,000) and business advice. SVP targets exclusively people living in poverty with no other access to seed funding. It also provides incubation space for early-stage and start-up businesses. It supports Action Tallaght's Enterprise programme.

Small Firms Association
The Small Firms Association represents and provides

economic, commercial, employee relations and social affairs advice and assistance to over 7,000 member companies. It provides training in the management of people and related topics for managers at all levels. Members are also entitled to access IBEC management training facilities and courses.

SPADE
SPADE opened in 1990 in the former St Paul's Church, offering incubator workspace for small businesses. Tenants have access to in-house secretarial services, central reception facility, fire insurance on buildings, use of the conference room, and off-street car parking. Space is available on a monthly licence.

TecNet
TecNet, the Technology Network, was established in 1999 by the Institutes of Technology and is jointly funded by Enterprise Ireland. Its mission is to enhance the research and development capacities of the Institutes of Technology through strategic networks in support of regional economic development. It provides industry with research & development, consulting services and technology transfers by using the skills and facilities available within the ITs. Examples of services provided include:

- Technical prototyping
- Commercial feasibility studies
- Technical feasibility reports
- Product scoping
- Market analysis
- Product testing
- Competitive analysis.

Telework Ireland
Telework Ireland represents the interests of Irish teleworkers (of whom there are estimated to be 15,000) and provides a teleworking information and advice service for members. It publishes a Manual for Employees and Business Start-Ups, as a book and on CD. Its website has an FAQ section on teleworking issues.

Terenure Enterprise Centre
The Terenure Enterprise Centre provides business incubator units, business advice and assistance with business plans, grant applications, etc. and an enterprise information library for small start-up projects unable to secure such support from other sources.

Tipperary Institute
TI provides locally responsive and interactive educational, training, communication, mentoring and support services to rural communities. It is piloting a distance learning competency training programme for owner/managers of SMEs.

Reducing Risk

This guide sets out what is probably the best way of reducing the risk involved in your start-up – producing a well-thought out Business Plan.

Next, you need to quantify the risks. The panel opposite helps you to do that. It shows you what is at risk (your personal investment and any borrowings), how long for, and other factors that help you assess the risk.

Sensitivity analysis

This technique looks at how sensitive your Business Plan projections are to changes – in sales, in costs, in the environment generally. Ask yourself these questions:

- What happens if sales do not take off until month 8, even though the Business Plan projects month 3? How likely is this?
- What happens if sales are half the level projected? How likely is this?
- What happens if ... ? How likely is this?

Break-even analysis

Another useful analysis tool is "break-even", the sales volume at which your business begins to make profit. This happens when Sales less Variable Costs (those that vary directly with output) covers Fixed Costs (costs that remain fixed over a wide range of activity).

Use the panel to calculate the break-even point for your business. If your sales expectations fall below this level, you have some work to do!

Other risks

The other risk is that things can just go wrong. You can be unlucky. Answer the questions in the second panel below to see how at risk your business may be.

Protection

When you have identified the risks to which you are (or may be) exposed:

- Reconsider your Business Plan and look at alternatives
- Review your insurance situation (personal and business)
- Review your dependency (if any) on specific suppliers
- Review your dependency (if any) on specific customers.

QUANTIFYING THE RISKS

Personal investment	€ ______
Total borrowing	€ ______
Annual cash flow	€ ______
Period personal investment is at risk	€ ______
Period borrowing is at risk	€ ______
Security given	€ ______
Time commitment over risk period	€ ______
Expected profit over risk period	€ ______
Salary required over risk period	€ ______

BREAK-EVEN

Sales price per unit	€ ______
Variable Costs per unit	€ ______
Fixed Costs (total)	€ ______
Break-even volume:	
Fixed Costs (total)	€ ______
divided by	
Sales – Variable Costs per unit	€ ______
equals Number of Units	______
Number of Units x Sales Price equals	
Break-even Sales value	€ ______

OBJECTIVES

- ☐ Be aware of risk in start-ups
- ☐ Be able to identify and reduce risk in your business

First ask yourself: What is the worst that can happen? Then prepare to accept it. Then proceed to improve on the worst.

DALE CARNEGIE

If your project doesn't work, look for the part you didn't think was important.

ARTHUR BLOCH

AT RISK?

What happens if:

You get sick for a long period?
Your spouse/partner gets sick?
Your computer breaks down?
Your machinery breaks down?
Your transport breaks down?
How dependent are you on specific suppliers?
How dependent are you on specific customers?

Consider both the probability of the situation happening AND its likely impact.

MENTORS

OBJECTIVES

- ☐ Understand the role of mentor
- ☐ Understand how to select a mentor
- ☐ Understand how to work with a mentor

Discover someone to help shoulder your misfortunes. Then you will never be alone ... neither fate, nor the crowd, so readily attacks two.

BALTASAR GRACIAN

Loneliness and a sense of isolation are the two most common complaints among entrepreneurs (after the difficulty in getting anyone to finance their business!). That's why it is so important to have the support of your family when you run your own business. But sometimes you need more than support – you need someone who has been there, done that, someone who has experienced what you are going through. This is where a mentor can be helpful.

A mentor is an experienced businessperson who makes available their experience and expertise to small businesses, usually for very modest reward. Most mentors are "putting something back into the system". There are several mentor schemes available – from Enterprise Ireland, the City/County Enterprise Boards and the Area Partnership Companies. Sometimes your bank may be able to suggest a suitable mentor.

Why a mentor? Then, who?

The first question to ask yourself is why you want a mentor. Use the questions in the panel below to help you answer the question.

Next, you need to build a profile. Use the second panel for this. Then, when you apply to the relevant agency, you will have a head-start.

When selecting a mentor, act as if you were interviewing for a vacancy with your business (you are – for a trusted adviser to yourself). Aim to meet about three potential mentors and prepare carefully (re-read "Recruiting Staff" again). Go through the skills/experience match carefully. You may not be able to judge how good the mentor is at his/her specialist area but you can judge the chemistry between the two of you. This will be important, especially if you are looking for a confidante rather than an expert to solve a problem.

Working with a mentor

Your mentor must keep totally confidential everything you say to him/her. If you don't trust them to keep your secrets, get rid of them. By the same token, you must be totally honest with your mentor. You are wasting your time (and theirs) if you are not telling them the full picture – and you may get wrong advice as a result. Structure the mentor/business relationship:

1. Express your expectations from the mentoring process. (Write them down.)
2. Allow the mentor to express their expectations. (If you have selected carefully, there will be no surprises.)
3. Agree on what the mentor will do and what they will not do. Confirm confidentiality.
4. Decide on what information the mentor needs to be able to help you.
5. Decide on the frequency and venue of meetings. Don't be too ambitious. Keep it practical.

WHAT DO YOU WANT IN A MENTOR?

A sounding-board for ideas?	☐ YES	☐ NO
Advice based on previous experience?	☐ YES	☐ NO
Hands-on assistance, perhaps in implementing something new in your business?	☐ YES	☐ NO
Contacts, to open doors that might otherwise be closed?	☐ YES	☐ NO
Expertise/experience in specific areas: Marketing, sales, finance, production, legal?	☐ YES	☐ NO
Market knowledge?	☐ YES	☐ NO

WHO DO YOU WANT AS A MENTOR?

Someone:

Older than yourself?	☐ YES	☐ NO
Younger than yourself?	☐ YES	☐ NO
With entrepreneurial experience?	☐ YES	☐ NO
With managerial experience?	☐ YES	☐ NO
With specific expertise?	☐ YES	☐ NO
With specific industry background?	☐ YES	☐ NO
From your own personal or business network?	☐ YES	☐ NO
A complete stranger?	☐ YES	☐ NO
Who will become more than a mentor (friendship as part of the mentoring)?	☐ YES	☐ NO

Professional Advisers

OBJECTIVES

- ☐ Understand how to work with, and what to expect from, professional advisers

An entrepreneur has to be a master of all trades. But, as your business expands, you may need to hire a consultant or specialist to assist in implementing a project or dealing with a problem that you are unable to solve on your own.

Choose carefully – a good consultant can add immeasurably to your business, while a bad one could cost you a lot of money with nothing to show for it. Ignore qualifications – they are necessary but not the basis for choosing a consultant. Look instead for experience. A good consultant will refer you to his/her previous clients. Ask other entrepreneurs whose opinions you value for recommendations.

Areas in which you should seriously consider employing a consultant (depending on your own skills, of course) include computers, accounting, taxation and law.

Reasons for hiring an outside consultant might be:

- To save time
- You need information, knowledge and expertise in a specific area
- You want an independent view
- You want a second opinion.

Selecting the right adviser is difficult. Just as with a mentor, before deciding on taking on an adviser, you should formulate some selection criteria.

Things to consider are:

- The consultant's knowledge of your business area and your specific project/problem
- His/her experience as a consultant and entrepreneur
- His/her way of working (dedicated to you until the project is done/available as necessary?)
- Ethics/confidentiality (can you trust him/her?)
- Costs (how/when will you be billed?)
- Time-frame (can the work be done when you want?).

Develop a clear briefing of what you expect from the adviser and ask for several quotes before you decide which one you are going to deal with.

Accountants

For information or advice on accounting or taxation matters, you are advised to consult your accountant.

If you do not know an accountant, check the Golden Pages or contact one of the following accounting bodies:

- Association of Chartered Certified Accountants
- Institute of Certified Public Accountants in Ireland
- Institute of Chartered Accountants in Ireland.

Any of these bodies will be happy to put you in touch with one of their members close to where you live/work. Ask other entrepreneurs whose opinions you value for recommendations to their accountants.

Most accountants will not charge you for a first meeting. Use this to help you decide whether you want to engage the accountant or look further.

Solicitors

You need a solicitor to:

- Check out any lease, loan agreement or contract you may be asked to sign
- Advise you on relevant legislation
- Act as the final step in your credit control process
- Act for you if you are sued.

If you do not know a solicitor, check the Golden Pages or contact the Law Society for a recommendation.

I don't want a lawyer who tells me what I can't do. I hire a lawyer to tell me how I can do what I want.
JP MORGAN

To spot the expert, pick the one who predicts the job will take the longest and cost the most.
MURPHY'S LAW, BOOK TWO

The Business Plan

OBJECTIVES

- ☐ Understand the process of business planning
- ☐ Combine work done on earlier sections of the guide into a Business Plan

The discipline you impose on yourself by writing things down is the first step towards getting them done.
LEE IACOCCA

A three sentence course on business management:
You read a book from the beginning to the end.
You run a business the opposite way.
You start with the end, and then you do everything you must to achieve it.
HAROLD GENEEN

It is always wise to look ahead, but difficult to look further than you can see.
SIR WINSTON CHURCHILL

A good business plan is nine parts implementation for every one part strategy.
TIM BERRY

All the research into success and failure factors of small businesses show that one of the most important success factors is business planning – over 70% of failures are due to bad planning.

Planning becomes even more important as the business develops. Business planning should be an ongoing process. All major companies have a business plan which is updated regularly. The same should apply for a small company.

A business plan has many functions, which change as the business develops:

- ☐ It makes an idea measurable
- ☐ It gives a complete picture of a business
- ☐ It gives insight into all the aspects of the business
- ☐ It is an exercise to assess the viability of an idea
- ☐ It helps people to familiarise themselves with all kinds of possible problems
- ☐ It is a communication tool for use with suppliers, clients, advisers, banks, funds, etc.
- ☐ It can be used as a reference point in history
- ☐ It is a planning tool for the future
- ☐ It is a teaching tool for the entrepreneur
- ☐ It provides a step-by-step approach towards reaching a decision
- ☐ It is a way of assessing an existing business
- ☐ It is a working manual for the entrepreneur
- ☐ It is a checklist for the entrepreneur, bank, funding agency, etc.

Which functions apply to your Business Plan? Tick them above.

As a business goes through various stages in its life, it has different needs (see panel). In each, the Business Plan plays a vital role.

Writing a Business Plan before starting a business reduces the trial and error factor (which is a very costly process) and will prevent obvious mistakes. The more you put into the Business Plan, the more you will get out of the plan.

Writing a Business Plan

The type of Business Plan you are going to write depends on the audience you are writing the plan for. It might be for:

- ☐ Yourself
- ☐ Your partner/spouse
- ☐ Potential business partner
- ☐ Private investors
- ☐ Suppliers
- ☐ Banks
- ☐ City/County Enterprise Boards
- ☐ Others.

A good Business Plan is:

- Practical
- Honest

BUSINESS PLANNING IN THE DIFFERENT STAGES OF A BUSINESS' LIFE CYCLE

1. Existence and survival

- Thinking it through
- Ensure solid base
- Check viability
- Convince yourself, your spouse/partner and investors

2. Consolidation and control

- Decide further direction
- Ensure progress
- Confidence
- Financing growth/survival

3. Control and planning

- Secure finance
- Communication tool to employees, partners and investors

4. Expansion

- Maximise potential
- Secure finance of growth

5. Stagnation

- Revitalise company
- Assess viability
- Convince investors

6. Selling off the company

- Sales document
- Maximise selling price
- Set terms of agreement

BUSINESS PLAN – STRUCTURE

I Executive Summary

II Introduction and Background
- Background to the company

III Project Outline
- Overview of what the business is proposing to do over the period of the business plan – sales increase, employment increase, turnover increase, profit level increase

IV Ownership, Management and Employment
- Founders/Management
- Employee levels

V Market and Marketing Strategy
- Overview of the market
- Projected share of the market
- Target markets
- Main competitors
- Key competitive advantages
- Marketing strategy
- Distribution

VI Production
- Products
- Increased capacity required
- New capital expenditure required
- Efficiency levels
- Skills and numbers of staff required
- Training requirements
- Quality
- Raw material sources

VII Financial
- Summary of projected performance

VIII Funding Proposal
- Funding requirements
- Proposed sources of funding

IX Detailed Projections
- Assumptions
- Profit and Loss account
- Balance Sheet
- Cash Flow

He hath made good progress in a business that hath thought well of it before-hand.
THOMAS FULLER (1654-1734)

Growth is the goal,
profit is the measure,
security is the result.
SIR OWEN GREEN, BTR

Think of these things:
whence you came, where you are going,
and to whom you must account.
BENJAMIN FRANKLIN

Sit down to write what you have thought and not to think about what you shall write.
WILLIAM COBBETT

Always keep in mind that your Business Plan tells your story to those reading it when you are not present.
ANON.

- Consistent
- Based on research and facts
- Complete
- Realistic
- Gives a clear picture of the personality and the quality of the entrepreneur
- Turn-key.

Structuring your Business Plan

Your Business Plan must have a structure that is easily followed and understood by the person reading it.

Use the structure set out in the panel on the previous page and work through the example layout on the following pages.

Executive Summary

This is the first part of a Business Plan to read – and the last to be written. Here, in less than a page, you summarise the key points of your plan. It's easiest if you can put them in bullet point, like this:

This Business Plan:
- *Explains how XYZ Company came to be*
- *Describes the products we intend to make*
- *Describes the market*
- *Shows how we will reach that market*
- *Costs the products*
- *Includes Operating Budgets and cash-flow projections*
- *Requests grant aid of €xxk, based on equity already committed of €xxk and loans agreed of €xxk.*

See page 116.

Introduction and Background

This is the start of your Business Plan. Here you set out the basic information that a reader will want to know about your business:
- The purpose of the Plan
- Business name and contact details
- Whether it is in operation or has yet to start
- The business objective
- The product/service range.

See page 116.

Project outline

Here you can go into more detail about the business:
- A description of the business
- Your Mission Statement
- Trends in the industry
- Targets that you have set.

This gives the reader a sense of what you are setting out to achieve.

See page 117.

Ownership, Management and Employment

You, the entrepreneur, are one of the critical success factors of the business. For this reason, the reader of your Business Plan will want to know about you. This is not a place for boasting – simply explain why you believe you are a good bet to make a success of the business, based on:
- Your education
- Your work experience
- Your other experience.

If you have business partners, they should also complete this section. If your start-up is big enough to have managers employed (or key staff whose presence or absence will be critical to the business), you should consider getting them to complete this section too.

If several people are included in this section, it may be best to summarise each person's details here and include the full information in an Appendix.

Since most of the State agencies, the City/County Enterprise Boards, Area Partnership Companies, etc. are focused on job creation, it makes sense to tell them about the extent to which your business will contribute to job creation. Even though the agencies cannot grant aid part-time jobs, include them in your calculations anyway. And, where you are sub-contracting manufacturing or other aspects of your business, (even though again these are not grant-aided) include them also as "downstream" employment.

See page 118.

Marketing and marketing strategy

A critical section that will be read carefully by any investor. Because readers are unlikely to be familiar with your market, you need to set the scene for them:
- An overview
- Key indicators
- Target groups/customers
- Competitors
- Your key competitive advantages
- Your marketing strategy
- Your distribution.

See page 119.

Production

Again, because your readers may have no experience of your market, you need to explain:
- Your product/service

- How it is made/delivered
- The experience you have with the process
- What equipment you need (this ties in with your financial projections later)
- How you will assure quality
- Where you will source supplies.

If there is too much detail, put it in an Appendix.
See page 123.

Financial
Most readers of business plans not only have a financial background, they are preparing to invest in your business. Therefore they pay special attention to your financial section.

Here, you set out your financial projections – profit and loss account and cash-flow. Whatever your own background, you need to be sufficiently sure of your financial projections to be able to withstand severe questioning. No one will invest or lend you money if you appear to be incapable of controlling it.
See page 125.

Funding proposal
This is the important bit – from your point of view. Here you lay out your stall. You have already explained what the business does, the market, the product, the financial projections. Now you are saying "I need €xxk, made up as follows. I have €xxk of my own. I have tied down €xxk more from these sources. I need €xxk, please".

Again, you need to be very sure of your calculations here. If some figures are loose – you think you need €10k but it could be as high as €12k for some item – say so. Don't get found out when you run out of money!
See page 127.

Detailed projections
Almost an Appendix, this is where the real number-crunching is put – out-of-the-way at the back. The critical part here are your assumptions. Expect to be quizzed on these when you make a presentation of your Business Plan to a City/County Enterprise Board or bank.
See page 129.

Almost finished
Your Business Plan is now almost finished – except that, just like your market research and testing of your product – you must test your Business Plan.

Perform the Reality Check in the panel. Then give it to a few trusted friends to read through. Ask them to pick holes in it. Don't be defensive. Use their comments to improve the plan.

A REALITY CHECK

You have finished your Business Plan. You are ready to submit it to your local City/County Enterprise Board, Area Partnership Company or bank. Before you do, run these final checks:

Is the Executive Summary:
- Short? ☐
- Relevant? ☐
- To the point? ☐
- Interesting? ☐
- Packed with "Ooomph"? ☐

Check the entire Business Plan (get help if you need it) for:
- **Spelling mistakes** – Use a spelling checker if your business plan has been word-processed ☐
- **Grammatical mistakes** – Use a grammar checker (but be careful) if your business plan has been word-processed ☐
- **Page numbering** – Are the pages all in order, with no gaps or duplication? ☐
- **Chapter/section numbering** – Are the chapters/sections all in order, with no gaps or duplication? ☐
- **Cross-references between sections/pages** – Are these correct? ☐
- **Logical structure** – Does the plan flow in a sensible order? ☐
- **Jargon/use of language** – Do you introduce concepts, explain jargon, demystify complicated things for the reader? ☐
- **Length** – Is it too long? Could you cut parts out, without damaging it? Could sections be moved into an Appendix? ☐
- **Type size/style** – Is it easy to read? Are headings clearly identifiable? ☐
- **Colour** – If you are using coloured type, does it help or does it distract? Keep it simple. ☐

I EXECUTIVE SUMMARY

Use this section to write a brief summary (no more than 1 page) of the whole Business Plan.

II INTRODUCTION AND BACKGROUND

Introduction

This Business plan is written to:

☐ Document strategy
☐ Act as a management tool in monitoring performance
☐ Raise € ________ k equity funding from ____________________
☐ Raise € ________ k grant aid from ____________________
☐ Other (specify):

Explain here the purpose of the Business Plan. Put it in your own words.

Background

Business name:
Address:

Telephone/Facsimile/E-mail:

Status:	☐ Sole trader	☐ Partnership	☐ Limited company	
Registered for:	☐VAT	☐ PAYE/PRSI	☐ Corporation tax	☐ Income tax
Formed as:	☐ Purchase of existing business		☐ Purchase of franchise	
	☐Start-up	☐ Other (specify)		

Business in operation? Yes, started on ____________
No, planned to start on ____________

Product/service range

Product/service	***Description***	***Price***
A ____________	____________	€ ________
B ____________	____________	€ ________
C ____________	____________	€ ________
D ____________	____________	€ ________
E ____________	____________	€ ________
F ____________	____________	€ ________

Copy this from "Products and Production", page 51.

III PROJECT OUTLINE

General description of proposed business

Mission statement

Copy this from "Developing a Mission Statement", page 26.

Trends in industry

Copy this from "Developing a Strategy", page 28.

Targets

Copy this from "Developing a Strategy", page 29.

IV OWNERSHIP, MANAGEMENT AND EMPLOYMENT

Founders/Management
Name:
Address:

Telephone/Facsimile/E-mail:
Date of birth:
Nationality:
Marital status:
Percentage shareholding:

The first four sections must be completed for EACH founder or key manager. Use additional pages, if necessary.

Education

Year(s)		*School/course*	*Degree/certificate*
From ______	to ______	______	☐ YES ☐ NO
From ______	to ______	______	☐ YES ☐ NO
From ______	to ______	______	☐ YES ☐ NO
From ______	to ______	______	☐ YES ☐ NO

Work Experience

Year(s)		*Organisation*	*Position*
From ______	to ______	______	______
From ______	to ______	______	______
From ______	to ______	______	______
From ______	to ______	______	______
From ______	to ______	______	______

Other Experience
Describe other significant experience that could be useful for your business

Employer and employees
Initially, how will your staffing be organised?

- You alone, while holding another wage-earning position ☐
- You alone, full-time ☐
- You and your partner: Full-time ☐
- You and your partner: Part-time ☐
- You and your business partner(s) ☐
- You and your business partner(s) with employees at a wage ☐
- How many employees full-time? ______
- How many employees part-time? ______

Copy this from section "Staff", page 53.

Have you drawn up clear job descriptions for your employees? ☐ YES ☐ NO
If yes, enclose job description(s) as an Appendix
Do you plan to expand your employee numbers quickly? ☐ YES ☐ NO
If yes, do you think you can attract enough qualified people? ☐ YES ☐ NO
Who will replace you during any required absences? ______

V MARKET AND MARKETING STRATEGY

Overview of the market

Describe the market in which you operate and the level of competition you face. Copy information from "Marketing", pages 34-46.

What are the leading indicators in your market sector?

- Average annual turnover per employee ________
- Average annual turnover per m^2 of selling space ________
- Average annual purchases per head of population ________
- Extent of the service area per outlet ______ m^2
- Other

What is your estimate of the Irish market for your product? ________

What part of this market do you intend to service? ________%

Have you contacted future customers? ☐ YES ☐ NO

What was their reaction?

Have you obtained any forward orders? ☐ YES ☐ NO

What comments did you receive with the forward orders?

If Yes, enclose copies as an Appendix.

The forward orders total approximately € ________ k

Market

Who are your target groups?

What do you have to offer them?

Competitors

	Competitor	*Description of product/service*	*Turnover*	*Employees*
A			€	
B			€	
C			€	
D			€	
E			€	
F			€	

Competitors' strengths compared to your own.
(Use + where you think your business is better, = where they are the same, and – where you think your competitors have an advantage.)

Competitor	*A*	*B*	*C*	*D*	*E*	*F*
Broad Range						
Guarantee						
Quality						
Price						
Service						
Delivery						
Proximity						
Other						

In what ways do your products/services differ from your competitors'?
(If you can, describe differences for each competitor)

A ______________________________

B ______________________________

C ______________________________

D ______________________________

E ______________________________

F ______________________________

Key competitive advantages

What extras do you offer compared to the competition?

A ______________________________

____

B ______________________________

____

C ______________________________

____

D ______________________________

____

E ______________________________

____

F ______________________________

____

Marketing strategy

How are you going to present your business?

- o Layout
- o Colours
- o Music
- o Atmosphere
- o Correspondence
- o Brochures
- o Business cards
- o Van signs

Rate those areas your customers are most interested in, and your relative strengths in those areas.

Buying Motive	*Customer Importance*	*Your Relative Strength*
Broad Range	☐ High ☐ Medium☐ Low	☐ Strong ☐ OK ☐ Weak
Guarantee	☐ High ☐ Medium☐ Low	☐ Strong ☐ OK ☐ Weak
Quality	☐ High ☐ Medium☐ Low	☐ Strong ☐ OK ☐ Weak
Price	☐ High ☐ Medium☐ Low	☐ Strong ☐ OK ☐ Weak
Delivery	☐ High ☐ Medium☐ Low	☐ Strong ☐ OK ☐ Weak
Service	☐ High ☐ Medium☐ Low	☐ Strong ☐ OK ☐ Weak
Proximity	☐ High ☐ Medium☐ Low	☐ Strong ☐ OK ☐ Weak
Other	☐ High ☐ Medium☐ Low	☐ Strong ☐ OK ☐ Weak
	☐ High ☐ Medium☐ Low	☐ Strong ☐ OK ☐ Weak

How are you going to approach your customers and what buying motives are you going to emphasise?

What marketing and promotion resources will you emphasise?

Resource	***Emphasis***				***Cost***
Brochures	☐ A lot	☐ A little	☐ Not at all	☐ Not yet	€ ______
Mailings	☐ A lot	☐ A little	☐ Not at all	☐ Not yet	€ ______
Advertisements	☐ A lot	☐ A little	☐ Not at all	☐ Not yet	€ ______
Sponsorship	☐ A lot	☐ A little	☐ Not at all	☐ Not yet	€ ______
Word-of-mouth	☐ A lot	☐ A little	☐ Not at all	☐ Not yet	€ ______
Personal selling	☐ A lot	☐ A little	☐ Not at all	☐ Not yet	€ ______
Notice boards	☐ A lot	☐ A little	☐ Not at all	☐ Not yet	€ ______
Public relations	☐ A lot	☐ A little	☐ Not at all	☐ Not yet	€ ______
Other	☐ A lot	☐ A little	☐ Not at all	☐ Not yet	€ ______
	☐ A lot	☐ A little	☐ Not at all	☐ Not yet	€ ______

Explain your promotion methods (how, where, frequency, why, etc.)

Distribution

How will your products/services be distributed?

Are product deliveries insured? ☐ YES ☐ NO

If yes, for how much? € ________ k

If your goods or services are supplied under standard terms of trade, summarise them here.

Enclose a copy of your full terms of trade with this plan, as an Appendix.

VI PRODUCTION

Copy this from page 51.

Products

Product/service	***Description***	***Price***
A ______	______	€ ______
B ______	______	€ ______
C ______	______	€ ______
D ______	______	€ ______
E ______	______	€ ______
F ______	______	€ ______

Describe your production process.

What experience do you have with this process?

Are you involved with (or will you be using) new techniques or new products in your production processes? ☐ YES ☐ NO
If yes, are you receiving assistance from experts? ☐ YES ☐ NO
If yes, who are they and how are they engaged?

New capital expenditure required
What equipment are you using in the production process?

List the equipment you intend to lease, buy new, or buy used.

Description	***New/Used?***	***If used, Age***	***Buy/Lease?***	***Cost***
____________________	☐ N ☐U	____ years	☐ B☐ L	€ ______
____________________	☐ N ☐U	____ years	☐ B☐ L	€ ______
____________________	☐ N ☐U	____ years	☐ B☐ L	€ ______
____________________	☐ N ☐U	____ years	☐ B☐ L	€ ______
____________________	☐ N ☐U	____ years	☐ B☐ L	€ ______
____________________	☐ N ☐U	____ years	☐ B☐ L	€ ______
____________________	☐ N ☐U	____ years	☐ B☐ L	€ ______
____________________	☐ N ☐U	____ years	☐ B☐ L	€ ______
____________________	☐ N ☐U	____ years	☐ B☐ L	€ ______
____________________	☐ N ☐U	____ years	☐ B☐ L	€ ______
____________________	☐ N ☐U	____ years	☐ B☐ L	€ ______

What guarantees do you have for this equipment in case of malfunction (re-purchase, service contract, insurance)?

Does the available production equipment provide enough capacity to achieve the revenue you have budgeted? ☐YES ☐ NO

Quality

Will your production process be accredited to a Quality Standard?

If yes, which? ☐Quality Mark ☐ Hygiene Mark
☐ISO 9000/2000 ☐ ISO 14000
☐ Other

Have you checked your products and production processes for environmental considerations? (pollution, noise, undesirable waste products) ☐YES ☐ NO

If yes, are there any environmental objections? ☐YES ☐ NO

If yes, what are you planning to do about it?

Raw material sources

Have you contacted your future suppliers? ☐YES ☐ NO

If yes, what are their terms of trade? (Payment conditions, delivery times, etc.)

Are there alternative suppliers? ☐YES ☐ NO

If yes, list them

What advantages do these alternative suppliers offer you?

VII FINANCIAL

Summary of projected performance

Profit and loss account

Copy this from page 88.

Revenue by product	***Year 1***	***Year 2***	***Year 3***
Cash sales			
A ____________	______	______	______
B ____________	______	______	______
C ____________	______	______	______
D ____________	______	______	______
E ____________	______	______	______
	______	______	______
Credit sales			
A ____________	______	______	______
B ____________	______	______	______
C ____________	______	______	______
D ____________	______	______	______
E ____________	______	______	______
	______	______	______
Total sales	______	______	______
Deduct			
Opening stock	______	______	______
Purchases	______	______	______
	______	______	______
Less Closing stock	______	______	______
Cost of goods sold	______	______	______
Gross profit	______	______	______
Gross profit percentage	____ %	____ %	____ %
Overheads			
Staff costs	______	______	______
Production overheads	______	______	______
Premises costs	______	______	______
Transport costs	______	______	______
Sales and promotion costs	______	______	______
General expenses	______	______	______
Finance costs	______	______	______
Depreciation costs	______	______	______
Total costs	______	______	______
Net profit	______	______	______
Less tax on profits	______	______	______
	______	______	______
Drawings	______	______	______
Profit retained	______	______	______

Copy this from page 130-131.

What effect will any shortfall in turnover have on your business and how do you plan to handle it?

What is your minimum required turnover? € ________ k

Cash flow

Copy this from page 132.

	Year 1	*Year 2*	*Year 3*
Opening bank balance	______	______	______
Cash in			
Cash sales	______	______	______
Debtors	______	______	______
VAT refunds	______	______	______
Other income	______	______	______
Total income	______	______	______
Cash out			
Cash purchases	______	______	______
Creditors	______	______	______
Overheads:			
Staff	______	______	______
Production	______	______	______
Premises	______	______	______
Transport	______	______	______
Selling and promotion	______	______	______
General expenses	______	______	______
Finance costs	______	______	______
Loan repayments	______	______	______
Private drawings	______	______	______
Fixed assets	______	______	______
VAT payable/(due)	______	______	______
Other taxes	______	______	______
Other expenditure	______	______	______
Total expenditure	______	______	______
Net cash flow	______	______	______
Final bank balance	______	______	______

VIII FUNDING PROPOSAL

Copy this from page 83.

Funding requirements

	Year 1
1. Fixed assets	
Property	________
Renovations	________
Fixtures and fittings	________
Transport	________
Machines and equipment	________
Goodwill, security deposits	________
Other	________
Total fixed assets	________
2. Current assets	
Stock of raw material	________
Stock of finished goods	________
Work in progress	________
Debtors	________
Other	________
Total current assets	________
3. Liquid assets	
Cash	________
Bank	________
Other	________
Total liquid assets	________
4. Start-up costs	
Prepaid expenses	________
Promotion, opening	________
Other	________
Total start-up costs	________
5. Margin for unforeseen costs	________
Total investment	________

Proposed sources of funding

Copy this from page 84.

Personal assets available:	€
Fixed assets	______
Car	______
Additional private mortgage	______
Savings	______
Deferred loans (family)	______
Other	______
Total personal assets	______

Introduced as:

Equity	______
Loans	______

External equity:

		Agreed?
Source	______	☐ YES ☐ NO

External debt:

Long/medium-term finance

	Term	Amount	Agreed?
Mortgage on company building	______ years	€ ______	☐ YES ☐ NO
Loans	______ years	€ ______	☐ YES ☐ NO
Leasing (cars, machines, etc.)	______ years	€ ______	☐ YES ☐ NO
Other	______ years	€ ______	☐ YES ☐ NO
	______ years	€ ______	☐ YES ☐ NO
Total long/medium term finance	______		

Short-term finance

	Amount	Agreed?
Overdraft	€ ______	☐ YES ☐ NO
Suppliers' credit	€ ______	☐ YES ☐ NO
Payments received in advance	€ ______	☐ YES ☐ NO
Other	€ ______	☐ YES ☐ NO
	€ ______	☐ YES ☐ NO
Total short term/other finance	**€** ______	

Subsidies/grants

	Amount	Agreed?
Agency	€ ______	☐ YES ☐ NO
Enterprise Board	€ ______	☐ YES ☐ NO
Area Partnership Company	€ ______	☐ YES ☐ NO
Other	€ ______	☐ YES ☐ NO
	€ ______	☐ YES ☐ NO
Total subsidies/grants	**€** ______	

Total available finance **€** ______

Can you support the required investment in fixed assets with quotations from suppliers? ☐ YES ☐ NO

If Yes, enclose quotations as an Appendix.

In your estimates, did you take seasonal business influences into account, and calculate based on your maximum requirements? ☐ YES ☐ NO

How did you estimate your stock levels?

How did you estimate the value of your work-in-progress?

How did you estimate the value of your debtors?

Do you have sufficient liquid assets to cope with disappointments, delays and unexpected expenses? ☐ YES ☐ NO

IX DETAILED PROJECTIONS

Assumptions

Copy this from page 88.

SCRIBBLE BOX

Copy this from page 87.

Analysis of Overheads

	Year 1	*Year 2*	*Year 3*
Staff costs			
Gross staff salaries	______	______	______
Employer's PRSI	______	______	______
Bonuses, etc	______	______	______
Staff training costs	______	______	______
Other staff costs	______	______	______
Total staff costs	______	______	______
Production overheads			
Use of auxiliary materials	______	______	______
Maintenance	______	______	______
Heat, light and power	______	______	______
Rent/lease equipment	______	______	______
Insurance equipment	______	______	______
Other costs	______	______	______
Total production costs	______	______	______
Premises costs			
Rent	______	______	______
Heat, light & power	______	______	______
Insurance	______	______	______
Cleaning	______	______	______
Maintenance	______	______	______
Equipment rent/lease	______	______	______
Other costs	______	______	______
Deduct: Rent received	€ <___>	€ <___>	€ <___>
Total premises costs	______	______	______
Transport costs			
Maintenance and repairs	______	______	______
Lease costs	______	______	______
Fuel	______	______	______
Insurance	______	______	______
Road Tax	______	______	______
Public transport	______	______	______
Air fares	______	______	______
Deduct: Private use	€ <___>	€ <___>	€ <___>
Total transport costs	______	______	______

Analysis of Overheads

	Year 1	Year 2	Year 3
Sales and promotion costs			
Advertising	______	______	______
Packaging	______	______	______
Promotion	______	______	______
Trade fairs	______	______	______
Commissions	______	______	______
Other costs	______	______	______
Total sales & promotion	______	______	______
General expenses			
Telephone	______	______	______
Postage	______	______	______
Subscriptions	______	______	______
Insurance	______	______	______
Stationery	______	______	______
Computer supplies	______	______	______
Office expenses	______	______	______
Accountancy fees	______	______	______
Legal & other fees	______	______	______
Bad debts	______	______	______
Profit/loss on sale of assets	______	______	______
Other costs	______	______	______
Total general expenses	______	______	______
Finance costs			
Interest on loans/overdraft	______	______	______
Mortgage interest	______	______	______
Charges/fees	______	______	______
Other	______	______	______
Total finance costs	______	______	______
Depreciation			
Property	______	______	______
Fixtures and fittings	______	______	______
Transport	______	______	______
Machines and equipment	______	______	______
Other	______	______	______
Total depreciation	______	______	______

SCRIBBLE BOX

SCRIBBLE BOX

Bring forward from pages 133-135.

Cash flow

	Year 1	*Year 2*	*Year 3*
Opening bank balance			
Income			
Cash sales			
Debtors			
VAT refunds			
Other income			
Total income			
Expenditure			
Cash purchases			
Creditors			
Overheads:			
Staff			
Production			
Premises			
Transport			
Selling and promotion			
General expenses			
Finance costs			
Loan repayments			
Private drawings			
Fixed assets			
VAT payable/(due)			
Other taxes			
Other expenditure			
Total expenditure			
Net cash flow			
Final bank balance			

Cashflow: Year 1

	M1 €	M2 €	M3 €	M4 €	M5 €	M6 €	M7 €	M8 €	M9 €	M10 €	M11 €	M12 €	Year 1 €
Opening balance													
Income													
Cash sales													
Debtors													
VAT refunds													
Other income													
Total income													
Expenditure													
Cash purchases													
Creditors													
Overheads:													
Staff													
Production													
Premises													
Transport													
Selling/promotion													
General expenses													
Finance costs													
Loan repayments													
Private drawings													
Fixed assets													
VAT payable													
Other taxes													
Other expenses													
Total outgoings													
Net cash flow													
Final balance													

Copy this from page 90.

Take Year 1 total to page 132.

SCRIBBLE BOX

Cashflow: Year 2

	M1 €	M2 €	M3 €	M4 €	M5 €	M6 €	M7 €	M8 €	M9 €	M10 €	M11 €	M12 €	Year 2 €
Opening balance	___	___	___	___	___	___	___	___	___	___	___	___	___
Income													
Cash sales	___	___	___	___	___	___	___	___	___	___	___	___	___
Debtors	___	___	___	___	___	___	___	___	___	___	___	___	___
VAT refunds	___	___	___	___	___	___	___	___	___	___	___	___	___
Other income	___	___	___	___	___	___	___	___	___	___	___	___	___
Total income	___	___	___	___	___	___	___	___	___	___	___	___	___
Expenditure													
Cash purchases	___	___	___	___	___	___	___	___	___	___	___	___	___
Creditors	___	___	___	___	___	___	___	___	___	___	___	___	___
Overheads:													
Staff	___	___	___	___	___	___	___	___	___	___	___	___	___
Production	___	___	___	___	___	___	___	___	___	___	___	___	___
Premises	___	___	___	___	___	___	___	___	___	___	___	___	___
Transport	___	___	___	___	___	___	___	___	___	___	___	___	___
Selling/promotion	___	___	___	___	___	___	___	___	___	___	___	___	___
General expenses	___	___	___	___	___	___	___	___	___	___	___	___	___
Finance costs	___	___	___	___	___	___	___	___	___	___	___	___	___
Loan repayments	___	___	___	___	___	___	___	___	___	___	___	___	___
Private drawings	___	___	___	___	___	___	___	___	___	___	___	___	___
Fixed assets	___	___	___	___	___	___	___	___	___	___	___	___	___
VAT payable	___	___	___	___	___	___	___	___	___	___	___	___	___
Other taxes	___	___	___	___	___	___	___	___	___	___	___	___	___
Other expenses	___	___	___	___	___	___	___	___	___	___	___	___	___
Total outgoings	___	___	___	___	___	___	___	___	___	___	___	___	___
Net cash flow	___	___	___	___	___	___	___	___	___	___	___	___	___
Final balance	___	___	___	___	___	___	___	___	___	___	___	___	___

Copy this from page 91.

Take Year 2 total to page 132.

SCRIBBLE BOX

Cashflow: Year 3

	M1 €	M2 €	M3 €	M4 €	M5 €	M6 €	M7 €	M8 €	M9 €	M10 €	M11 €	M12 €	Year 3 €
Opening balance													
Income													
Cash sales													
Debtors													
VAT refunds													
Other income													
Total income													
Expenditure													
Cash purchases													
Creditors													
Overheads:													
Staff													
Production													
Premises													
Transport													
Selling/promotion													
General expenses													
Finance costs													
Loan repayments													
Private drawings													
Fixed assets													
VAT payable													
Other taxes													
Other expenses													
Total outgoings													
Net cash flow													
Final balance													

Copy this from page 91.

Take Year 3 total to page 132.

SCRIBBLE BOX

Downloads for this section available @
www.startingabusinessinireland.com

Presenting your Business Plan

OBJECTIVES

- ☐ Understand the importance of presentation
- ☐ Understand the importance of preparation
- ☐ Prepare to present your Business Plan

The minute you start talking about what you're going to do if you lose, you have lost.
GEORGE SCHULTZ

The Business Plan is your ticket to financing your business. It should communicate your ability to make your business a success. Therefore, when you are asked to make a presentation of your Business Plan, there are two critical aspects:

- The Business Plan itself
- You.

Of these, at this stage, the Business Plan is the least important. If you have worked through this guide to this point and put into practice its suggestions, your Business Plan should be an effective communication tool.

If you have been asked to make a presentation on it, you know that it has worked. It's now up to you!

You must show:

- Credibility
- Willingness to work and prepare
- Ability to sell
- A positive attitude
- Professionalism.

Remember, the people you are presenting to are asking themselves, "Should we be lending/investing our money with this person?"

Start with the Executive Summary from your Business Plan. Put it on an overhead projector slide. If it won't fit, it's too long. If you can't make it shorter, break it up and put it on two slides.

Make your business idea real. Bring it to life. Show your product or a prototype. Demonstrate it. Show its features, particularly the ones that your market research has shown are important to customers. Explain why these are important. "Sell" the product to your listeners.

When you come to discuss the financial aspects of your Business Plan, make sure that you know every single figure, its origin, its calculation, the reason it is in the plan, the impact it has on other figures – all of this off by heart.

You must **BE** the business plan. If you cannot explain and defend its contents, it reflects badly on you as a potential business partner.

Prepare your presentation carefully. This is no time for a few notes scribbled out on a scrap of paper. Write out what you want to say.

Anticipate questions that you might be asked. Try and build the answers into your presentation, so that you have answered them before they can be asked.

Rehearse your presentation in front of family and friends. Ask them to be critical and to shoot as many holes in the plan as they can. Build their reactions into your presentation. And practise, practise, practise.

On the day, make sure you are at the appointed venue in plenty of time – not too early and definitely not late.

Try to find out in advance who you will be meeting. Ask around to find out what their preferences are – use this information in your presentation.

If you can, see the room a day or so before the presentation and check (and double-check) that any equipment you need, like overhead projectors, etc., will be available.

If you are using your own technology, check, double and triple-check that it works – and bring a back-up with you anyway.

And then relax. It's your business. You know more about it than any investor, Enterprise Board officer or banker will ever learn. You are a self-confident, capable, well-organised entrepreneur with a good Business Plan. Go for it!

Business Plans: The Bankers' View

Understanding how the banks assess business plans is critical to success in raising finance. Below, some bankers give their views.

Caroline Tully of AIB's Enterprise Development Bureau explains that the bank is looking for evidence of market research in the business plan. It is easier for the bank to assess a promoter already known to them. If you can't handle all aspects of the business, recognise the fact and get professional assistance. Bear in mind that banks are cash-flow lenders rather than equity investors, therefore an approach to a bank should be for working capital or asset finance.

Michael Gannon, Manager of the Enterprise Support Unit at Bank of Ireland, suggests that to succeed, entrepreneurs must believe in themselves – though their belief must be based on reality. The Business Plan is an excellent way to map out tangible, achievable and realistic goals for your business. The major weakness of Business Plans is over-optimism. Do carry out some sensitivity analysis when producing financial projections and look at "What if?" scenarios.

David McGee of National Irish Bank gives some of the reasons why banks will not finance a business idea:

- **Lack of research** – Would **you** lend to a restaurant with a high dependency on passing traffic when you know a bypass is scheduled in a year's time?
- **Inexperienced management** – The pub business is a classic example. Everybody fancies that they have the necessary expertise – not always so
- **Repayment capacity** – Projections always show repayment capacity but the optimism of promoters is sometimes difficult to justify
- **No planning for setbacks** – Most loan applications fail to recognise that real life does have setbacks.
- **Value of asset dependent on trading success** – This is obvious but not always appreciated. It is particularly relevant in investment property but applies to most fixed assets (say, machinery)
- **Grants** – Sometimes mask the true viability (or lack of it) of an enterprise.

Michael Bradley, Small Business Manager at Ulster Bank, suggests these acronyms:

CAMPARI applies to the business:

- **C** – Character of the promoter
- **A** – Ability
- **M** – Means: How much is the promoter risking?
- **P** – Purpose: Not just vague "expansion"
- **A** – Amount
- **R** – Repayment
- **I** – Insurance: Security for the bank, in case things go wrong.

SODA applies to individuals:

- **S** – Self-starting
- **O** – Open-minded
- **D** – Determined
- **A** – Approachable.

David McGarry at NCB Corporate Finance offers these suggestions:

- **A clear concise Executive Summary** – The reader must know what the plan is trying to achieve and how it holds together
- **Figures** – Clearly state assumptions
- **Business** – An overview of how the business works is required. The quality of the business must be evident
- **Business model must be clear** – How functional areas interact/support each to sell product/service
- **Product** – Clearly defined and customer uses clarified. Competitive advantage must be evident
- **Sales** – Based on firm orders, not letters of intent. Must be deliverable
- **Market information** – Must be included to demonstrate growth potential
- **Industry overview** – Show business in context. Show that business is a winner
- **Money** – Where does business make its money? Pinpoint exactly
- **People** – Note past achievements
- **Layout** – Spaces, easy to read and get a handle on key messages.

As a specialist agency, Cork Business Innovation Centre focuses on the promoter. If he/she is prepared to do the leg-work, in particular to go out and sell their product, Cork BIC will back them. The BIC favours teams over individuals, in order to make sure that the start-up has the necessary mix of skills.

OBJECTIVES

- ☐ Understand banks'/agencies' reasoning
- ☐ Avoid common mistakes

REASONS FOR DECLINING LOAN APPLICATIONS

	%
Repayment capacity	38
100% Finance/ Low equity	21
Pricing	8
Poor track record	5
Inadequate security	5
Customer dependence	5
Start-up	5
Non-core	3
Other	10

Source: National Irish Bank

Smell the Flowers

OBJECTIVES

- ☐ Appreciate balance in life

Don't hurry, don't worry.
You're only here for a short visit.
So be sure to stop and smell the flowers.
WALTER HAGEN

TWELVE THINGS TO REMEMBER

1. The value of time.
2. The success of perseverance.
3. The pleasure of working.
4. The dignity of simplicity.
5. The worth of character.
6. The power of kindness.
7. The influence of example.
8. The obligation of duty.
9. The wisdom of economy.
10. The virtue of patience.
11. The improvement of talent.
12. The joy of origination.

MARSHALL FIELD

Starting and running your own business is all-consuming. Everything falls back on you. And you are doing it for yourself – so there is a temptation to do too much.

Certainly, it is hard (and may even be damaging to your business) to turn down work but, at some point, you need to take time out to decide what is really important to you, what you are achieving at present and what you need to do about it. This is where time management comes in.

Time management

An average working week for an entrepreneur is between 70 and 80 hours. As well as handling all aspects of the business – book-keeping, selling, clients, networking, etc. – you also must know how to handle your time and how to maintain your entrepreneurial drive.

You, the entrepreneur, are the most important success factor in the business. It is vital that this success factor is maintained. An entrepreneur needs to know when to peak and when to rest and take it easy. It is impossible to go full throttle all the time.

Go back to the first chapter, **READY**, and ask yourself how much time you are willing to spend on the business. Discuss it with your partner/spouse.

Go back to your assessment of your strong and weak points. Then go back to your market research and your identification of the critical success factors for your business.

Next, decide whether you are a morning person or an evening person. When do you function best? Whenever it is, aim to do your best work then. Start late and keep your heavy thinking till late at night if that suits – or start at six in the morning and knock off at four in the afternoon.

As an entrepreneur, you can choose your hours. Choose them to make the most of yourself.

Now some tips for managing your time:

- Make a daily "To Do list"
- Learn to say "NO"
- Protect yourself, take time off regularly
- A healthy mind in a healthy body
- Never handle documents more than once (no paper shuffling, deal with and get it off your desk)
- Keep things simple
- Do the things you hate first
- Manage your stress levels (meditate, exercise)
- Delegate
- To handle paperwork – **TRAF**: Toss, Refer, Act or File – only do one, and only once!

Make time for yourself

However pressured your business, you need to take some time out to unwind – to "smell the flowers". Without it, you will burn out.

Add time to your diary – every day, every week, every month – for yourself. Cut yourself free from the business and the other demands on your life. Allow your batteries to recharge – and you will come back to the business better able to make it succeed.

INTRODUCTION

In the earlier chapters in this guide, you:

- Assessed your own suitability (and that of your business partners) for business and decided to proceed to the next stage
- Considered all the many factors that impact on the success of a start-up – from a Mission Statement and strategy, through marketing, finance and budgeting – and took these into account in developing your Business Plan.

This section takes you onwards from the Business Plan, into the detail of starting and running your new business.

It starts with sample documents, designed to save you time and difficulty, including:

- Sample accounts pages
- Sample Job Application
- Sample Job Description
- Sample Employment Contract
- Sample Safety Statement
- Sample Advertising Control Sheet.

These documents can be downloaded at **www.startingabusinessinireland.com**.

The chapter then covers topics whose importance only becomes apparent once a business is up and running. They have been touched upon in the **STEADY** chapter, but here they are considered in a little more detail.

However, most could fill a book on their own and so further research and reading is recommended, depending on your own specific circumstances.

Unlike the other chapters, there are no Key Questions here – just a genuine wish to see you succeed. Keep going!

OBJECTIVES

- ☐ To assist in establishing a business by providing sample documents
- ☐ Understand core topics relevant to the continued success and development of a business

Completing the Accounts Pages

The accounts pages shown opposite are based on the discussion in "Accounting" in the previous chapter, **STEADY**. This section explains how to use them.

Purchases on credit

This page records all the goods and services that you buy on credit and will have to pay for later.

The core information you are recording is:

- The date – in the first column
- The type of transaction – on the top of the page (Purchases on credit)
- The other person involved – the supplier, in the second column
- The amount involved – in the third column, headed up "Total".

Next, if your business is registered for VAT, you need to analyse the Total amount for VAT purposes – between the VAT itself and the "net" amount. (If your business is not registered for VAT, ignore the fourth and fifth – VAT and Net – columns).

Last, you need to analyse your purchases across the overhead categories defined earlier. This analysis will help you manage your business better by showing how your money is being spent. Write the net amount of the transaction in one of the remaining columns – Staff, Production, Premises, Transport, Selling, General, Finance or Other – according to where it belongs.

At the end of each week, or month, depending on the number of transactions, total the page and start a new one.

Sales on credit

Sales on credit accounts for all sales which you invoice and have to wait to get paid for. You complete the page in much the same way as the Purchases on credit page.

Write the date in the first column, and the customer in the second. The total amount of the transaction goes in the third, with a breakdown between VAT and "net" in the next two columns.

Then analyse your sales on credit across product categories to suit your information needs. Any unusual sales can go in the "Other" column.

Total the page at the end of the month and start a new one.

Receipts

It is critically important that you account for all cash coming into the business. You do this by writing all incoming cash transactions in a Receipts page. For one, the taxman will want this information and you need it anyway to protect yourself from loss.

Again, similar information is required. The date and name of the other party involved, the total amount, split between VAT and "net" where it is a new transaction (not if it has been accounted for earlier, as happens when you receive payment for sales on credit).

It is useful to know the breakdown of where cash comes from:

- Are your debtors building up or paying on time?
- How much of your business is from cash sales?
- What other sources of cash have you? Record these in the appropriate columns.

Total the page at the end of the week or month and start a new one.

Payments

Just as it is important to record cash in, it's also important to record cash out. The Payments page helps here.

Again, date and the other party to the transaction, as well as the amount, are essential information. Again, also only account for VAT on new transactions. In some cases here, you will be paying for purchases made earlier on credit – record these in the "Suppliers" column. Other purchases made for cash should be analysed into the appropriate category.

Petty Cash

This is like the Payments page but on a smaller scale of spending. This should be totalled and checked every week, so that money does not go astray. You also need receipts for all Petty Cash expenditure – set this as a habit from the start.

Bank balance book

The operation of this page is explained in the previous chapter, page 64.

Summary

These are very simple "books", which give you the absolute basics of information that you need to control your business.

Talk to your own accountant about the specific needs of your business but always keep in mind that book-keeping is a means (to information for management purposes) not an end in itself.

Accounts Pages: Purchases on Credit

Date	Supplier	Total	Net	VAT	Staff	Production	Premises	Transport	Selling	General	Financial	Other
Total												

Accounts Pages: Sales on Credit

Date	Customer	Total	Net	VAT	A	B	C	...	X	Y	Z	Other
Total												

Accounts Pages: Receipts

Date	Received From	Total	Net	VAT	Debtors	Cash Sales	Loans	Other
Total								

Accounts Pages: Payments

Date	Paid To	Total	Net	VAT	Suppliers	Staff	Production	Premises	Transport	Selling	General	Financial	Other
Total													

Accounts Pages: Petty Cash

Date	Paid To	Total	Net	VAT	Postage	Stationery	Office Exp.	Transport	Other
Total									

Accounts Pages: Bank Balance Book

Date	Transaction	In	Out	Balance

Downloads for this section are available @
www.startingabusinessinireland.com

Job Application Form

POSITION ____________________

NAME (Mr/Mrs/Miss/Ms) ____________________
ADDRESS ____________________
____
____
TELEPHONE (Home/Work) ____________________
DATE OF BIRTH ____________________
STATUS [] Single [] Married [] Divorced [] Separated
CHILDREN (Number/Ages) ____________________
HEALTH (Illnesses/Disabilities) ____________________
____

EDUCATION

Year(s)	*School/course*	*Degree/certificate*
From ______ to ______	____________________	o Yes o No
From ______ to ______	____________________	o Yes o No
From ______ to ______	____________________	o Yes o No
From ______ to ______	____________________	o Yes o No

WORK EXPERIENCE

Year(s)	*Organisation*	*Position*
From ______ to ______	____________________	__________
From ______ to ______	____________________	__________
From ______ to ______	____________________	__________
From ______ to ______	____________________	__________
From ______ to ______	____________________	__________

OTHER EXPERIENCE
Describe other significant experience that could be useful in this position
____
____
____

HOBBIES/INTERESTS
____
____
____

OTHER INFORMATION
____
____
____
____

I wish to apply for the position of ____________________ .
I declare the information above to be correct to the best of my knowledge and belief.

Signed ____________________ Date __________

JOB DESCRIPTION

POSITION ______________________

NAME ______________________

DATE APPOINTED __________

REPORTING TO ______________________

SUBORDINATES ______________________

____

____

CORE RESPONSIBILITY

____

____

____

KEY TASKS

Daily ______________________

____

Weekly ______________________

____

Monthly ______________________

____

Yearly ______________________

____

TARGETS

____

____

____

Employment Contract

(Name)
(Address)
(Date)

Company Letterhead

Dear

The following are the terms and conditions of your employment, which I am required to give you. Should you require clarification on any point, please feel free to ask me.

Position
You will be employed primarily as (POSITION), commencing on (DATE). A job specification for the position is attached. You will be required to be flexible in this position and to undertake such other work as may be assigned to you by the company from time to time, outside the area of your normal duties. This work may be for such subsidiary or associate companies of the company as the company may require.

Hours of work
Your normal working week will be ______ days, ___day to _______day. Your normal working hours will be ___ am to _____ pm on those days, with _____ hour for lunch. Your position may require you to work in excess of these hours from time to time, especially when deadlines have to be met.

Remuneration
You will be paid monthly in arrears by credit transfer. Your salary at commencement will be €________ pa and will be reviewed on (DATE). There is no payment for overtime. If additional responsibilities or working hours in excess of normal working hours become part of your regular work, your salary may be reviewed before the review date above.

Annual leave
The company's holiday year runs from 1 January to 31 December. Your annual holiday entitlement will be 20 working days and shall be given in accordance with the Organisation of Working Time Act, 1997. Your entitlement in 200__ will be ____ days. Holiday dates must be agreed in advance with the Managing Director and are subject to management discretion. Public holidays shall also be given in accordance with the Organisation of Working Time Act, 1997.

Maternity Leave (female staff only)
You have a statutory entitlement to Maternity Leave and Maternity Benefit as provided for under the Maternity Protection Act, 1994 and the Social Welfare Acts. You are also entitled to have your existing job, or a suitable alternative, held open for you pending your return to work following maternity leave, which is calculated as four weeks before the expected date of the birth of your child and 14 weeks following that date. To ensure your entitlement, you must:

- Provide a letter from your doctor, certifying that you are pregnant and the expected date of birth of your child
- Write a letter to the Managing Director, stating that you are pregnant, advising the dates you intend to be absent on maternity leave and stating whether you intend to return to work following your maternity leave.

Maternity Benefit is paid by the Department of Social, Community and Family Affairs on a weekly basis throughout your maternity leave. The amount paid is not taxable, and is based on your earnings in the previous tax year. The maximum benefit payable is currently € _____ per week. In addition, you have a statutory entitlement to an additional four weeks' unpaid leave immediately following the end of your statutory maternity leave. No benefit is payable by the Department of Social & Family Affairs during these four weeks which must be taken entirely at your own expense. You must advise the Managing Director of your intention to take this unpaid leave at least four weeks before the end of your statutory maternity leave.

Sick Pay
If you are sick and unable to attend at work, you must notify the Managing Director or another senior member of staff before 10 am on the first day of non-attendance, to advise of your absence and to state how long you expect to be absent. Medical certificates must be provided to the Managing Director for absences of more than 2 days.

The company will pay you your normal salary, less PAYE and PRSI, for up to ____ weeks' sick leave in any calendar year. You must claim Social Welfare benefits, where applicable, during such sick leave and must pay any such benefits received to the company immediately on receipt. The company reserves the right to reduce the period of paid sick leave or withdraw the scheme at any time.

Retirement

Normal retirement age is ___. A pension/No pension is payable at retirement.

Grievances

If you have a grievance in relation to any aspect of your employment, you have a right to a hearing by your immediate superior. If you are unhappy with the outcome of that hearing, you may appeal to the Managing Director. You may be accompanied by a fellow employee at this appeal meeting. Where the circumstances warrant it, you may refer your grievance directly to the Managing Director. If the matter cannot be resolved within the company, it shall be referred through procedures, which shall include, as appropriate, reference to a Rights Commissioner, the Labour Relations Commission, the Labour Court, the Employment Appeals Tribunal or the Equality Officer.

Notice of Termination

Except in circumstances justifying immediate termination of your employment by the company, you are entitled to receive _____ month's notice of termination of your employment. The company reserves the right to pay you _____ month's salary in lieu of notice. Your employment may be terminated without notice for serious misconduct or unreasonable failure to carry out such duties as may be assigned to you from time to time.

You must give the company _____ month's notice of your intention to terminate your employment. The company reserves the right to pay you _____ month's salary in lieu of this period of notice.

Dismissal

The company hopes that it will not be necessary to dismiss you. However, you may be dismissed for: Incompetence or poor work performance, serious or persistent misconduct, incapacity, failure to carry out reasonable instructions, redundancy, or some other substantial reason. The following procedures will be carried out before a decision to dismiss you from the company's employment is taken:

- A full investigation will be carried out by the company. You may be suspended, with or without pay at the company's discretion, during this investigation
- You will be informed of the reasons for the proposed dismissal
- You will have a right to state your case and may be accompanied by a fellow employee at any meeting that you are asked to attend concerning your proposed dismissal.

If you wish to challenge your dismissal, it shall be referred in accordance with normal procedures to a Rights Commissioner, the Labour Court, the Labour Relations Commission or the Employment Appeals Tribunal, as appropriate.

Health and safety

The company is committed to fulfilling its obligations under applicable health and safety legislation and has prepared a Safety Statement. It is a condition of your employment that you sign the Health and Safety Statement and abide by its requirements.

On behalf of (BUSINESS NAME), I wish you well in your employment. Please sign one copy of this letter to indicate your acceptance of the terms and conditions of your employment and return it to me as soon as possible.

Signed ______________________________ Managing Director

I accept and agree to be bound by the above terms and conditions of employment.

Signed ______________________________ (EMPLOYEE)

SAFETY STATEMENT

BUSINESS NAME: ______________________________

ADDRESS: ______________________________

____

____

____

BUSINESS ACTIVITY:

____

____

____

NAME/TEL NO of:

Doctor: ______________

Hospital: ______________

Ambulance: ______________

Fire: ______________

Garda: ______________

Safety Rep: ______________

First Aider: ______________

HSA: ______________

"This Safety Statement is aimed at protecting our employees from workplace accidents and ill-health at work. It is our programme in writing to manage health and safety. We provide protective equipment, guards, etc., as well as information, training and supervision necessary to protect our employees. The Safety Statement is available to our employees, outside contractors and inspectors of the Health and Safety Authority. We will update it as necessary and it will be reviewed at least once a year."

Signed: ______________________________ **Date:** ______________

(Proprietor/Manager)

Deputy: ______________________________

CHECKLIST OF HAZARDS AND RELATED ISSUES

Is your workplace safe, clean and tidy?
Are your work systems safe?
Is your equipment and machinery safe (guarded if necessary and maintained regularly)?
Are machinery and equipment suppliers' instructions followed?
Is portable equipment (such as ladders, welders, electrical tools, etc) properly maintained?
Are boilers, air receivers, lifts and cranes examined and maintained?
Can manual lifting, pushing, pulling or dragging of heavy weights be avoided?
Is care taken with chemicals? Remember to read the labels and chemcial safety sheets.
Are there health hazards – processes giving rise to dust or fumes?
Have you made arrangements for emergencies and fire-fighting? Are escape routes clear?
Is there safe means of access to heights?
Are goods safely stacked?
Is there training, consultation, information and supervision of employees in health and safety?
Are records kept of safety training?
Is ventilation adequate?
Is personal protective equipment provided and used?
Do your VDUs comply with safety standards?
Are First Aid provisions adequate?
Is there any history of accidents/ill-health in the business?
Are accidents reported to the Health and Safety Authority?
Are there any other hazards in the workplace?
Are employees adhering to all remedial steps to avoid injury?
Are the welfare facilities (toilets/washing/eating/drink) adequate?
Are employees and outside contractors aware of this Safety Statement?
Have you displayed your Health and Safety poster?

Reproduced by permission of the Health and Safety Authority

Advertising Control Sheet

ADVERTISING OBJECTIVE:							
Media selected	Ad	Timing	Responsibility Whose?	Budget cost	Actual cost	Criteria by which success will be judged	Evaluation

Downloads for this section are available @
www.startingabusinessinireland.com

QUALITY

OBJECTIVES

- ☐ Understand the importance of quality
- ☐ Be aware of quality standards

It goes without saying that your product is top quality.
HARRY CROSBIE, on developing a brand

Quality is no longer a competitive advantage. It is a minimum entry requirement in any market.
BRIAN TRACY

Quality is in – big time! Quality has always been important as a means of differentiating products and delivering higher value-added but there is no escaping the current management focus on quality as a means of achieving higher profits through customer satisfaction.

What is quality?

Quality is an attitude of mind that results in everyone in a business working together towards:

- Eliminating (or minimising) errors and faults
- Meeting deadlines
- Mapping out clear lines of responsibility
- Continuous improvement.

Think about what quality means to you. What does it mean for your customer? What does it mean for your product/service?

Write your answers in the space below.

Quality systems

Quality systems help ensure that quality is delivered every time.

Quality certification provides independent assurance that the quality systems meet approved standards. Surveys show that quality assurance marks/logos give customers valued guidance when buying products and services and influence their decision to buy at point of sale. However, few companies trading in Ireland have either the Q-Mark or ISO 9000 certification.

Quality standards

The key quality standards in Ireland are:

- **The Q-Mark** – Excellence Ireland's most successful programme to date and one of the most coveted brands on the Irish market. The Q-Mark is regarded as the national symbol of quality and is essentially a framework through which a business can continually improve
- **Hygiene Mark Certification**
- **The Triple Hygiene Mark**
- **ISO 9000** – The Quality Standard, the most successful international standard ever produced and currently in use in over 70 countries world-wide
- **ISO 14000** – The Environmental Standard.

The Q-Mark

The Quality Systems Q-Mark is a systems and processes framework used to help continuously improve the practices that underpin the way an organisation operates. As well as giving internal confidence to organisations, enabling them to consistently deliver good product/s and/or services, the Q-Mark also enhances the organisation and its products as a brand, thus sustaining customer confidence.

The granting of the Q-mark is based on a two-fold asessment of an organisa-

What does quality mean to you?

What does it mean to your customer?

What does it mean for your product/service?

tion's quality system. First, the business completes a questionnaire from Excellence Ireland, which evaluates the quality system. This is followed by an in-depth, interactive, on-site audit of the system. The business is audited annually to ensure that its operations and systems are being improved upon.

The Q-Mark is only given to organisations that demonstrate to Excellence Ireland's independent auditors that their standards of quality management are rigorous and consistent. Benefits include:

- Increased management control through service delivery system
- A constructive audit
- Public recognition through display of the Q-Mark logo
- Motivational impact on employees
- Deepened understanding of customer needs and requirements
- Independent feedback to assist the organisation's development.

The Hygiene Mark

This mark provides recognition to hygiene-conscious firms within the Irish food and catering industry. It is an assurance to customers that the company pursues a rigorous and consistent hygiene programme based on an independent substantiation of hygiene standards.

A hygiene systems audit assesses (on a surprise basis):

- Structural hygiene
- Operational hygiene
- Food storage and protection
- Staff facilities and personal hygiene
- Hygiene management systems.

Successful companies can display the Hygiene Mark on their premises and use it to maximise marketing and promotional activities. They can also go on to try for the Triple Hygiene Mark and Excellence Ireland's National Awards scheme.

ISO 9000

ISO 9000: 2000 (a revised standard introduced in 2000) is a strategic management tool, facilitating effective control over design, manufacturing and service delivery processes. Applying an ISO 9000 system for Quality Management within an organisation can result in significant benefits including:

- **Management effectiveness** – Through structured, organised and defined authorities, responsibilities and reporting structures
- **Operating efficiency** – Through clearly documented practices and procedures
- **Cost reduction** – Through the identification and elimination of potential system deficiencies and product failures
- **Increased marketability** – Through the identification of a registered company with a quality philosophy and international standard
- **Customer satisfaction** – Through the receipt of enhanced service or product quality levels.

As ISO 9000 is a harmonised European and international standard, certification to the standard opens up international markets to companies where previously technical trade barriers may have been a major impediment.

It requires an organisation to implement a documented quality management system addressing all organisational activities from the definition of its quality policy and objectives to the detailing of the various methodologies and controls applicable to its service delivery or product manufacturing processes.

This takes the form of a Quality Manual, supported by procedures manuals, work instructions, etc, defining:

- **What** must be done
- **Who** is to do it
- **When** it is to be done
- **How** it is to be done.

The business' Quality Manual is assessed to ensure that it adequately and completely conforms to the requirements of the relevant standard. The assessment is conducted on the applicant's premises by an experienced team of assessors. On approval, the business is awarded "Registered Firm" status and can use the mark on advertising material, letterheads and for other promotional purposes. Once registered, on-going inspections ensure that quality standards are maintained.

ISO 14000

ISO 14000 is a standard for the management of the environment and a business' relationship with it. It is applicable mainly to larger process and chemical industries.

Environmental Concerns

OBJECTIVES

- ☐ Be aware of environmental trends
- ☐ Be aware of environmental management systems

As explained in "Developing a Mission Statement" in the **STEADY** chapter, customers increasingly expect companies to be concerned about their impact on the environment, both socially and physically. At the same time, EU regulations on environmental issues are becoming stricter.

Businesses tend to react in three ways:

- **Do nothing** – Wait to be pushed into complying with emerging regulations
- **Act now** – Identify potential environmental hazards and take steps to eliminate them. Use this as a "competitive edge"
- **Identify new businesses** that will be created by these trends and get in first.

Areas to consider include:

- Materials used, both in manufacture and packaging (toxic, recyclable, replaceable)
- Machines used
- Odour
- Noise
- Risks (health, fire, etc.)
- Waste.

In the meantime, control over the impact of your activities on the environment is an important part of the management of your business. There are, of course, legal requirements in this area, but more than that, good environmental management can lead to cost savings, enhanced customer relations and a positive product image. If you are interested in exporting your product, you will find that compliance with an environmental management standard is invaluable, especially when dealing with other European businesses.

Environmental Protection Agency

The Environmental Protection Agency was established under the Environmental Protection Agency Act, 1992. The Agency has a wide range of statutory duties and powers. Its main responsibilities include:

- The licensing and regulation of large/complex industrial and other processes with significant polluting potential, on the basis of integrated pollution control (IPC) and the application of best available technologies for this purpose
- The monitoring of environmental quality, including the establishment of databases to which the public will have access, and the publication of periodic reports on the state of the environment
- Advising public authorities in respect of environmental functions and assisting local authorities in the performance of their environmental protection functions
- The promotion of environmentally sound practices through, for example, the encouragement of the use of environmental audits, the setting of environmental quality objectives and the issuing of codes of practice on matters affecting the environment
- The promotion and co-ordination of environmental research
- The licensing and regulation of all significant waste recovery activities, including landfills and the preparation and updating periodically of a national hazardous waste plan for implementation by other bodies
- Preparation and implementation of a national hydrometric programme for the collection, analysis and publication of information on the levels, volumes and flows of water in rivers, lakes and groundwaters
- Generally overseeing the performance by local authorities of their statutory environmental protection functions.

Environmental Management Systems

An environmental management system can take many forms:

- **The Irish Standard 310, Environmental Management Systems** – Published by the NSAI
- **ISO 14000** – See "Quality Certification"
- **Self-audited systems** – Such as that outlined in *A guide to environmental self-auditing* published by the Chambers of Commerce in Ireland
- **EU Eco-Management & Audit Scheme.**

Enterprise Ireland's Information Desk can help client companies to find a suitable standard for environmental management.

Health and Safety

Health and safety in the workplace has become a major issue in industry in recent years, driven largely by EU regulations and by an increasing awareness of employers' social responsibilities.

Put simply, an employer is responsible in so far as is reasonably practicable for the safety, health and welfare of his/her employees. Employees also have a duty to ensure their own health and safety as well as that of other staff and others in the workplace.

Safety, Health and Welfare at Work Act, 1989

This Act applies to all places of work, regardless of size or activity, all employers and self-employed persons, manufacturers, suppliers and importers.

Under the Act, an employer must:

- Consult with employees on health and safety issues and allow employees to select a Safety Representative to represent them in these discussions
- Prepare a Safety Statement (see **GO**), which outlines the hazards identified in the place of work and details how they are controlled in order to safeguard the health and safety of employees
- Ensure that working practices and procedures, means of access and exit, and articles or substances used at the workplace or provided for use at work are safe and not dangerous to employees' health. This duty extends beyond the company's own employees to include employees of other businesses who happen to be in the workplace
- Test plant, equipment or materials he/she manufactures, designs, imports or supplies and give adequate information on associated hazards.

Other legislation

Where the 1989 Act forms the skeleton, the detail is provided by the Safety, Health and Welfare at Work (General Application) Regulations, 1993 and the Safety, Health and Welfare at Work (Miscellaneous Welfare Provisions) Regulations, 1995 and other industry-specific legislation.

Areas covered include:

- Risk assessment
- Design of the workplace
- Use of work equipment
- Manual handling methods
- Use of visual display units
- Electricity
- Protective equipment
- The availability of first aid
- Notification of accidents and dangerous occurrences.

Specific legislation covers hazards such as noise, chemicals and certain named substances, asbestos, lead, infection, and biological risks, safety signs and conditions for pregnant employees, etc.

The Health & Safety Authority (see **Appendix 1** for address) has a range of publications that provide guidance on the 1989 Act and subsequent regulations, though industry-specific legislation is outside its remit.

The Health & Safety Authority

The Health and Safety Authority (HSA) is an autonomous body which reports to the Minister for Enterprise, Trade & Employment. Its functions include:

- Providing advice and information
- Promoting safety
- Undertaking research
- Enforcing health and safety laws generally.

HSA inspectors may visit any workplace at any time to inspect documents, books, registers, and the physical environment.

Various enforcement mechanisms may be used such as improvement directions and plans, improvement notices, and prohibition notices.

NOTE:
New legislation, in the form of the Safety, Health and Welfare at Work Act 2005 was introduced with effect from September 2005.

OBJECTIVES

- ☐ Understand the law relating to health & safety
- ☐ Understand the application of health & safety in the workplace

Intellectual Property

OBJECTIVES

- ☐ Understand the different types of intellectual property
- ☐ Be aware of application/ registration procedures

Inventors are warned that it is unwise to make any public disclosure of an invention or to put it into use publicly before an application for a patent has been made, as such action may prejudice the obtaining of a valid patent.
THE PATENTS OFFICE

Patents

A patent is an exclusive right given by the State and enforceable in the Courts. It gives the "patentee" a monopoly to make, use and sell the invention for a fixed period of time and the right to stop others manufacturing, using or selling the patented invention during that period unless they have obtained the patent owner's authorisation to do so. In return for this monopoly, the patentee pays fees to cover the costs of processing the patent application and granting the patent. Annual renewal fees are also paid in order to keep the patent in force. A patent can last for 10 years (short term) or 20 years. A patent granted in Ireland gives no rights in other countries.

To be eligible for the grant of a valid patent, an invention must be:

- New
- Involve an inventive step
- Capable of industrial application.

Not all inventions qualify for the grant of a patent. The Patents Act 1992 specifically excludes:

- A discovery, scientific theory or a mathematical method
- An aesthetic creation
- A scheme rule or method for performing a mental act, playing a game or doing business or a programme for a computer
- The presentation of information
- Methods of treatment of the human or animal body by surgery or therapy
- Plant and animal varieties or essentially biological processes for their production
- Inventions which are contrary to public order or morality.

An example of a well-known patented invention is the "widget" at the bottom of a Guinness can which promotes froth on canned beer similar to that of draught beer.

European Patents

The European Convention (EPC) came into force in 1977 and established the European Patent Office (EPO). A European patent application can be filed either with the Irish Patents Office or directly with the Hague Branch of the EPO and the applicant can choose to designate any of the 18 contracting states including Ireland. When granted, a European patent has the effect of a national patent in each of the countries designated. Therefore, an applicant may find it considerably cheaper to lodge a single patent application to the EPO, designating a number of contracting states, as opposed to lodging individual patent applications with each of the countries.

Patent Co-operation Treaty (PCT)

The Patent Co-operation Treaty (PCT) came into effect in 1978. Its main aim is to streamline patent application filing and novelty search procedures for applicants wishing to obtain patent protection in a wide number of countries around the world. The PCT provides a system whereby a single international application in one of the contracting states allows for the designation of up to 80 other countries in which one wishes to have patent protection. The applicant designates those in which a patent is desired and eventually the relevant national authority may grant a patent. The Patents Office acts as a receiving office for PCT applications.

Trade Marks

Once a business has a product to sell, it needs something which distinguishes its goods and services from those of competitors. A trade mark is a sign which is capable of being represented graphically (in words or pictures written down) and which is capable of distinguishing the goods or services of one business from those of other businesses. It may consist of words (including personal names), designs, letters, numerals, or the shape of the goods or of their packaging. An applicant is required to pay fees to register a trade mark and renewal fees to keep it in forcc.

The Trade Marks Act 1996 allows for the first time registration of a trade mark for a service.

A trade mark should be:

- Distinctive
- Not deceptive
- Not descriptive
- Not among certain excluded items listed in the Act (such as national emblems, immoral or offensive language).

When registered, a trade mark is valid for 10 years and may be renewed every 10 years. Validity is effective from the date of application.

Well-known Irish trade marks are Guinness, Kerrygold and Aer Lingus.

You apply for registration of a trademark to:

- (For Ireland) Patents Office, Government Buildings, Hebron Road, Kilkenny
- (For EU) Office for Harmonisation in the Internal Market, Avenida de Europa 4, Apartado de Correos 77, E-03080, Alicante, Spain.

Industrial Designs

A design is a new idea or a conception of the external "shape, configuration, pattern or ornament" intended to be assumed by any article. Designs may be registered in respect of such diverse items as toys, lamps, articles of furniture, containers, clothes, fabrics and wallpaper.

A design applied to an article should not be confused with what may be a patentable invention, or a "device" trademark (a trademark containing or consisting of a picture or drawing). A trademark is only used for the purpose of indicating the origin of the goods/service on which it is used.

To be eligible for registration, a design must be new or original and must not have been published previous to the application.

A design may be registered initially for five years and may be renewed for further periods of five years, subject to a maximum of 15 years.

A new Industrial Designs Bill was published in Ireland in July 2000, to update and enhance Irish industrial design law. It broadens the civil and criminal remedies available in respect of infringements of design rights, implements the EU Directive on the legal protection of designs and enables future access for Irish designs to an international system of design protection under the Geneva Act of the Hague Agreement.

Copyright Protection

Copyright is the creator's (or legal owner's) rights in creative works like paintings, writings, computer software, photographs, drawings, sound recordings, films and television broadcasts. No formality such as registration or deposit of the work or payment of fees is required in order that copyright may subsist in a work.

The author of a work is the first owner of copyright in the work, except in the case of a work made under a contract of service in the course of employment. Subject to any agreement with the author, copyright in Government publications belongs to the Government.

To avoid others copying your work, it is essential to be able to show proof of ownership. It is advisable for an author to sign, date and witness his/her work as proof of ownership and to display the international copyright symbol © prominently on his/her work.

The law relating to copyright was updated by the Copyright and Related Rights Act, 2000. This is a complex area, and it is advisable to seek legal advice on any matter of doubt or dispute.

Information and Advice

The Patent Office has Libraries at its Dublin and Kilkenny offices. Both contain various legal and technical reference works which may be of interest to inventors. In addition to providing access to a wide range of patent and trademark information in paper form, the Library also offers some electronic patent information services through CD-ROM computer terminals and also provides a document delivery service to the public.

The laws relating to intellectual property are complex and it is advisable for intending applicants to consult a registered patent or trade mark agent in advance.

General advice on the protection, technical development and commercialisation of inventions is available to client companies from Enterprise Ireland under the Inventions Assistance Scheme. In certain cases, Enterprise Ireland can give financial assistance with patenting expenses and can assist in finding suitable manufacturers. Full details of the scheme are available from Enterprise Ireland.

Application forms, information leaflets and lists of registered patent/trademark agents are available free of charge from the Patents Office (**www.patentsoffice.ie**).

Monitoring Performance

OBJECTIVES

- ☐ Understand the importance of monitoring performance
- ☐ Be aware of monitoring techniques

It is important that you monitor the progress of your business against your business plan forecasts on a quarterly, monthly, even weekly basis. If you do not, there is a danger that things will go wrong without you knowing about it. In particular, if you do not watch your cash-flow carefully, you could run into difficulties very quickly.

Most lenders are keen to have regular financial information on the performance of the businesses to which they lend money. How they get it depends on the local manager and the arrangements he makes, since few small businesses have the capacity or ability to supply monthly or quarterly accounts.

The panel below provides a simple system both for you to monitor the financial performance of your business and to communicate it to your bank manager.

The first column is taken from your business plan and represents your forecast performance. The second is your actual performance to date, which you will get from your accounts. Calculate the difference between budget and actual, both in money terms and in percentages.

If it's working, keep doing it.
If it's not working, stop doing it.
If you don't know what to do, don't do anything.
MEDICAL SCHOOL ADVICE

WHAT STAGE IS YOUR BUSINESS AT?

1. **Existence and survival**
   - Owner is business
   - Problem is finding customers and cash flow
2. **Consolidation and control**
   - Developing systems
   - Problem is to generate repeat sales and financial control
3. **Control and planning**
   - Taking on staff
   - Focus on management
   - Problem is fighting competition, development of new markets and control of margins and costs
4. **Expansion**
   - Delegation and decentralisation
   - Market expansion (new products and/or markets)
   - Tight financial control

Month/Quarter/Year ended ________________________________

	Budget	Actual	Difference		Comment
Revenue by product					
A ____________	€ _____	€ _____	€ _____	_____%	____________
B ____________	€ _____	€ _____	€ _____	_____%	____________
C ____________	€ _____	€ _____	€ _____	_____%	____________
D ____________	€ _____	€ _____	€ _____	_____%	____________
E ____________	€ _____	€ _____	€ _____	_____%	____________
Total revenue	**€** _____	**€** _____	**€** _____	_____%	____________
Gross profit	**€** _____	**€** _____	**€** _____	_____%	____________
Gross profit % of turnover	_____%	_____%	_____%	_____%	____________
Staff costs	€ _____	€ _____	€ _____	_____%	____________
Production costs	€ _____	€ _____	€ _____	_____%	____________
Premises	€ _____	€ _____	€ _____	_____%	____________
Transport costs	€ _____	€ _____	€ _____	_____%	____________
Sales and promotion	€ _____	€ _____	€ _____	_____%	____________
General expenses	€ _____	€ _____	€ _____	_____%	____________
Finance costs	€ _____	€ _____	€ _____	_____%	____________
Depreciation	€ _____	€ _____	€ _____	_____%	____________
Total overheads	**€** _____	**€** _____	**€** _____	_____%	____________
Net profit	**€** _____	**€** _____	**€** _____	_____%	____________
Net cash flow	**€** _____	**€** _____	**€** _____	_____%	____________

Appendix 1: Addresses

Key:		
	T:	Telephone
	F:	Facsimile
	E:	E-mail
	C:	Contact

ACT Venture Capital Ltd, Jefferson House, Eglinton Road, Dublin 4 T: (01) 260 0966 F: (01) 260 0538 E: info@actvc.ie W: www. actventure.com C: Niall Carroll

Action Tallaght, 80 Killinarden Heights, Tallaght, Dublin 24 T: (01) 452 6098 F: (01) 452 6441 C: Tony Nolan

AIB Bank Enterprise Development Bureau, Bankcentre, Ballsbridge, Dublin 4 T: (01) 641 3090 F: (01) 641 3045 E: business.banking@ aib.ie W: www.aib.ie/roi/business/businessbanking.asp C: John Kelly, Caroline Tully

Area Development Management Ltd, Holbrook House, Holles Street, Dublin 2 T: (01) 240 0700 F: (01) 661 0411 E: enquiries@adm.ie W: www.adm.ie C: Dr Tony Crooks, CEO

Arts Council, 70 Merrion Square, Dublin 2 T: (01) 618 0200 F: (01) 676 1302 E: reception@artscouncil.ie W: www.artscouncil.ie C: Tara Byrne

Association of Chartered Certified Accountants, 9 Leeson Park, Dublin 6 T: (01) 496 3144 F: (01) 496 3615 E: edgelyl@accaglobal. com W: www.acca.ie C: Roger Acton

Athlone Institute of Technology, Dublin Road, Athlone, Co Westmeath T: (0902) 24400 F: (0902) 24417 E: pmulhern@ait.ie W: www.ait.ie C: Dr Patrick J Mulhern, Industrial Liaison Officer

AWG Investment Fund, Deal Management Ltd, 74 Pembroke Road, Ballsbridge, Dublin 4 T: (01) 660 9313 F: (01) 668 7904 E: dealman@eircom.net C: Joe Doddy

Balbriggan Enterprise Development Group, Enterprise House, 13 Drogheda Street, Balbriggan, Co Dublin T: (01) 841 5141 F: (01) 841 1010 E: info@ balbrigganenterprise.ie W: www.balbrigganenterprise.ie C: Adrian Brown

Ballyfermot Partnership, 290 Ballyfermot Road, Dublin 10 T: (01) 626 9222 F: (01) 626 3416 E: bpart@indigo.ie W: www.planet.ie C: Liz O'Brien, Manager

Ballymun Partnership, North Mall, Ballymun Town Centre, Dublin 11 T: (01) 842 3612 F: (01) 842 7004 E: bmunpart@indigo.ie W: www. planet.ie C: Terence Kavanagh, Business Adviser

Bank of Ireland Enterprise Support Unit, 40 Mespil Road, Dublin 4 T: (01) 665 3466 F: (01) 665 3482 E: tom.meally@boimail.com W: www.bankofireland.ie/sbb C: Tom Meally

Bank of Ireland Entrepreneurs Fund, Delta Partners, South County Business Park, Leopardstown, Dublin 18 T: (01) 294 0870 F: (01) 294 0877 E: venture@delta.ie W: www. deltapartners.com C: Frank Kenny

Bank of Scotland (Ireland) Ltd, Canada House, 65–68 St Stephen's Green, Dublin 2 T: (01) 408 3500 F: (01) 475 3219 E: barry.walshe @bankofscotland.ie W: www. bankofscotland.ie C: Barry Walshe

Blanchardstown Area Partnership, Deanstown House, Main Street, Blanchardstown, Dublin 15 T: (01) 820 9550 F: (01) 820 9551 E: blancpar@iol.ie W: www.planet.ie C: Derek Hanway

Bolton Trust, Docklands Innovation Park, 128-130 East Wall Road, Dublin 3 T: (01) 855 2333 F: (01) 855 2380 E: michael.drennan@docklands-innovation.com W: None C: Michael Drennan

Bord Bia — The Irish Food Board, Clanwilliam Court, Lower Mount Street, Dublin 2 T: (01) 668 5155 F: (01) 668 7521 E: colette.shannon@bordbia.ie W: www.bordbia.ie C: Colette Shannon, Small Business; Michael Duffy, Chief Executive

Bord Glas — The Horticultural Development Board, 8-11 Lower Baggot Street, Dublin 2 T: (01) 676 3567 F: (01) 676 7347 E: info@bordglas.ie W: www.bordglas.ie

Bord Iascaigh Mhara — Irish Sea Fisheries Board, PO Box 12, Crofton Road, Dun Laoire, Co Dublin T: (01) 214 4100 F: (01) 284 1123 E: info@bim.ie W: www.bim.ie C: Imelda Bradley

Bray Partnership, 4 Prince of Wales Terrace, Quinsboro Road, Bray, Co Wicklow T: (01) 286 8266 F: (01) 286 8700 E: info@braypartnership.org C: Peter Brennan

Business Expansion Scheme, Office of the Revenue Commissioners, Dublin Castle, Dublin 2 T: (01) 674 8426 F: (01) 671 0012 E: mgalvin@revenue.ie W: www.revenue.ie C: Jim Barry

Business Information Centre, Central Library, ILAC Centre, Henry Street, Dublin 1 T: (01) 873 4333 F: (01) 872 1451 E:dubcilib@iol.ie W: www.iol.ie/ dublincitylibrary/ C: Margaret Conroy, Caroline Clery

Business Innovation Fund, Dublin Business Innovation Centre, The Tower, TCD Enterprise Centre, Pearse Street, Dublin 2 T: (01) 671 3111 F: (01) 671 3330 E: bif@dbic.ie W: www.dbic.ie C: Alex Hobbs

Campus Companies Venture Capital Fund, Molesworth House, Moleworth Street, Dublin 2 T: (01) 679 0818 F: (01) 679 9014 E: info@campuscapital.com W: www.campuscapital.com C: Pat Ryan

Canal Communities Partnership, 197 Tyrconnell Road, Inchicore, Dublin 8 T: (01) 473 2196 F: (01) 453 4857 E: canalcp@iol.ie W: www.planet.ie C: Brian Kenny

Carlow County Enterprise Board, Enterprise House, O'Brien Street, Carlow T: (059) 913 0880 F: (059) 913 0717 E: info@carlow-ceb.com W: www.carlow-ceb.com; www.carlow-directory.com C: Michael P. Kelly, CEO

Carréfour Cahirciveen, Community Office, IDA Industrial Estate, Caherciveen, Co Kerry T: (066) 947 2724 F: (066) 947 2725 E: mdoherty@skdp.net W: www.kerrygems.ie/carrefour C: Majella Doherty

Carréfour Dublin, Rural Dublin LEADER Company, 11 Parnell Square, Dublin 1 T: (01) 787 0564 F: (01) 878 0572 E:eohara@ruraldublin.ie W: None

Carréfour Galway, Department of Economics, National University of Ireland, Galway T: (091) 524411 x3042 F: (091) 524130 E: caoilinn.orourke@nuigalway.ie W: www.nuigalway.ie/ecn/carrefour/ C: Caoilinn De Bairéad, Manager

Carréfour Waterford, See *South East European Centre*

Cavan County Enterprise Board, 17 Farnham Street, Cavan T: (049) 433 2427 F: (049) 433 1384 E: cceb@eircom.net C: Vincent Reynolds, CEO

Central Statistics Office, Skehard Road, Mahon, Cork T: (021) 453 5000 F: (021) 453 5555 E: information@ cso.ie W: www.cso.ie C: Kevin Moriarty Also at: Ardee Road, Rathmines, Dublin 6 T: (01) 497 7144 F: (01) 497 2360

Centre for Co-operative Studies, O'Rahilly Building, University College Cork, Cork T: (021) 490 2570 F: (021) 490 3358 E: ccs@ucc.ie W: www.ucc.ie/acad /foodecon/centre_b.html C: Michael Ward

Centre for Entrepreneurial Studies, University of Limerick, Limerick T: (061) 202 183 F: (061) 338 171 E: patricia.fleming@ul.ie W: www.ul.ie C: Patricia Fleming, Professor Barra O Cinnéide

Chambers of Commerce of Ireland, 22 Merrion Square, Dublin 2 T: (01) 661 2888 F: (01) 661 2811 E: info@chambersireland.ie W: www. chambersireland.ie C: John Dunne

City of Dublin Vocational Education Committee, Town Hall, Merrion Road, Ballsbridge, Dublin 4 T: (01) 668 0614 F: (01) 668 0710 E: jim.boland@cdvec.ie W: www.cdvec.ie C: Jim Boland, Management Services; WJ Arundel, CEO

Clare County Enterprise Board, Enterprise House, Mill Road, Ennis, Co Clare T: (065) 684 1922 F: (065) 684 1887 E: cceb@iol.ie W: www.clare-ceb.ie C: Eamonn Kelly

Clondalkin Partnership, Camac House, Unit 4, Oakfield Industrial Estate, Clondalkin, Dublin 22 T: (01) 457 6433 F: (01) 457 7145 E: clonpart@indigo.ie W: None C: Aileen O'Donoghue, Manager

Comhair Chathair Chorcaí — Cork City Partnership, Sunbeam Industrial Park, Millfield, Mallow Road, Cork T: (021) 430 2310 F: (021) 430 2081 E: partnershipcork@eircom.net C: Jim O'Flynn

Companies Registration Office, Parnell House, 14 Parnell Square, Dublin 1 T: (01) 804 5200 F: (01) 804 5222 E: info@cro.ie W: www.cro.ie

Co-operation Ireland, 37 Upper Fitzwilliam Street, Dublin 2 T: (01) 661 0588 / 676 3608 F: (01) 661 8456 E: info@cooperationireland.org W: www.cooperationireland.org C: Maurice Inglis

Co-operative Development Society Ltd, Dominick Court, 41 Lower Dominick Street, Dublin 1 T: (01) 873 3199 F: (01) 873 3612 E: coopsoc@tinet.ie W: www. ablaze.ie/cds C: Dermot McKenna

Cork Business Innovation Centre, NSC Campus, Mahon, Cork T: (021) 230 7005 F: (021) 230 7005 E: postmaster@corkbic.com W: www.corkbic.com C: Michael O'Connor, Chief Executive

Cork City Enterprise Board, 1-2 Bruach na Laoi, Union Quay, Cork T: (021) 496 1828 F: (021) 496 1869 E: corkceb@iol.ie W: www.corkceb.ie C: Dave Cody, CEO

Cork Institute of Technology, Rossa Avenue, Bishopstown, Cork T: (021) 432 6100 F: (021) 454 5343 E: jsomullane@cit.ie W: www.cit.ie C: Josette O'Mullane, Industrial Liaison Officer

Cork North County Enterprise Board, The Enterprise Office, 26 Davis Street, Mallow, Co Cork T: (022) 43235 F: (022) 43247 E: corknent@iol.ie C: Rochie Holohan

County Cavan Partnership, 28A Bridge Street, Cavan T: (049) 433 1029 F: (049) 433 1117 E: cavpart@iol.ie C: Orla Brady, Enterprise Officer; Brendan Reilly, Manager

County Leitrim Partnership Board, Church Street, Drumshambo, Co Leitrim T: (078) 41740 F: (078) 41741 E: clpdr@eircom.net W: www.planet.ie C: Tom Lavin, Manager

County Monaghan Partnership, Monaghan Road, Castleblaney, Co Monaghan T: (042) 974 9500 F: (042) 974 9504 E: reception@monaghanpartnership.com W: www.planet.ie C: Lorraine McKenna

County Wexford Partnership, Millpark Road, Enniscorthy, Co Wexford T: (054) 37033 F: (054) 37026 Also at: Gorey T: (055) 22477, New Ross T: (051) 425 028 E: info@wexfordpartnership.ie W: www.wexfordpartnerhsip.ie C: John Nunn

Crafts Council of Ireland, Castle Yard, Kilkenny T: (056) 61804 F: (056) 63754 E: info@ccoi.ie W: www.ccoi.ie C: Leslie Reed, CEO

Cross Atlantic Capital Partners, 3006 Lake Drive, Citywest Business Campus, Dublin 24 T: (01) 241 6100 F: (01) 241 6132 E: gmccrory@xacp.com W: www. xacp.com C: Gerry McCrory

Cross Border Technology Enterprise Start-up Programme, Enterprise Ireland North-West Region, Finisklin Industrial Estate, Sligo T: (071) 59700 F: (071) 59701 E: startup@enterprise-ireland.com W: www.enterprise-ireland.com C: Brian O'Malley

Dairy Products Research Centre, Moorepark, Fermoy, Co Cork T: (025) 42222 F: (025) 42340 E: elehane@moorepark.teagasc.ie W: www.teagasc.org/research/research_centres.htm C: Dr WJ Donnelly, Head of Centre

Delta Partners, South County Business Park, Leopardstown, Dublin 18 T: (01) 294 0870 F: (01) 294 0877 E: venture@delta.ie W: www.deltapartners.com C: Frank Kenny

Department of Agriculture & Food, Agriculture House, Kildare Street, Dublin 2 T: (01) 607 2802 (Information section) F: (01) 678 5214 E: information@daff.irlgov.ie W: www.irlgov.ie/daff

Department of Enterprise, Trade and Employment, Head Office, Kildare Street, Dublin 2 T: (01) 631 2121 F: (01) 631 2827 E: webmaster@entemp.ie W: www.entemp.ie C: Information Section

Department of Social & Family Affairs, Information Unit, 5th Floor, Store Street, Dublin 1 T: (01) 874 8444 F: (01) 704 3868 E: info@welfare.ie W: www.welfare.ie

Department of the Environment and Local Government, Custom House, Dublin 1 T: (01) 888 2000 F: (01) 888 2888 E: pressoffice@environ.irlgov.ie W: www.environ.ie

Donegal County Enterprise Board, Enterprise Fund Business Centre, Ballyraine, Letterkenny, Co Donegal T: (074) 916 0735 F: (074) 916 0783 E: info@donegalenterprise.ie W: www.donegalenterprise.ie C: Michael Tunney, CEO

Donegal Local Development Company, 1 Millennium Court, Pearse Road, Letterkenny, Co Donegal T: (074) 27056 F: (074) 21527 E: dldclk@iol.ie W: www.dldc.org C: Caoimhín Mac Aoidh, Manager

Drogheda Partnership Company, 12 North Quay, Drogheda, Co Louth T: (041) 984 2088 F: (041) 984 3358 E: drogpart@iol.ie W: www.iol.ie/~drogpart C: Mary-Ann McGlynn, Manager

Dublin Business Innovation Centre, The Tower, TCD Enterprise Centre, Pearse Street, Dublin 2 T: (01) 671 3111 F: (01) 671 3330 E: info@dbic.ie W: www.dbic.ie C: John McInerney

Dublin City Enterprise Board, 17 Eustace Street, Dublin 2 T: (01) 677 6068 F: (01) 677 6093 E: info@dceb.ie W: www.dceb.ie C: Greg Swift, CEO

Dublin City University, Glasnevin, Dublin 9 T: (01) 700 5000 F: (01) 836 0830 E: tony.glynn@dcu.ie W: www.dcu.ie C: Dr Tony Glynn, Director, Office of Innovation and Business Relations

Dublin Inner City Partnership, Equity House, 16-17 Upper Ormond Quay, Dublin 7 T: (01) 872 1321 F: (01) 872 1330 E: office@dicp.ie C: David Connolly, Director

Dublin Institute of Technology, Central office: Fitzwilliam House, 30 Upper Pembroke Street, Dublin 2 T: (01) 402 3379 F: (01) 402 3393 E: rea.oneill@dit.ie W: www.dit.ie C: Rea O'Neill, Industrial Liaison Officer

Dublin Seed Capital Fund, Dublin Business Innovation Centre, The Tower, TCD Enterprise Centre, Pearse Street, Dublin 2 T: (01) 671 3111 F: (01) 671 3330 E: dscf@indigo.ie W: www.dbic.ie C: Alex Hobbs

Dundalk Employment Partnership Ltd, Partnership Court, Park Street, Dundalk T: (042) 933 0288 F: (042) 933 0552 E: partnership@dep.ie W: www.dep.ie C: John Butler, Chief Executive

Dundalk Institute of Technology, Dublin Road, Dundalk, Co Louth T: (042) 937 0200 F: (042) 933 3505 W: www.dkit.ie C: Gerard Carroll, Industrial Liaison Officer

Dún Laoire/Rathdown County Enterprise Board, Venturepoint, Dundrum Office Park, Main Street, Dundrum, Dublin 16 T: (01) 205 1100 F: (01) 298 6827 E: ventur1@venturepoint.ie W: www.venturepoint.ie C: Michael Johnson, CEO

eircom Enterprise Fund Ltd, eircom plc, 114 St Stephens Green West, Dublin 2 T: (01) 701 5130 F: (01) 679 7253 E: mmoore@eircom.ie W: www.eircom-enterprise-fund.ie C: Maura Moore

Electronic Commerce Association of Ireland, PO Box 6247, Dublin 9 T: (01) 838 7255 F: None E: info@ecai.ie W: www.ecai.ie

ENFO — Environmental Information Service, St Andrew's Street, Dublin 2 T: (01) 888 2001 F: (01) 888 3946 E: info@enfo.ie W: www.enfo.ie

Enterprise 2000 Fund, 43 Pearse Street, Dublin 2 T: (01) 677 5570 F: (01) 677 5588 E: capital@enterprise2000fund.ie W: www.enterprise2000fund.ie C: Clare Shine

Enterprise Equity, Dublin Road, Dundalk, Co Louth T: (042) 933 3167 F: (042) 933 4857 E: info@enterpriseequity.ie W: www.eeirl.com C: Conor O'Connor

Enterprise Ireland, Wilton Park House, Wilton Place, Dublin 2 T: (01) 808 2000 F: (01) 808 2802 W: www.enterprise-ireland.com Also at: Glasnevin, Dublin 9 T: (01) 808 2000 F: (01) 808 2020; Merrion Hall, Strand Road, Sandymount, Dublin 4 T: (01) 206 6000 F: (01) 206 6400 Regional Offices in Athlone, Cork, Dublin, Dundalk, Galway, Letterkenny, Killarney, Sligo, Waterford

Enterprise Link, Wilton Park House, Wilton Place, Dublin 2 T: (01) 808 2000 F: (01) 808 2802 W: www.enterprise-ireland.com

Environmental Protection Agency, P.O. Box 3000, Johnstown Castle Estate, Co Wexford T: (053) 60600 F: (053) 60699 E: info@epa.ie W: www.epa.ie

Europa, W: europa.eu.int

European Commission, European Union House, 18 Dawson Street, Dublin 2 T: (01) 634 1111 F: (01) 634 1112 E: eu-ie-info-request@cec.eu.int W: www.euireland.ie C: Library

European Information Centre Athlone, Athlone Chamber of Commerce & Industry, Jolly Mariner Marina, Coosan Road, Athlone, Co Westmeath T: (0902) 73173 F: (0902) 74386 E: athcci@iol.ie W: www.athlonechamber.ie/europe C: Siobhan Bigley

European Information Centre Cork, Cork Chamber of Commerce, Fitzgerald House, Summerhill North, Cork T: (021) 450 9044 F: (021) 450 8568 E: eic@corkchamber.ie W: www.corkchamber.ie/euro_info.htm C: Kate Geary

European Information Centre Galway, Galway Chamber of Commerce and Industry, Commerce House, Merchants Road, Galway T: (091) 563536 F: (091) 561963 E: info@galwaychamber.com W: www.galwaychamber.com/euro.htm C: Elaine Wakely

European Information Centre Sligo, Sligo Chamber of Commerce, 16 Quay Street, Sligo T: (071) 61274 F: (071) 60912 E: sligoeic@eircom.net W: None C: Laura Caslin

European Information Centre Waterford, Waterford Chamber of Commerce, 8 George's Street, Waterford T: (051) 872639 F: (051) 876002 E: eic@indigo.ie W: www.waterford-chamber.ie C: Fiona Robbins

Excellence Ireland, Merrion Hall, Strand Road, Sandymount, Dublin 4 T: (01) 269 5255 F: (01) 269 8053 E: a.kelly@excellence-ireland.ie W: www.excellence-ireland.ie C: Seán Conlan, CEO

Fáilte Ireland - The National Tourism Development Authority, 88/95 Amiens Street, Dublin 1 T: 1890 525525 E: info@failteireland.ie W: www.failteireland.ie

FÁS — The Training & Employment Authority, Services to Business, 27–33 Upper Baggot Street, Dublin 4 T: (01) 607 0500 F: (01) 607 0600 E: stb@fas.ie W: www.fas.ie C: John McGrath

FÁS Co-operative Development Unit, FÁS Training Centre, Baldoyle Industrial Estate, Baldoyle, Dublin 13 T: (01) 816 7418 F: (01) 816 7419 E: cdu@fas.ie W: www.fas.ie C: Colm Hughes

Fingal (Dublin North) County Enterprise Board, Upper Floor Office Suite, Mainscourt, 23 Main Street, Swords, Co Dublin T: (01) 890 0800 F: (01) 813 9991 E: ceb@fingal.ie W: www.fingal.ie C: Oisin Geoghegan, CEO

Fingal Employees Youth Business Fund, c/o Fingal County Hall, Main Street, Swords, Co Dublin T: (01) 840 0149, 890 5000 F: (01) 840 5175 W: www.fingalcoco.ie C: Sean Ring

Finglas Business Initiative, Rosehill House, Finglas Road, Dublin 11 T: (01) 836 1666 F: (01) 864 0211 E: info@ fcp.ie W: www.planet.ie C: Paul Ring

Finglas/Cabra Partnership, Rosehill House, Finglas Road, Dublin 11 T: (01) 836 1666 F: (01) 864 0211 E: info@fcp.ie W: www.planet.ie C: Michael P Bowe

First Step, Jefferson House, Eglinton Road, Donnybrook, Dublin 4 T: (01) 260 0988 F: (01) 260 0989 E: firststep @eircom.net

Food Product Development Centre, 31 Marlborough Street, Dublin 1 T: (01) 814 6080 F: (01) 874 857 E: fpdc@dit.ie W: www.dit.ie/tour/fpdc C: Mary Dineen

Food Safety Authority of Ireland, Abbey Court, Lower Abbey Street, Dublin 1 T: (01) 817 1300 F: (01) 817 1301 E: info@fsai.ie W: www.fsai.ie

Forfás, Wilton Park House, Wilton Place, Dublin 2 T: (01) 607 3000 F: (01) 607 3030 E: tom.odwyer@forfas.ie W: www.forfas.ie C: Tom O'Dwyer, Press Office

Galway Business Innovation Centre, See *WestBIC*

Galway City Partnership, Townpark, Tuam Road, Galway T: (091) 773466 F: (091) 773468 E: info@gcp.iol.ie C: Declan Brassil

Galway County and City Enterprise Board, Woodquay Court, Woodquay, Galway T: (091) 565269 F: (091) 565384 E: lynchc@iol.ie W: www.galwayenterprise.ie C: Charles Lynch, CEO

Galway–Mayo Institute of Technology, Dublin Road, Galway T: (091) 753161 F: (091) 751107 E: andrew.darcy@gmit.ie W: www.gmit.ie C: Andrew D'Arcy, Head of Development

Galway Rural Development Company, Church Street, Athenry, Co Galway T: (091) 844335 F: (091) 845465 E: grdc@iol.ie W: www.galway-leader.com C: Bríd Hynes, Manager

Gorann Technology Venture Catalyst Ltd, 25–26 Great Strand Street, Dublin 1 T: (01) 874 8188 F: (01) 289 1236 E: info@gorann.com W: www.gorann.com

Government Publications, 4/5 Harcourt Road, Dublin 2 T: (01) 647 6839 F: (01) 475 2760 E: patricia.ward @opw.ie C: Patricia Ward, Customer Liaison Officer Also at: Sales Office: Sun Alliance House, Molesworth Street, Dublin 2

Growcorp Innovation Centre, 3015 Lake Drive, Citywest Business Campus Park, Dublin 24 T: (01) 466 1000 F: (01) 466 1002 E: grow@growcorp.net W: www.growcorp.net

Guaranteed Irish Ltd, 1 Fitzwilliam Place, Dublin 2 T: (01) 661 2607 F: (01) 661 2633 E: info@guaranteed-irish.ie W: www.guaranteed-irish.ie

Guinness Enterprise Centre, Taylor's Lane, Dublin 8 T: (01) 410 0600 F: (01) 410 0602 E: info@guinness-enterprisectr.com W: www.guinness-enterprisectr.com C: Dolores Dempsey, Administration Manager

Guinness Ulster Bank Equity Fund, NCB Ventures Ltd, 3 George's Dock, IFSC, Dublin 1 T: (01) 611 5611 F: (01) 611 5987 W: www.ncb.ie C: Michael Murphy, michael.murphy@ncb.ie; Mark Mulqueen, mark.mulqueen@ncb.ie

Guinness Workers' Employment Fund Ltd, St James's Gate, Dublin 8 T: (01) 453 6700 F: (01) 408 4967 C: Rowena Thornburgh, Andy Shirran (Part-time)

Health & Safety Authority, 10 Hogan Place, Dublin 2 T: (01) 614 7000 F: (01) 614 7020 E: infotel@hsa.ie W: www.hsa.ie

Hibernia Capital Partners Ltd, 88 St Stephen's Green, Dublin 2 T: (01) 475 4725 F: (01) 475 4728 E: equity @hcp.ie W: www.hcp.ie C: John Bolger, Luke Crosbie

HotOrigin, Richmond Business Campus, North Brunswick Street, Dublin 7 T: (01) 809 0484 F: (01) 872 6252 E: ventures@hotorigin.com W: www.hotorigin. com C: David Dalton

IBEC, Confederation House, 84–86 Lower Baggot Street, Dublin 2 T: (01) 660 1011 F: (01) 660 1717 W: www.ibec.ie

IDA Ireland, Wilton Park House, Wilton Place, Dublin 2 T: (01) 603 4000 F: (01) 603 4040 W: www. idaireland.com

IE Domain Registry Ltd, Windsor House, 14 Windsor Terrace, Sandycove, Co Dublin T: (01) 230 0797 F: (01) 230 0365 E: hostmaster@domainregistry.ie W: www. domainregistry.ie

Info Point Europe Athlone, Athlone Chamber of Commerce & Industry, Jolly Mariner Marina, Coosan Road, Athlone, Co Westmeath T: (0902) 73173 F: (0902) 74386 E: athcci@iol.ie W: www. athlonechamber.ie/europe/ C: Siobhan Bigley

Info Point Europe Mullingar, Mullingar Chamber of Commerce, Market House, Mullingar, Co Westmeath T: (044) 44044 F: (044) 44045 E: info@mullingar-chamber.ie W: www.mullingar-chamber.ie C: Marina Swarbrigg

Info Point Europe North East, Dundalk Institute of Technology, Dublin Road, Dundalk, Co Louth T: (042) 937 0492 F: (042) 933 8313 E: eu-info@dkit.ie W: www.dkit.ie/eu-info C: Ronan Gingles

Inishowen Partnership Board, 2 Victoria Villas, St Mary's Road, Buncrana, Co Donegal T: (077) 62218 F: (077) 62990 E: inishpar@indigo.ie C: Fionnuala McGeever, Manager

Inner City Enterprise, 56–57 Lower Gardiner Street, Dublin 1 T: (01) 836 4073 F: 836 3742 E: ice@iol.ie W: None C: Eamon Brady, Development Manager

Innovation Centre, Shannon Development, Innovation Centre, National Technological Park, Limerick T: (061) 338177 F: (061) 338065 E: corcoranj@shannon-dev.ie W: www.shannon-dev.ie/innovation/ C: J Corcoran

Innovation Relay Centre for Ireland, Enterprise Ireland, Glasnevin, Dublin 9 T: (01) 808 2305 F: (01) 808 2376 E: irc@enterprise-ireland.com W: www.enterprise-ireland.com/irc/ C: Greg Treston

Institute of Business Advisers (Irish branch), T: (01) 833 4806 C: Willie Maxwell

Institute of Certified Public Accountants in Ireland, 9 Ely Place, Dublin 2 T: (01) 676 7353 F: (01) 661 2367 E: cpa@cpaireland.ie W: www.cpaireland.ie C: Eamonn Siggins, Chief Executive

Institute of Chartered Accountants in Ireland, CA House, 87–89 Pembroke Road, Ballsbridge, Dublin 4 T: (01) 637 7200 F: (01) 668 0842 E: ca@icai.ie W: www.icai.ie C: John McCarthy

Institute of Directors in Ireland, 89 James Street, Dublin 8 T: (01) 408 4548 F: (01) 408 4550 E: info@iodireland.ie W: www.iodireland.ie C: Susan Thornber, Chief Executive

Institute of Technology Blanchardstown, Blanchardstown Road North, Blanchardstown, Dublin 15 T: (01) 885 1000 F: (01) 885 1001 E : info@itb.ie W: www.itb.ie C: Tom Doyle, Head of Development

Institute of Technology Carlow, Kilkenny Road, Carlow T: (0503) 70400 F: (0503) 70500 E: info@itcarlow.ie W: www.itcarlow.ie C: Jim McEntee, Head of External Services

Institute of Technology Sligo, Ballinode, Sligo T : (071) 55222 F: (071) 44096 E: info@itsligo.ie W: www. itsligo.ie C: Des McConville, Head of Development

Institute of Technology Tallaght, Tallaght, Dublin 24 T: (01) 404 2000 F: (01) 404 2700 E: eamon.tuffy@it-tallaght.ie W: www.it-tallaght.ie C: Eamon Tuffy, Head of Development and External Services

Institute of Technology Tralee, Clash, Tralee, Co Kerry T: (066) 714 5600, 714 5611 (Development) F: (066) 714 5636 E: brenda.clifford@ittralee.ie W: www.ittralee.ie C: Brenda Clifford, Development Dept

International Fund for Ireland, PO Box 2000, Dublin 2 T: (01) 478 0655 F: (01) 475 1351 W: www.intl-fund-ireland.org C: Paddy Purcell, Director General

IRD Duhallow Ltd, James O'Keeffe Institute, Newmarket, Co Cork T: (029) 60633 F: (029) 60694 E: duhallow@ eircom.net C: Maura Walsh, Manager

IRD Kiltimagh, Enterprise House, Aiden Street, Kiltimagh, Co Mayo T: (094) 81494 F: (094) 81884 E: info@ird-kiltimagh.ie, ird@iol.ie W: www.ird-kiltimagh.ie C: Joe Kelly

Irish BICs Seed Capital Fund, Dublin BIC, The Tower, TCD Enterprise Centre, Pearse Street, Dublin 2 T: (01) 671 3111 F: (01) 671 3330 E: dscf@indigo.ie W: www.indigo.ie/dbic C: Alex Hobbs

Irish Co-operative Society Ltd, Plunkett House, 84 Merrion Square, Dublin 2 T: (01) 676 4783 F: (01) 662 4502 E: info@icos.ie W: None

Irish Energy Centre, Enterprise Ireland, Glasnevin, Dublin 9 T: (01) 808 2070, 836 9080 F: (01) 837 2848 E: info@irish-energy.ie W: www.irish-energy.ie C: Tom Halpin, Manager

Irish Exporters Association, 28 Merrion Square, Dublin 2 T: (01) 661 2182 F: (01) 661 2315 E: iea@irishexporters.ie W: www.irishexporters.ie C: John Whelan, Chief Executive

Irish Internet Association, PO Box 6118, Dublin 8 T: (01) 416 9191 F: (01) 473 6258 E: info@iia.ie W: www.iia.ie C: Lorna O'Callaghan (Membership), Sinead Murnane (Events T: (01) 664 3505)

Irish League of Credit Unions, 33-41 Lower Mount Street, Dublin 2 T: (01) 614 6700 F: (01) 614 6701 E: info@creditunion.ie W:www.creditunion.ie

Irish Productivity Centre, Block 4B-5, Blanchardstown Corporate Park, Blanchardstown, Dublin 15 T: (01) 822 7125 F: (01) 822 7116 E: ipc@ipc.ie W: www.ipc.ie C: Tom McGuinness, Chief Executive

Irish Small and Medium Enterprises Association, 17 Kildare Street, Dublin 2 T: (01) 662 2755 F: (01) 661 2157 E: info@isme.ie W: www.isme.ie C: Mark Fielding

Kerry County Enterprise Board, County Buildings, Ratass, Tralee, Co Kerry T: (066) 718 3522 F: (066) 712 6712 E: kerryceb@kerrycoco.ie W: www.kerryceb.ie C: Martin Collins, CEO

Kerry Technology Park, Dromtacker, Tralee, Co Kerry T: (066) 712 4988 F: (066) 712 4267 E: lynchm@shannon-dev.ie W: www.shannon-dev.ie/ktp/ C: Marie Lynch, Projects Executive

Kildare County Enterprise Board, The Woods, Clane, Co Kildare T: (045) 861707 F: (045) 861712 E: info@ kildareceb.ie W: www.kildareceb.ie C: Donal Dalton, CEO

Kilkenny County Enterprise Board, 42 Parliament Street, Kilkenny T: (056) 52662 F: (056) 51649 E: kceb@ kceb.ie C: Sean McKeown, CEO

Kimmage/Walkinstown/Crumlin/Drimnagh Partnership, Unit 9, Ashleascentre, Crumlin Cross, Dublin 12 T: (01) 405 9300 F: (01) 405 9359 E: info@kwcd.ie W: www.kwcd.ie C: Brian Nugent

Laois County Enterprise Board, IBS House, Dublin Road, Portlaoise, Co Laois T: (0502) 61800 F: (0502) 61797 E: admin@laoisenterprise.com W: www.laoisenterprise.com C: Maria Callinan, CEO

Law Society of Ireland, Blackhall Place, Dublin 7 T: (01) 672 4800 F: (01) 672 4801 E: general@lawsociety.ie W: www.lawsociety.ie C: Ken Murphy, Director General

LEADER Programme, Department of Agriculture & Food, Agriculture House, Kildare Street, Dublin 2 T: (01) 678 9011 F: (01) 661 6203 E: leader@daff.irlgov.ie W: www.leaderii.ie

Leitrim Enterprise Board, Carrick-on-Shannon Business Park, Dublin Road, Carrick-on-Shannon, Co Leitrim T: (078) 20450 F: (078) 21491 E: leitceb@iol.ie W: www.leitrimenterprise.ie C: Joe Lowe, CEO

Letterkenny Institute of Technology, Port Road, Letterkenny, Co Donegal T: (074) 64100 F: (074) 64111 E: jack.oherlihy@lyit.ie W: www.lyit.ie C: Jack O'Herlihy, Head of Development

Limerick Business Innovation Centre, Innovation Centre, National Technological Park, Limerick T: (061) 338177, 338118 F: (061) 338065 E: dillonj@shannon-dev.ie W: www.shannon-dev.ie/innovation C: John Dillon, Manager

Limerick City Enterprise Board, The Granary, Michael Street, Limerick T: (061) 312611 F: (061) 311889 E: info@limceb.ie W: www.limceb.ie C: Eamon Ryan, CEO

Limerick County Enterprise Board, County Buildings, 79–84 O'Connell Street, Limerick T: (061) 319319 F: (061) 319318 E: lcoeb@lcoeb.iol.ie W: www.lcoeb.ie C: Ned Toomey, CEO

Limerick Enterprise Development Partnership, Limerick Enterprise Development Park, Roxboro Road, Limerick T: (061) 316833, 316083 F: (061) 319318 C: Liam McElligott

Limerick Food Centre, Raheen Industrial Park, Limerick T: (061) 302033 F: (061) 301172 E: kehellyo@shannon-dev.ie W: www.shannon-dev.ie/foodcentre C: Oliver Kehelly

Limerick Institute of Technology, Moylish Park, Limerick T: (061) 208803 F: (061) 208209 E: iso@lit.ie W: www.lit.ie C: Dr John Donovan, Industrial Services Manager

Longford Community Resources Ltd, 6 Earl Street, Longford T: (043) 48554 F: (043) 48675 E: enquiries@ lcrl.ie W: www.lcrl.ie C: Monica O'Malley, Manager

Longford County Enterprise Board, New Street, Longford T: (043) 42757 F: (043) 40968 E: longfordceb@eircom.net W: www.longenterprise.ie C: Michael Nevin, CEO

Louth County Enterprise Board, Enterprise House, The Ramparts, Dundalk, Co Louth T: (042) 932 7099 F: (042) 932 7101 E: info@lceb.org W: www.lceb.org C: Ronan Dennedy, CEO

M50 Enterprise Platform Programme, Institute of Technology Tallaght, Tallaght, Dublin 24 T: (01) 404 2000/ 404 2376 F: (01) 404 2700 E: m50@ it-tallaght.ie W: www.it-tallaght.ie/external_services C: Patricia O'Sullivan

MAC (National Microelectronics Application Centre), UL Building, National Technological Park, Plassey, Limerick T: (061) 334699 F: (061) 338500 E: mac@ ul.ie W: www.mac.ie C: Dr John J. O'Flaherty, MD

Marine Institute, 80 Harcourt Street, Dublin 2 T: (01) 476 6500 F: (01) 478 4988 W: www.marine.ie

Mayo County Enterprise Board, Spencer Street, Castlebar, Co Mayo T: (094) 24444 F: (094) 24416 E: f.fullard@mayoceb.iol.ie W: www.mayoceb.com C: Frank Fullard, CEO

Meath County Enterprise Board, Navan Enterprise Centre, Trim Road, Navan, Co Meath T: (046) 78400 F: (046) 27356 E: mhceb@meath.com W: www.meath.com C: Hugh Reilly, CEO

Meitheal Forbartha na Gaeltachta Teo, Baile an Fheirtéaraigh, Trá Lí, Co Chiarraí T: (066) 915 6400 F: (066) 915 6199 E: mfgciarrai@eircom.net W: www.mfg.ie C: Antaine M Ó Sé

Meitheal Mhaigh Eo, Lower Main Street, Foxford, Co Mayo T: (094) 56745 F: (094) 56749 E: meithealm@eircom.net C: Justin Sammon, Manager

Millennium Entrepreneur Fund, Enterprise Ireland, Merrion Hall, Strand Road, Sandymount, Dublin 4 T: (01) 206 6375 F: (01) 206 6376 E: tony.shiels@enterprise-ireland.com W: www.millennium-fund.com C: Tony Shiels, Karen Price

Monaghan County Enterprise Board, Courthouse, Monaghan T: (047) 71818 F: (047) 84786 E: info@mceb.ie W: www.mceb.ie C: John McIntaggart, CEO

National Association of Building Co-operatives Ltd, 50 Merrion Square, Dublin 2 T: (01) 661 2877 F: (01) 661 4462 E: admin@nabco.ie

National Food Centre, Dunsinea, Castleknock, Dublin 15 T: (01) 805 9500 F: (01) 805 9550 E: v.tarrant@nfc.teagasc.ie W: www.teagasc.org/research/research_centres.htm C: Dr Vivion Tarrant, Head of Centre

National Irish Bank Ltd, 7–8 Wilton Terrace, Dublin 2 T: (01) 638 5000 F: (01) 638 5198 W: www.nib.ie C: Brian Leydon

National Microelectronics Application Centre, See *MAC*

National Microelectronics Research Centre, University College Cork, Lee Maltings, Prospect Row, Cork T: (021) 490 4177 F: (021) 427 0271 E: admin@nmrc.ie W: www.nmrc.ie C: Professor Gabriel Crean, Director

National Software Centre, NSC Campus, Mahon, Cork T: (021) 230 7005 F: (021) 230 7020 E: postmaster@corkbic.com W: www.corkbic.com C: Michael O'Connor, Cork BIC

National Software Directorate, Enterprise Ireland, Merrion Hall, Strand Road, Sandymount, Dublin 4 T: (01) 206 6310 F: (01) 206 6278 E: info@nsd.ie W: www.nsd.ie C: Jennifer Condon, Director

National Standards Authority of Ireland, Glasnevin, Dublin 9 T: (01) 807 3800 F: (01) 807 3838 Also at: The Granary, Michael Street, Limerick T: (061) 411872 E: delaneyv@nsai.ie W: www.nsai.ie C: Vincent Delaney, Business Development Manager

National Technological Park, Limerick T: (061) 336555 F: (061) 336545 E: parkhouse@shannon-dev.ie W: www.shannon-dev.ie/ntp/ C: Orla Kelly, Marketing Executive

National University of Ireland Galway, Galway T: (091) 524411 F: (091) 525700 E: joe.watson@mis.nuigalway.ie W: www.nuigalway.ie C: Dr Joe Watson, Industrial Liaison Officer

NCB Ventures, 3 George's Dock, IFSC, Dublin 1 T: (01) 611 5611 F: (01) 611 5766 E: info@ncb.ie W: www. ncb.ie C: Michael Murphy, michael.murphy@ncb.ie; Mark Mulqueen, mark.mulqueen@ncb.ie

Network Ireland, Gardiner House, 64-66 Lower Gardiner Street, Dublin 1 T: (01) 855 2932, 855 2922 F: (01) 855 2931 E: info@networkireland.ie W: www.networkireland.ie C: Elaine Dowdall, National Director

North West Kildare/North Offaly Partnership (OAK), Edenderry Business Park, Edenderry, Co Offaly T: (0405) 32688 F: (0405) 32690 E: oakpart@iol.ie W: www.offaly.ie/oak/ C: Pat Leogue, Manager

Northside Partnership, Coolock Development Centre, Bunratty Drive, Coolock, Dublin 17 T: (01) 848 5630 F: (01) 848 5661 E: nsp@iol.ie W: www.northsidepartnership.ie C: Denise Brennan

OAK Partnership, See *North West Kildare/North Offaly Partnership*

Oak Tree Press, 19 Rutland Street, Cork T: (021) 431 3855 F: (021) 431 3496 E: brian.okane@oaktreepress.com W: www.oaktreepress.com C: Brian O'Kane, Managing Director

Offaly County Enterprise Board, Cormac Street, Tullamore, Co Offaly T: (0506) 52971/2 F: (0506) 52973 E: offalyceb@eircom.net W: www.offaly.ie/oceb C: Seán Ryan, CEO

Páirtíocht Chonamara & Árann, Ionad Fiontar, Rosmuc, Co na Gaillimhe T: (091) 574353 F: (091) 574047 E: cumas@eircom.net C: Máire Uí Ghiobúin, Manager

Páirtíocht Gaeltacht Thír Chonaill, MFG Teo, Aonad Earagail 1, An t-Eastát Tionsclaíoch, Na Doirí Beaga, Leitir Ceanainn, Co Dún na nGall T: (075) 32017 F: (075) 32428 E: mfgtc@eircom.net C: Eithne Nic Lochlainn

Partas, Enterprise Centre, Main Road, Tallaght, Dublin 24 T: (01) 459 9159 F: (01) 452 6708 E: djones@partas.ie W: www.partas.ie C: Darren Jones, Manager - Special Projects

Partnership Trá Lí, 37 Ashe Street, Tralee, Co Kerry T: (066) 718 0190 F: (066) 712 9562 E: mail@partnershiptrali.com W: www.partnershiptrali.com C: Seamus O'Hara, Manager

Patents Office, Government Buildings, Hebron Road, Kilkenny T: (056) 20111 F: (056) 20100 E: patlib@entemp.irlgov.ie W: www.patentsoffice.ie C: Fiona O'Dea, Bill Walsh

Patents Information Office, Earlsfort Centre, Lower Hatch Street, Dublin 2 T: (01) 631 2603 F: (01) 631 2551 C: Rose Johnson, Clodagh O'Reilly

PAUL Partnership Limerick, Unit 25, The Tait Centre, Dominic Street, Limerick T: (061) 419388 F: (061) 418098 E: jackiew@aonad.iol.ie W: www.planet.ie C: Ann Kavanagh

permanentTSB, Corporate Centre, Blackrock, Co. Dublin T: (01) 212 4000 W: www.permanenttsb.ie Contact: Local branch manager

PLATO Ireland, Confederation House, 84-86 Lower Baggot Street, Dublin 2 T: (01) 605 1677 F: (01) 638 1677 E: gary.rynhart@ibec.ie W: www.plato.ie C: Gary Rynhart

Project Development Centre, Docklands Innovation Park, 128-130 East Wall Road, Dublin 3 T: (01) 240 1300 F: (01) 240 1310 E: info@pdc.ie W: www.pdc.ie C: Margaret Whelan

Rabobank, Business Banking Unit, Charlemont Place, Dublin 2 T: (01) 418 4052 F: (01) 418 4809 E: padraig. kiernan@ accbank.ie W: www.accbank.ie C: P. Kiernan

Rathmines Information Centre, See *Terenure Enterprise Centre*

Regional Development Centre, Dundalk Institute of Technology, Dublin Road, Dundalk, Co Louth T: (042) 933 1161 F: (042) 935 1412 E: info@rdc.ie W: www. dkit.ie/rdc C: Gerard Carroll, Head of Development

Registry of Business Names, Companies Registration Office, Parnell House, 14 Parnell Square, Dublin 2 T: (01) 804 5200 F: (01) 873 5298 W: www.cro.ie

Registry of Friendly Societies, Parnell House, 14 Parnell Square, Dublin 1 T: (01) 804 5499 F: (01) 804 5498

Revenue Commissioners, Dublin Castle, Dublin 2 T: (01) 679 2777 F: (01) 679 2035 W: www.revenue.ie Personal Callers: Central Revenue Information Office, Cathedral Street, off O'Connell Street, Dublin 1; Central Telephone Information Office: (01) 878 0000; Forms and leaflets: (01) 878 0100 (24 hours a day, 7 days a week)

Richmond Business Campus, North Brunswick Street, Dublin 7 T: (01) 809 0400 F: (01) 872 6252 E: richmond@iol.ie W: www. richmondbusinesscampus.com C: Rory O'Meara

Roscommon County Enterprise Board Ltd, Library Buildings, Abbey Street, Roscommon T: (0903) 26263 F: (0903) 25474 E: ceb@roscommon.ie W: www. roscommon.ie/enterprise/ C: Anne Flynn, CEO

Roscommon Partnership Company, The Square, Castlerea, Co Roscommon T: (0907) 21337/8/9 F: (0907) 21340 E: roscommonptnship@eircom.net W: www.planet.ie/partners/roscommon.html C: Patricia Murphy-Byrne, Manager

Seed Capital Scheme, Office of the Revenue Commissioners, Dublin Castle, Dublin 2 T: (01) 702 4107 F: (01) 671 0012 E: mgalvin@revenue.ie W: www.revenue.ie C: John Cheasty, Marie Galvin

Shannon Development, Town Centre, Shannon, Co Clare T: (061) 361 555 F: (061) 361 903 E: info@shannon-dev.ie W: www.shannon-dev.ie Also offices in Birr, Ennis, Limerick, Nenagh and Tralee

Sligo County Enterprise Board, Sligo Development Centre, Cleveragh Road, Sligo T: (071) 44779 F: (071) 46793 E: sceb@iol.ie W: www.sligo.ie/local/ceb/sligoceb.htm C: John Reilly, CEO

Sligo LEADER Partnership Company Ltd, Sligo Development Centre, Cleveragh Road, Sligo T: (071) 41138 F: (071) 41162 E: slpc@iol.ie W: www.sligo.ie C: Michael Quigley

Small Enterprise Seed Fund, Project Development Centre, Docklands Innovation Park, 128-130 East Wall Road, Dublin 3 T: (01) 240 1300 F: (01) 240 1310 E: info@pdc.ie W: www.pdc.ie C: Joanne Campbell

Small Firms Association, Confederation House, 84–86 Lower Baggot Street, Dublin 2 T: (01) 660 1011 F: (01) 638 1668 E: info@sfa.ie W: www.sfa.ie C: Pat Delaney, Director

Society of Saint Vincent de Paul, New Cabra Road, Dublin 7 T: (01) 838 4164 F: (01) 838 7355 E: info@svp.ie W: www.svp.ie

South Cork Enterprise Board, Unit 6A, South Ring Business Park, Kinsale Road, Cork T: (021) 497 5281 F: (021) 497 5287 E: info@sceb.ie W: www.sceb.ie C: Jim Brennan, CEO

South Dublin County Enterprise Board, 3 Village Square, Old Bawn Road, Tallaght, Dublin 24 T: (01) 405 7073/4 F: (01) 451 7477 E: webmaster@sdenterprise.com W: www.sdenterprise.com C: Loman O'Byrne, CEO

South-East Business Innovation Centre, Unit 1 B, Industrial Park, Cork Road, Waterford T: (051) 356300 F: (051) 354415 E: info@sebic.ie C: Patrick Munden, Director

South East European Centre (Carréfour Waterford), Waterford LEADER Partnership Ltd, 21 Church Street, Dungarvan, Co Waterford T: (058) 44279 F: (058) 45238 E: abradley@iol.ie W: www.amireland.com/waterford_partnership/partpage/carrefour.html C: Antonia Bradley, Julie O'Donnell

South Kerry Development Partnership, Valentia Road, Caherciveen, Co Kerry T: (066) 947 2724 F: (066) 947 2725 E: bthorne@skdp.net W: www.southkerry.net C: Bill Thorne

Southside Partnership, 24 Adelaide Street, Dun Laoire, Co Dublin T: (01) 230 1011 F: (01) 202 0630 E: info@ship.ie W: None C: Neal Newman

SPADE Enterprise Centre, St Paul's, North King Street, Dublin 7 T: (01) 617 4800 F: (01) 677 1558 E: spade @eircom.net, kenprice@eircom.net C: Ken Price

Tallaght Partnership, Unit 19, The Village Green, Tallaght, Dublin 24 T: (01) 459 7990 F: (01) 459 7991 E: tallpart@eircom.net W: None C: Anna Lee

Teagasc — The Agriculture Food and Development Authority, 19 Sandymount Avenue, Ballsbridge, Dublin 4 T: (01) 637 6000 F: (01) 668 8023 E: pr@ hq.teagasc.ie W: www.teagasc.ie C: PR & Information: Michael Miley; Advisory Services: Tom Kirley

TecNet – The Technology Network, Crestfield Centre, Glanmire, Co Cork T: (021) 485 8060 F: (021) 482 3725 E: info@tecnet.ie W: www. tecnet.ie C: Eugene O'Leary, Chief Executive

Telework Ireland, Ballaghana, Mountnugent, Co Cavan T: 1800 421 426, (049) 854 0416 W: www.telework.ie C: Siobhán Duffy, Riona Carroll

Terenure Enterprise Centre, 17 Rathfarnham Road, Terenure, Dublin 6W T: (01) 490 3237 F: (01) 490 3238 E: info@tereneure-enterprise.ie W: www.terenure-enterprise.ie C: Pauline Doyle Also at: Rathmines Information Centre, 11 Wynnefield Road, Rathmines, Dublin 6 T: (01) 496 5558 F: (01) 496 5590 E: info@rathminesinformationcentre.com C: Nollaig Hannaway

Tipperary Institute, Nenagh Road, Thurles, Co Tipperary T: (0504) 28000 F: (0504) 28001 E: info@tippinst.ie W: www.tippinst.ie Also at Cashel Court, Clonmel, Co Tipperary T: (0504) 28000 F: (0504) 28001

Tipperary North County Enterprise Board, Connolly Street, Nenagh, Co Tipperary T: (067) 33086 F: (067) 33605 E: info@tnceb.ie W: www.tnceb.ie C: Rita Guinan, CEO

Tipperary South Riding County Enterprise Board, 1 Gladstone Street, Clonmel, Co Tipperary T: (052) 29466 F: (052) 26512 E: ctaylor@southtippcoco.ie C: Thomas Hayes, CEO

TradeNetIreland Ltd, 41 Lisburn Enterprise Centre, Ballinderry Road, Lisburn BT28 2BP T: (028) 9266 1160 F: (028) 9260 3084 E: info@tradenetireland.com W: www.tradenetireland.com C: Tracey Walsh, eBusiness Manager/Una O'Kane, Internet Marketing Executive

Trinity Venture Capital Ltd, Dunleary House, Dun Laoire, Co Dublin T: (01) 202 0420 F: (01) 202 0421 E: info@tvc.com W: www.tvc.com C: John Tracey, CEO

Údarás na Gaeltachta, Na Forbacha, Gaillimh T: (091) 503100 F: (091) 503101 E: eolas@udaras.ie W: www. udaras.ie C: Mairtin O Cadhain Also offices in Dingle, Donegal, Dublin and Mayo

Ulster Bank, Small Business Office, 33 College Green, Dublin 2 T: (01) 702 5225 F: (01) 702 5350 E: michael.bradley@ulsterbank.com W: www. ulsterbank.com C: Michael Bradley, Manager, Small Business

University College Cork, Cork T: (021) 490 3000 F: (021) 490 3612 E: tony.weaver@ucc.ie W: www.ucc.ie C: Tony Weaver, Industrial Liaison Officer

University College Dublin, University Industry Programme, Industry Centre, Belfield, Dublin 4 T: (01) 716 1676 F: (01) 283 8189 E: pat.frain@ucd.ie W: www.ucd.ie C: Dr Pat Frain, Director, University Industry Programme

University of Dublin, Trinity College, College Green, Dublin 2 T: (01) 608 1155 F: (01) 679 8039 E: innovation-centre@tcd.ie W: www.tcd.ie C: Eoin O'Neill, Director

University of Limerick, Limerick T: (061) 202700 F: (061) 330316 E: john.mcginn@ul.ie W: www.ul.ie C: Dr John McGinn, Industrial Liaison Officer

VenturePoint, See *Dun Laoire/Rathdown County Enterprise Board.*

Waterford Area Partnership, Westgate Business Centre, Tramore Road, Waterford T: (051) 841740 F: (051) 843153 E: areapart@iol.ie W: www.planet.ie C: Joe Stokes, Manager

Waterford City Enterprise Board, Enterprise House, New Street Court, Waterford T: (051) 852883 F: (051) 877494 E: info@waterfordceb.com W: www. waterfordceb.com C: Bill Rafter, CEO

Waterford County Enterprise Board, Court House, Dungarvan, Co Waterford T: (058) 44811 F: (058) 44817 E: waterfordceb@cablesurf.com C: Gerard Enright, CEO

Waterford Institute of Technology, Development Office, Cork Road, Waterford T: (051) 302039 F: (051) 378292 E: enquiries@wit.ie W: www.wit.ie C: Kathryn Kiely, External Services Officer

Waterford LEADER Partnership Ltd, Teagasc Centre, Lismore, Co Waterford T: (058) 54646 F: (058) 54126 E: wlp@eircom.net, seec@iol.ie W: www. amireland.com/waterford_partnership/partpage/partnership.html C: Julie O'Donnell, Jimmy Taafe, General Manager

WestBIC (Business Innovation Centre, Galway), Galway Technology Centre, Mervue Business Park, Galway T: (091) 730 850 F: (091) 730 853 E: info@westbic.ie W: www. westbic.ie C: Joe Greaney, Director

West Cork Enterprise Board, 8 Kent Street, Clonakilty, Co Cork T: (023) 34700 F: (023) 34702 E: enterprise@ wceb.ie W: www.wceb.ie C: Michael Hanley, CEO

West Limerick Resources Ltd, The Weigh House, Market Yard, Newcastlewest, Co Limerick T: (069) 62222 F: (069) 61870 E: wlr@eircom.net W: www. westlimerickresources.ie C: Brenda Cahill, Manager

Westmeath Community Development Ltd, Presentation House, Harbour Street, Mullingar, Co Westmeath T: (044) 48571 F: (044) 48441 E: westcd@iol.ie W: www.planet.ie C: Joe Potter

Westmeath County Enterprise Board Ltd, Business Information Centre, Church Avenue, Mullingar, Co Westmeath T: (044) 49222 F: (044) 49009 E: info@westmeath-enterprise.ie W: www.westmeath-enterprise.ie C: Christine Charlton, CEO

Wexford Area Partnership, Cornmarket, Mallin Street, Wexford T: (053) 23994 F: (053) 21024 E: paulaw@wap.iol.ie C: Bernard O'Brien, General Manager

Wexford County Enterprise Board, 16–17 Mallin Street, Cornmarket, Wexford T: (053) 22965 F: (053) 24944 E: info@wexfordceb.ie W: www.wexfordceb.ie C: Sean Mythen, CEO

Wicklow County Enterprise Board, 1 Main Street, Wicklow T: (0404) 67100 F: (0404) 67601 E: enterprise@wicklowceb.ie W: www.wicklowceb.ie

Updates to Appendix 1 are available on www.startingabusinessinireland.com

Appendix 2: Further Information

BOOKS

Clicking, Faith Popcorn and Lys Marigold, Thorsons
Creativity for Managers, Alan Barker, The Industrial Society
European Handbook of Management Consultancy, Oak Tree Press
Handbook of Modern Manufacturing Techniques, William Jones, Oak Tree Press
How to Form a Limited Company, PDF eBook, Brian O'Kane, Oak Tree Press
Managing & Marketing Your Website, Jim Hutchinson, Oak Tree Press
Look Before You Leap, Ron Immink, Oak Tree Press
Multipreneuring, Gorman, Fireside Press
Planning for Success: A Business Plan Workbook for Start-ups, Ron Immink, Oak Tree Press
Simpson Xavier Guide to The Family Business in Ireland, Smyth and Leach, Blackwater Press
Small Business Start-Up Pack, Ulster Bank
Starting a Business in Ireland, Brian O'Kane, 5th edition, Oak Tree Press
Starting on a Shoestring — Building a Business without a Bankroll, Goldstein, Ronald Press
The Mind of the Strategist, Ken Ohmae, McGraw-Hill
The Spirit of Enterprise, George Gilder, Penguin
The Women's Business Resource Guide, Barbara Littman, Contemporary Books

MAGAZINES

Running Your Business, Small Firms Association
Business Plus, www.bizplus.ie

WEB-SITES

www.americanexpress.com/small business – A section within American Express' site devoted to small business matters
www.ask-ireland.com
www.basis.ie – Business Access to State Information Services, a new Government web-site
www.bizplus.ie – Business Plus magazine
www.chambersireland.ie – Chambers of Commerce
www.cro.ie – Companies Registration Office
www.cso.ie – Central Statistics Office
www.entrepreneurmag.com
www.enterprise-ireland.ie
www.enterpriseboards.ie.com – a central point for access to the City/County Enterprise Boards
www.franchisedirect.com
www.iia.ie – Irish Internet Association
www.irlgov.ie – the Irish Government web-site
www.isme.ie – ISME
www.managementdirect.com
www.morebusiness.com
www.pdc.ie – Product Development Centre, Dublin
www.revenue.ie – Revenue Commissioners
www.ros.ie – Revenue Services On-line
www.sbaonline.sba.gov – US Small Business Administration
sbinformation.about.com
www.sfa.ie – Small Firms Association
www.sfediuk.com
www.startingabusinessinireland.com – where you will find updates for this guide and will be able to download spreadsheets and templates for use with your business plan
www.startups.co.uk
www.tradenetireland.com
uksmallbusiness.about.com

EVALUATION FORM

PLEASE COMPLETE AND RETURN THIS FORM TO:
STARTING YOUR OWN BUSINESS: A WORKBOOK EVALUATION
OAK TREE PRESS, 19 RUTLAND STREET, CORK. Fax: 021 431 3496.

How did you receive a copy of this guide?
☐ City/County Enterprise Board
☐ Area Partnership Company
☐ Enterprise Ireland
☐ Department of Enterprise, Trade and Employment
☐ Department of Social, Community & Family Affairs
☐ Other (specify)

When you received the guide, were you:
☐ Thinking about starting a business?
☐ Actively working towards starting a business?
☐ Doing a Feasibility Study?
☐ About to start a business?
☐ Running a business?

How long ago was this?
_________ months

What is your present situation?
☐ Thinking about starting a business
☐ Actively working towards starting a business
☐ Doing a Feasibility Study
☐ About to start a business
☐ Running a business

On a score of 0 (very poor) to 10 (excellent), please rate the guide for:

Readability	_____
User-friendliness	_____
Practicality	_____
Usefulness	_____
Clarity	_____
Relevance	_____

What improvements would you suggest for future editions of the guide?

Would you recommend the guide to someone you know who is planning to start a business?
☐ YES
☐ NO

If NO, why not?

(OPTIONAL)
Name

Address

☐ Male
☐ Female

Age _______

Thank you for taking the time to complete this evaluation form.

Snap
PRINTING
making you look good

Need a Nationwide Supplier of
Design, Print &
Promotional Products
to help you get started?

Snap do it.
So Snap to it.

Need to find out more?
Call 01 466 0525 for your nearest centre or log on to
www.snapprinting.ie

PaloAltoSoftware

www.paloalto.ie

Always dreamed of starting your own business?

Producing a business plan is easier than you think.

- No. 1 Recommended
- Saves Time
- 500+ Sample Plans
- Step-by-Step Help
- Available as download
- RRP: €120 (VAT incl.)

SPECIAL OFFER

Get 10% off Business Plan Pro 2007

To avail of this offer call us on 061 702035

Terms and Conditions Apply. Valid until December 31st, 2007.